LIFE BEYOND DEATH

A CRITICAL STUDY OF SPIRITUALISM

SWAMI ABHEDANANDA

The Vedanta Center of St. Petersburg
216 19th Ave. S.E., St. Petersburg, FL 33705
www.vedantaflorida.com

RAMAKRISHNA VEDANTA MATH
19A & B, RAJA RAJKRISHNA STREET
KOLKATA-700006 : INDIA

Published by :
Swami Satyakamananda
Ramakrishna Vedanta Math
19A & B, Raja Rajkrishna Street, Kolkata-700 006
Email : ramakrishnavedantamath@vsnl.net
Website : www.ramakrishnavedantamath.org

First Published : December 1944
Second Edition : November 1948
Third Edition : November 1960
Fourth Edition : December 1965
Fifth Edition : July 1971
Sixth Edition : April 1978
Seventh Edition : November 1984
Reprint : January 1989, April 1996, April 2000
Eighth Edition : April 2005

ISBN 81-88446-38-6

Printed at :
East India Photocomposing Centre
69, Sisir Bhaduri Sarani
Kolkata-700 009

PREFACE TO THE FIRST EDITION

Swāmi Abhedānanda delivered from time to time a number of lectures on spiritualism in response to the invitations from some well-known institutions of culture during his long stay in America. These lectures have now been published together in book form under the name of *Life Beyond Death* as the first contribution of the *Abhedananda Memorial Series* to the reading public. Three of these lectures, formerly published as separate pamphlets, have also been incorporated in this volume.

Unlike many of the books on spiritualism, the present work has a special feature of its own. Its pages do not narrate the legends and tales of ghosts and other supernatural beings, as one in most cases finds in such books that claim to unveil the mystery of the world beyond the grave. The treatment of the subject is purely a scientific one, and it has taken a new departure from the prevailing methods and systems of presentation of this subject.

For some reasons or other a great majority amongst the learned people in modern times do not view spiritualism with favour and appreciation. Their attitude towards spiritualism is one of indifference. There are again others who are credulous, and they, without any question or investigation, like to believe its everything to be true. The present work is fully free from both these prejudices, and never subscribes to any of these blindly biased views. It has given an impartial or dispassionate view on spiritualism, showing wisely and ably its merits and demerits, its bright and dark sides as well. Spiritualism, in these lectures, has never been upheld, nor totally denied. One, going through these lectures, realizes to what extent spiritualism should

3

be accepted and to what extent it ought to be rejected. Even those who are not in favour of spiritualism or who delight to scoff at it, will find in these lectures many things instructive and valuable.

Whether spiritualism is really helpful or injurious to men as regards their religious perfection, whether there is any way other than spiritualism, more certain, systematic and rational in order to reach the state of Self-realization, should be known by every inquisitive mind. And these knotty problems have been clearly solved by the philosopher-saint in these lectures with the remarkable characteristics of his own.

One thing should be made clear. The repetitions of a few instances have crept in some of the lectures. But their omission, in our humble opinion, will be of no avail, as the idea conveyed in these will lose much of its force and the addresses will appear somewhat mutilated.

Besides the lectures mentioned above, the Swami's view on the soul-life revealed in the process of questions and answers, his discussions with eminent American scholars on soul's preexistence, immortality, reincarnation and eternality, have also been reprinted from some leading journals of America as to form the appendices of the book.

In addition to these, the extracts from the Vedic passages, the utterances of some mystics, poets and philosophers and several notes have been annexed by the editor to it, for the convenience of the readers.

Ramakrishna Vedanta Math   THE PUBLISHER
           Calcutta-6
      December, 1944.

PREFACE TO THE SECOND EDITION

The second edition of *Life Beyond Death* is offered to the reading public with some corrections and new additions. All the notes and footnotes in it have been added by Swāmi Prajñānānanda, the editor. Some new plates of ectoplasm and spirit materialised are also added to this new edition from B. V. Schrenck Notzing's *Phenomena of Materialization*, and for this we are indebted to its Publisher. We are glad to see that the first edition of this book got a warm reception from all corners of the globe, and we hope that this present edition will also be appreciated by seekers of truth and knowledge.

Ramakrishna Vedanta Math   THE PUBLISHER
19B, Raja Rajkrishna Street
        Calcutta-6
November, 1948.

CONTENTS

7

The heaven and the hell—The Persians—The
Egyptians—The Chaldeans—The Christian idea—
Prof. Huxley—The soul.

CHAPTER III

The *Mahabharata* on death—The mystery of death is
not solved by mythology—Different scriptures—The
Genesis—Adam and Satan—Scientific researches—
Deaths of the conscious life and the cellular life—
Prof. Charles Minot—Causes and signs of death—
Trance, catalepsy and ecstasy—The old Babylonian
method of embalming the body—The cremation
method—The belief of the Egyptians—Mind as a
factor in the case of death—Dr. John Hunter—
Tourtelle, the French Physician—Extreme anger
generates poison—Grief produces a havoc—*Prana*
the life-force—Mind and the *Prana*—Mind is the
creator—Who is the conductor of the organs—
Ectoplasm—Materializing medium—Soul at the time
of death—C. Flammarion—What is materialization—
Subtle body—Body, the instrument—Death is no
longer mysterious—Nothing is destroyed—There is
something unchangeable in the midst of changes.

CHAPTER IV

Different views of death and soul—*Katha
Upanishad*—The Vedas—*Brahmaloka*—Law of
Karma—*Pitriyana*—*Devayana*—The heavens—

Higher conception of Vedanta—Zend Avesta on Spiritualism—Old and New Testaments—The Persians—The Egyptians—The Chaldeans—Pythagoras and Plato—What Palto believed—Vedanta on transmigration—Power exists in nature—The views of the so called scientists—Race or species—Evolution—Soul is immortal—Vedanta cares not for heaven or hell.

CHAPTER V

The term soul—Materialistic thinkers—Everything is subject to the law of cause and effect—Scientific thinkers—A germ of life—Mind and its functions—Psychic powers—Rebirth of the soul does not mean the same thing as transmigration—Metempsychosis and reincarnation—Births according to the merits and demerits of deeds—What is transmigration—Migrating substance—Mythological theory of transmigration—The belief of the Hindus—Rational minds do not believe in the retrogression of the human souls into animal forms—Doctrine of reincarnation is based upon the theory of evolution—The passages of the *Upanishads*—Reincarnation of the soul does not mean the same thing as expressed by the Buddhist philosophers—One-birth theory—The Christian theologians on reincarnation—The followers of Judaism, Christianity and Mohammedanism—Time has no absolute existence—What nature teaches—The Greek philosophers about doctrine of incarnation—One-birth theory and heredity do not explain the mystery of rebirth—The protoplasmic cell—Theories against heredity—Illustrations of reincarnations.

CHAPTER IX

CHAPTER X

CHAPTER XI

of our thoughts and deeds—The Hindus believe in the existence of the soul from time immemorial—The fraudulent spirits—Spirits borrow powers from the subconscious mind of anybody—The funeral ceremonies of the Hindus are different from that of the Christians—We can help spirits more than they can help us—Good thoughts or prayers help the spirits—Present *karma*, the seed of the future—The conditions of the souls in their slumbers—Astral shells—Those are the planes which we call heaven—Law of cause and sequence—The realm of thought—How do the spirits see, touch, hear in the world beyond grave—Sleep after death is like the sleep before birth—The second sleep—The souls seek conditions and environments before their birth—The occupations may be according to the beliefs—There is none to mould our future—Desires are the cause of our sufferings—The wise ones will never be afraid of death.

CHAPTER XVI

APPENDICES

A summary of the Swami Abhedananda's speech at an Anniversary Meeting of the Psychical Research Society of Calcutta.

An interesting discourse under the auspices of the Calcutta Psychical Society presided over by Swami Abhedananda.

PREFACE

Unlike many of the books on spiritualism, the present work has a special feature and beauty of its own. Its pages do not narrate the chief legends and tales of the departed spirits and the wondering ghosts and also of the supernatural beings of the unknown etherial sphere, as one in most cases finds in such books that claim to unveil the mystery of the world beyond the grave. The treatment of the chapters of this book is purely a scientific and rational one, and it has taken a new and novel departure from the prevailing methods and systems of the presentation of this subject.

Swami Abhedananda delivered from time to time a number of lectures on spiritualism in response to the invitations from many institutions like the Free Religious Association of America, The Psychical Research Society of America and the President of the Psychical Research Society of America, the American Institute of Science, etc. The Swami was once the President of the Psychical Research Society of America. He was also well-acquainted with the leading scientists, spiritualists, mediums and spirit-communicators, during his long stay in America. He had many personal experiences about the departed spirits, seances, spirit-communications and other subjects on spiritualism; he believed that most of the spirits are earth-bound, as they are not free from desires and passions. Regarding the mediums, he has said that in most cases, the mediums are deprived of their mental and physical powers. Regarding the seances, the Swami is of opinion that though the departed spirits communicate with the seance-holders and with near and dear ones, and furnish information of their earthly and etherial worlds, yet, in most cases, it has been found that all the information and talks, received from them, are not genuine or correct. So the

17

Swami says that everything of the spirits should be examined with logical and scientific mind.

Regarding this present work, it can be said that it is absolutely free from prejudices and blindly biased views. It is a critical study of the science and practice of spiritualism with impartial or dispassionate views. It has shown wisely and ably the merits and the demerits and also the bright and dark sides of the fact and science of spiritualism. At the same time the learned Swami clearly solved all the controversial points and problems of the theory of birth and rebirth of the souls, existence and pre-existence of the souls, and immortality and eternality of the souls. In short, all the knotty problems of spiritualism or spiritism have been clearly explained and solved by this philosopher-saint in the chapters of this book with remarkable characteristics of his own.

It can be said that Swami Abhedananda has neither blindly upheld, nor has totally deny or rejected the facts of the aspects of spiritualism. As for example, the Swami has said : "Although many of the professional mediums have been pitifully exposed as frauds, still there are genuine mediums and authentic manifestations which cannot be explained by telepathy or any other theory than that of the communications of the discarnate spirits. In many cases the audience is deceived by the earth-bound spirits. The manifestations on the material plane, such as the table turning, the ropping knocks of the spirits, are ordinarily understood by spiritualism, but all such phenomena belong to the lower class of spiritualism or spiritism, as it is called by many. Spiritism can only satisfy our curiosity and does not explain any of our vital questions. But true spiritualism should be distinguished from that phase which is called spiritism. Higher spiritism, therefore, is the name for that which starting from the belief in a life after death, reveals the nature of the soul and its relation to God".

Further the Swami has said : "Within the last fifty years modern spiritualism has given wonderful demonstrations regarding the existence of the disembodied spirits who continue to live even after the dissolution of their gross material forms. It has brought comfort and consolation to the hearts of many people, who were suffering from the the evil effects of scepticism and unbelief, concerning the future life, caused by the dry theories of the atheistic, agnostic, and materialistic thinkers of the last century". But it is true, the Swami says, that though the disembodied spirits satisfy some of the curiosities of the questioning people, yet they cannot do any real good or they cannot help in any way in the path of spiritual progress. As for example, the Swami said : "The genuine phenomena of spiritism may do some good in the way of satisfying the curiosity of certain people or of bringing the assurance that there is a life after death. They may foretell some petty, trivial events in connection with our business or daily life, but they cannot bring to us the highest wisdom and happiness which come to the soul through Divine communion. These spirits are not angels, as the spiritualism may encourage the hope of meeting the departed spirits of our friends and relatives, and may bring consolation in the mind of those that doubt their existence, but it cannot give us the realization of the absolute Truth, or the attainment of God-consciousness".

Swami Abhedananda, being a true philosopher and a man of realization, surveyed everything of spiritualism or spiritism from the viewpoint of logic, reasoning, and science. He says that death is inevitable for all the living beings, and they are involved in the cycle of birth and death, until they realize their immortal soul or *Atman*. Spiritualism is only an open passage for receiving the informations of the existence and pre-existence of the soul and also of their eternality and immortality, but it cannot assure anyone the blessings of knowledge of the absolute Brahman.

The Swami says that when a man passes from the material plane, he lives in the mental plane, and does everything through his mind with the impressions (*samskaras*) of the works he performed in the material plane and also with the countless impressions that are hoarded in the subconscious lair of the mind. The departed soul sleeps there as it were in the spirit or mind world, and, regarding this sleep after death, Swami Abhedananda says : "The sleep after death is like the sleep before the birth. Then they (departed souls) have a second sleep before they come to this plane (material plane), they go into the sleep, and gravitate towards proper environment. If I have a strong desire to be the best artist, and if I do not succeed or pass away before I fulfil my desire, that desire will remain in me even in that soul-slumber. It will sprout again". Now, from this it is evident that the departed souls gravitate again and again in this world of desire and fulfilment, because their souls exist and the souls take births until and unless they reach the absolute Truth by cutting asunder the knots of desires and passions. The law of *karma* is predominant in the lives of all living creatures. They do works in this world of duties and reap their results. Swami Abhedananda says : "So this law of cause and sequence which is called the law of *karma*, does not wait for widow's tears, or orphan's cries. What we have sown, we must reap either on this plane, or in some other realm. So after death we may enjoy the pleasures of our thoughts and deeds in the heavenly regions".

From the law of *karma* it is also proved that our soul is immortal and will not be extinguished after death. But it should be remembered, the Swami says, that the life after death, or the life in this material world, is liable to change and also subject to the law of cause and sequence. So we shall have to transcend the realm of cause and effect, which is dominated by time and space, the ingredients of nescience or *maya*. And this transcendance is possible only by the realization of our true existence which is the immortal *Atman*.

There are sixteen chapters and five appendices in the book. If we briefly survey different chapters, we find that Chapter I has dealt with "modern science and the higher spiritualism". In this chapter, the Swami has said that during the last sixty years, spiritualism made a considerable progress, convincing many scientific minds who were earnestly seeking for the truth of man's survival after death. The experimental spiritualism began in America in 1870. For the scientific study of the phenomena of spiritualism, the Psychical Research Society was established in London in 1886, and many savants like Dr. Myers, Frank Podmore, Mr. Home, Sir William Crookes, Sir Oliver Lodge, Prof. William James, Alfred Russell Walace, Dr. Hedgeson and others were interested in the research work of the science of spirit. Camille Flammarion, W. T. Stead, Prof. Hyslop were also interested in the subject of spiritualism. Swami Abhedananda says that the higher spiritualism is at the root of all great religions of the world, and so the followers of different religions and also different great thinkers devoted their times for discovering some truths in the science and practice of spiritualism.

Chapter II deals with the problem of the existence of the soul after the dissolution of the material body. In this chapter, Swami Abhedananda says that from ancient times, there existed some belief that the psyche or soul is non-different from the material body, and so after the dissolution of the body, the soul also dies. This faith mainly prevailed among the Charvakas, who were the disciples of Vrihaspati and were out and out materialistic in thinking and doing. Besides them, there were dormant questions about the soul among ordinary men, who were generally guided by blind faith. But Swami Abhedananda says that the disbelief in the existence of the soul after death prevails among the modern physiologists, the anatomists, the pathologists and a host of other materialistic and agnostic thinkers. They believe that the combinations of matter produce thought, intelligence, consciousness, mind and soul. "They teach that thought or intelligence or consciousness is nothing but a function of the brain.** The brain brings into existence the

material of consciousness of which our minds consist**. As
the materials of food, after falling into the stomach, change and
assume new qualities, so the impressions of the brain are
metamorphosed into the ideas, thought, emotion, will,
impressions of the face, speech, disposition, etc. through the
nerves. Thus thought or soul is the secretion of the brain, and
when the brain is gone, the soul cannot exist". The Swami has
quoted some lines in support of this materialistic theory from
the writings of Buchner, Luys, Percival Lowell, Herbert Spencer,
Prof. Clifford, Romanes and others. In fact, the writings of these
materialistic thinkers are similar to those of the Charvakas of
India. But Vedanta does not admit this theory of the materialists.
Swami Abhedananda says that according to Vedanta "knowledge
of matter is nothing but the knowledge of that change of mind,
of which we are conscious.** Even our knowledge that the soul,
or the mind, is a function of the brain, presupposes the existence
of another mind or knower". This another mind or knower is
the self or the soul, which is different from the mind and the
body, but the substratum or ground of the mind and the body.
Dr. Schiller, Immanual Kant, Fichte, Schelling and others also
subscribe to a similar view, though David Hume, like the
Vijnanavadin Yogachara Buddhists, does not admit it, because
according to Hume and the Yogachara Buddhists, the soul is a
bundle of sensations or ideas.

Now Swami Abhedananda efficiently dealt with the
problem of the existence of the soul after death. He says that
the most ancient writers of the vedic ages believed in the spirits
of the *pitris* or departed fathers. The Egyptians, the
Mesopotemians, the Chaldeans and other ancient nations of the
world also believed in the 'double' or soul, devoid of the material
form. The Hindus believed that after death, the departed souls
live in the mental world with the sleeping impressions
(*samskaras*) of his desires (*vasanas*) which existed and were
not mitigated during life-time. The souls are subject to the cycle

of birth and rebirth, until they go beyond the nescience (*ajnana*) and realize their immortal nature. "The Hindus", says the Swami, "do not mean destruction or annihilation by death. They mean by it a change of body, or the form". The *Bhagavad Gita* says that the soul or *Atman* is deathless and birthless; it is eternal by its nature. So it is a proved fact that the soul exists after death, and its true nature is the *Atman*, or the *Brahman*, which is the background of the changing world-appearance.

Chapter III deals with the scientific view of death. In this chapter, the Swami Abhedananda says that the mystery of death is not to be solved by mere mythology or mythological beliefs of the ancient people which have been handed down to us through generations, but to be solved by scientific enquiry and investigation. The duty of science is to disclose truths which are genuine and real, and so those who wish to unveil the mystery of the unknown spirit-world, should study the details of spiritualism with a scientific mind. Swami Abhedananda says : "Scientific researches toward tracing the causes of death have brought out many truths and many laws which were unknown tó the writers of the Genesis and other scriptures of different nations". But it is a fact that the orthodox science, or the materialistic science, is quite unfit to discover the real truth that is behind spiritualism or spiritism. But it requires an open mind and reason backed by the scientific enquiry into the truth. The Swami has given some instances of the embalming process of the dead bodies of the old Babylonians and Egyptians, and has said that the very process or method proves the existence of the soul beyond the grave. They believed in a 'double' and that means, they maintained the belief of pre-existence of the soul. The Indians believe in the indestructibility of the life-force; and, that life-force or *prana* is not the product of any chemical actions of any material thing. It is all-intelligent and all-conscious, and it is the *Atman*, which transcends the cycle of birth and rebirth.

Now, in support of the existence of the soul as the life-force or the life-principle, the Swami has forwarded an argument which is beautiful and very rational. He says : "Thus we see that there are two principal factors in the body : the one is the mind and the other is the vibration of the *prana*, or the vibratory state of the cells and the tissues of the body. But the vibratory state of the cells and the tissues are governed by the mind". In fact, the mind is the director of all the organic functions of the body. But there is another principle which directs also the mind, and that director is the life-force, or the *prana*, or the soul. The Swami says : "It is the individual self-conscious life-force which is called** the living soul. The living soul means the self-conscious individualized life-force with the sense of 'I', and the sense of 'I' holds them together. This sense of 'I' holds all together, unifies them, and makes the separate parts vibrate and produce a perfect harmony. That harmony is life.** But advanced science tells us that there is a director and this director has the absolute control over the whole organism. He is the living soul. At the time of death, he disconnects himself from the organs and leaves the body."

The Swami has given in this chapter some interesting information of spiritualism. He says that a fine substance emanates from the body at the time of death. It is luminous, and is called the *ectoplasm*. The French Astronomer, Camille Flammarian has reports about this *ectoplasm* in his famous book, *The Unknown,* and he has said that "this ectoplasm is a substance, which contains finer matter in vibration, and this finer matter forms the under-garment of the soul, and the gross physical body is the outer garment. So we have two bodies : the gross physical body and the finer or etherial body which exists in each one of us." The *ectoplasm* is a vapourlike substance and has no particular form. It is like a cloud and can take a shape or a form and can be photographed, says Swami Abhedananda. The disembodied souls or spirits who desire to be materialized and to communicate with the near and dear ones in the phenomenal world, generally take the help of this *ectoplasm* which remains in the body of everyone. The Swami says : "Our human bodies are emanating that substance all the time. It can be seen especially at the time when there is a mediums in a trancelike condition. The materializing mediums emanate that very strongly". In fact, the *ectoplasm* is the under-garment of the soul, and the gross physical body is the outer garment. Now, the Hindu scriptures say that there is also a causal body (*karana-sharira*), which forms the background of the finer or etherial body (subtle or *sukshma-sharira*) and the real soul or the *Atman* is above all these bodies, gross, subtle and causal. The scientific study of spiritualism will disclose this truth.

Chapter IV deals with the soul after death. The Swami has given here many references from the *Upanishad, Gita* and other Hindu scriptures. He has said that the Hindus believe that the righteous and good souls pass through the *devayana* or the path of the *devas,* whereas the sinners pass through the *pitriyana* or the path of the departed fathers. The *Upanishad* has described that the departed spirits pass through the principal stages like smoke, night, dark, fifteen days, and each of the departed souls has a spirit as its ruler. Each of these spirits introduces them to the other spirits and thus they go very quickly to their proper destinations. Now, from these references-cum-evidence we come to know that the souls of the living beings, exist after death, and come under the sway of the cycle of birth and rebirth until they reach their final shapes, the immortal self. Swami Abhedananda says that death means the change of forms. "Death of one form reproduces or gives birth to another form, as death of the seed form produces the tree-form and so forth. Again that which is reproduced, will die and then reproduce another and so on".

Chapter V deals with rebirth of the soul. The Swami says : "Rebirth of the soul presupposes its existence as an intelligent entity and it is separable and independent of the gross physical body. By the term *Atman*, we mean that centre of the self-conscious activity which thinks, reacts on the personal or external phenomena, and consciously performs the functions of life". Regarding rebirth of the soul Swami Abhedananda says that reappearance of the germs of life in gross physical forms, whether animal or human, is called 'manifestation', which is known and understood by the theory of rebirth of the soul, or the doctrine of reincarnation, as it is called in the Vedanta philosophy. (Cf. the Swami's book, *Reincarnation*). By rebirth of the soul, Vedanta does not mean the theory of transmigration or metempsychosis which is quite different from the theory of reincarnation. The theory of reincarnation can nicely be explained by the theory of evolution (*abhivyaktivada* or *srishtivada*), as advanced by the *Sankhya* philosophy or Kapila. The *Sankhya* says that evolution means the projection of something which exists in a seed form. Something cannot come out of nothing. The entire universe comes out from the *Prakriti*, which is the sum total of all the individual soul and all the matters. When the unmanifested form comes out as the manifested form, then we call evolution, or projection, or creation. Vedanta also admits this theory. The soul or the life-force of all the sentient and insentient objects are uncreated and immortal, and it appears with a manifested body from its unmanifested causal form. So rebirth of the soul presupposes the idea of immortality of the soul. Swami Abhedananda has, therefore, refuted the one-birth theory and the theory of heredity. He says that "the whole human nature must have existed in that germ of life in some form or other".

Chapter VI deals with the soul and its destiny. Swami Abhedananda says : "The souls, which have desires for earthly things, will have to come down to earth. Some souls will remain earth-bound for a certain length of time, say one hundred or a thousand years.** They will be born again. So the destiny of the human soul is determined by the thoughts and desires and tendencies. We create our own destiny by our thoughts and desires and deeds.** God is not responsible for our conditions. We ourselves are responsible, **"

Chapter VII deals with the problems of pre-existence and immortality. In this Chapter, Swami Abhedananda has forwarded a very strong and unrefutable argument in support of pre-existence, reincarnation and immortality of the soul. The Swami has refuted the theories of heredity and one-birth, as believed by the old Christian theologians, and says that both the theory of heredity and that of one-birth cannot explain or solve the problems of life and death. He says that according to Vedanta, immortality means the continued existence in the eternal future, whereas pre-existence means the continued existence in the eternal past. "The one cannot exist without the other. Each of these only expresses the one-half of our life which is eternal, and both of these together make a complete whole and that is the soul-life". The soul-life is the uncreated and unborn life-principle that connects the threads of past, present and future, and also connects life and death. In fact, rebirth and reincarnation of the individual soul are based upon the truth of the eternality of the soul-life which is expressed by pre-existence and immortality. According to Vedanta, says the Swami, immortality includes the meaning of progress i.e., progress of growth and evolution of the soul from the lower to the higher stages of development. "It also includes the ideas that each individual soul will manifest the powers which are already latent in the soul by going through different stages of growth and development until perfection and omniscience and omnipresence are acquired. **This idea leads to the theories of rebirth and reincarnation of the individual soul which is expressed by pre-existence and immortality".

Chapter VIII deals with pre-existence and immortality and though these theories or problems have been discussed elaborately in Chapter VII, yet the Swami discussed them in a separate chapter by giving more facts and arguments, which are also supported by science. The Swami says in course of his argument : "Pre-existence and immortality are so closely related to each other that if we deny one, we cannot accept the other". Vedanta says that each individual soul existed before the birth of the body, and so if we believe that we shall continue to exist after death, we shall have to admit that we existed in the past, otherwise we cannot have immortal life in future."

Chapter IX deals with the subject-matter of science and immortality. In the beginning of this Chapter, Swami Abhedananda has refuted the belief of the orthodox Christians that Jesus the Christ for the first time brought the eternal life and immortality to light. The Swami says that the idea of immortality or the immortal life existed in India some thousands of years before Christ ; and the sacred scriptures of the Hindus, including the Vedas, have proved to the world the truth that the *Atman* or the real life-principle of the soul is eternal and immortal. The students of comparative religion as well as those of history know well that Egypt, Greece, Chaldea, Mesopotemia and other ancient and most civilized countries preached the theory or idea of resurrection of the body and also of the belief in a 'double' or soul from the time between 12,000 and 8,000 B.C. The Greeks believed that the righteous ones who went to the Elysium Fields would continue to enjoy the celestial pleasures throughout eternity. The Hindus also believe in the heavens or the *svargalokas* where the religious and righteous ones go and enjoy celestial pleasures, but they hold that the heavenly pleasures are not permanent and eternal ; and so after enjoying fruits of pleasures of the heavens for a definite period, the souls come back again to this material universe, and this is the difference between the Greeks and the Hindus regarding their heavens and the celestial pleasures. However, the ideas of heaven, life after death and immortality also prevail among the

Jews, Parsees, Zoroastrians, Chinese, Scandinavians and others.

Now regarding science and immortality, Swami Abhedananda says that it is a common belief that science has nothing to do with the problems of life after death and immortality, as it is absolutely concerned with the repeated observations and investigations upon the raw materials of the changing phenomena of the universe. But that is not the fact, as modern science "has resolved the whole phenomenal world into three states, and has explained that they are matter, energy and consciousness. These three things are the fundamental principles of the universe. If you study science or any of the philosophies of the world, you will find these three things, matter, energy and consciousness. But, in truth, matter, force or energy are inseparable ; they are the different states of the same substance. Then there comes the third thing, consciousness". Consciousness is indestructible and eternal. So science which resolves the three main principles of matter, energy and consciousness as the fundamental principles of the universe, is quite eligible for discussing about the doctrine of immortality, and the mystery of life beyond death held much science to the unifying truth of the universe.

Chapter X deals with the spiritualism. The Swami explains in this chapter the main principles and methods of spiritualism, with a scientific outlook. He has refuted the popular belief and the theories of production, combination and transmission. The upholders of the production theory are the atheists, agnostics, materialists and evolutionists. They believe that the material body produces the soul, which is really absurd. The upholders of the combination theory explain that the neural current is a stream which produces a stream of feelings. The feelings are different units of feeling which are loose and disconnected, and there is no intelligent something which can connect those units of feeling. This theory echoes the theory of the *vijnanavadin* Buddhists, who maintain that in a stream of consciousness (*vijnana*), the units of consciousness are separate from one another, and are momentary. This theory is untenable, as it admits no intelligent something which can bind or unite together the momentary units of consciousness.

Now we find that the transmission theory proves that the soul, or the mind, or the consciousness, is outside of the brain. It is not the result or product of the brain, "but is something like a self-conscious entity, which is using the brain, just as a musician uses the piano and plays on the keys". Now the transmission theory "tells us that the 'double' or the soul is the astral self of the individual, and this astral self is something which can live independent of the gross material body, and this astral self can pass out and can appear in the etherial form and perform many acts, which our ordinary self cannot do. The astral doubles are sometimes perceived by the relatives and the friends of the dying persons". Now, somehow or other, Vedanta accepts the transmission theory to prove that the matter is not percieved as an object, and is, therefore, meaningless, until there remains the mind as the subject. From this it is proved that the matter is different from the mind, as the mind forms the ground as well as the cause of the matter.

Swami Abhedananda also discussed in this chapter the problems of personality and individuality. The personality is that particular consciousness which is related to the physical body. But individuality is something which is beyond the material body and is indivisible. Personality is changing and might be held in an earth-bound condition but individuality is constant, unchanging and infinite. Personality is a kind of mask; it is the garment of the mind. Personality may be double, triple, and quadruple. But it is not a certain state of consciousness, it is like an assumed character. In other words, it can be said that different ideas and different tendencies and desires create different personalities which are supported by unchanging and eternal individuality. The Swami has elaborately discussed about individuality and personality in his book, *True Psychology.*

Chapter XI deals with spiritualism and Vedanta. In this chapter Swami Abhedananda has discussed about the ancestor-worship which is prevalent among the civilised nations like the ancient Indians, Egyptians, Babylonians, Chaldeans, Assyrians, Chinese, Parsees and other nations. The belief in the 'double' has been mentioned before and this 'double' is like the *sukshma-sharira* of the departed soul. The ancient Parsees used to call the departed souls of the ancestors, the *fravtshis* and the Hebrews called them *elohim.* The Hindus perform the *shraddha* ceremony for the satisfaction of the departed soul, and they believe that anything offered with devotion and regard to the departed souls, brings contentment and peace among the disembodied spirits. The realm of the fathers or ancestors is called the *Pitriloka,* where departed fathers enjoy heavenly life and celestial pleasures. The *Katha Upanishad* has related the story of Nachiketa and Yama, the Ruler of Death, and the story proves the existence of the soul after death. The Hindu scriptures say that the souls in this phenomenal plane and the souls in the astral plane are directed by the law of *karma,* or the law of action and reaction. The Buddhists also admit the theory. And this law of *karma* also proves the existence of the soul after death.

Swami Abhedananda has also described about the mediums through whom the spirits can communicate with their friends and relatives in this phenomenal world with their astral bodies, and Swami Abhedananda personally witnessed those materialized spirit-bodies when he attended some of the interesting seances in America. The Swami says that the earth-bound souls may take the form of his previous material bodies for his intense will, but they cannot hold those astral or subtle bodies for a long time, because they are not really conscious of their material bodies, and those bodies are melted away after a short time.

Chapter XII deals with the problems of spiritualism and ancestor-worship. This Chapter can be said to be the supplementary one of the Chapter XI. It is interesting to mention that Swami Abhedananda has explained in this Chapter many things about spiritualism including the miserable state of the disembodied spirits and of the mediums, together with the ancestor-worship in different scriptures of different nations of the world. He also related some of his personal experiences he gathered in the seances with the spirit-communication. He says : "Having spent sometime with the mediums of all kinds that exist in America, I wish to say a few words regarding my experiences. I have been invited by the spiritualists to speak for them and to attend their seances. I had accepted their invitations with great pleasure in order to make some investigations for my own satisfaction. I have seen many materialized spirits and have spoken with them. I have had long conversations with some who spoke through the tin trumphets, and have asked them many questions, but I have not found a single spirit in any seance and not a single medium who could answer my questions satisfactorily. I have asked them about the life after death, ** on many occasions they have confessed their ignorance and have said : 'We do not know ; you know better than what we can tell you'. Some spirits have often referred to me for my approval of their answers to the questions which they were asked by other sitters. A few years ago, I was amused to hear from a materializing spirit in a public seance : 'Oh, here is a thinking-box; what can we say before him ?' This exclamation came from an American Indian spirit. I was sitting next to the husband of the medium and, as he was a friend of mine, I asked him the meaning of such a remark. He said : 'She refers to you'. I inquired : 'Why ?' He replied : 'She thinks you are very wise, and she cannot show her power'. I am sorry to say that the seance was not successful that evening. On another occasion, I had a long talk with a spirit, and asked her many questions regarding the mode of living in the spirit world, and her answers to my questions were perfectly idiotic.** Sometimes, however, I noticed that telepathically my own thoughts and my own ideas and very expressions were reproduced as perfectly as if I was answering my own question.** Some of them congratulated me and said : 'My spirit-guides have taught me exactly what you have explained'."

Chapter XIII deals with the spiritualistic mediumship. The Swami says : "We are all familiar with the process of developing mediumship.** Those who wish to become the mediums, seek the company of other friends who have the same desire. They form themselves into a circle which is known as the *developing circle*. They are told by other mediums, or by their spirit-guides, to select a definite room, where they should sit as often as possible, at least once a week, but the sittings must be at the same hour and in the same evening of the week**". The sitters sit in the developing circle with their negative mind, and must not ask any questions, but surrender themselves to the will of their invisible control, and calmly wait for the wonderful results of the developing process.

Regarding the mediums, the Swami says that "a medium, who appears to be inspired in a semi-trance or full trance condition, does not show any power of his or her, which may be called a gift or inspiration**. A medium who becomes absolutely negative or passive in mind and body, becomes subject to all the surrounding influences of the earth-bound spirits who are constantly seeking opportunity to control, and make some victims, and thus through ignorance a medium opens a psychic field which is dominated by the will of these earth-bound spirits". And for this reason, Swami Abhedananda has not encouraged them who wish to be the mediums. Because the mediums in many cases lose their physical and mental powers, and sometimes become invalid.

Chapter XIV deals with the automatic slate-writing. In this Chapter, the Swami has related the story of his departed *gurubhai*, Jogen (Swami Jogananda), who appeared before the seances, and wrote with a blue pencil his name in four classical languages, Sanskrit, English, Bengali and Greek. Mr. Keeler was the medium, and it happened on August 5th at 10 o'clock in America. The photograph of this slate-writing with the spirit-hand has been included in this book, *Life Beyond Death*. The Swami says : "In another seance when I wanted to see Jogen materialized, he replied that he did not like it. But I was surprised to see the spirit of Babu Balaram Basu of 57, Ramakanta Bose Street, Calcutta.** After blessing me the whole materialized figure of Balaram Babu melted away in a mist like white substance (*ectoplasm*) and disappeared".

Chapter XV or the last chapter deals with 'what is there beyond the grave'. In this Chapter, Swami Abhedananda has elaborately and scientifically dealt with many important problems of spiritualism. He says that Jesus the Christ brought eternal life into light, and the Christians believe in the resurrection of the spiritual body, which continues to live after the gross physical body is destroyed, and this belief proves the immortality of the soul among the Christian nations of the world. The similar belief is seen also among the Zoroastrians, Egyptians, Chaldeans, Babylonians, Chinese, Hindus and all other ancient nations like the Romans, the Greeks, and the Scandinavians. They all had a belief in an eternal life.

The Swami says that when a soul goes out of the material body after death, it sleeps without consciousness or knowledge of his passing away, and he wakes up after a long time. Then he finds himself in an unknown world in an unfavourable circumstance with which he is not familiar. Then his sleeping and unfulfilled desires become very acute. He tries to mitigate his desires, but fails, and so he suffers much, and this suffering of the departed soul has been described as the suffering of the hell (*naraka-yantrana*). But the good souls enjoy peace and happiness in the after-world. An earth-bound spirit further suffers for his failure in communicating with the near and dear ones. It has been recorded that many disembodied souls try to rush in the open passage of the mediumistic current, but many of them cannot materialize themselves for their lack of will-power, and so they suffer. But the spirits can materialize themselves either with the help of the mediums, or without the help of any medium. B. V. Schrenck Notzing, Sir Oliver Lodge, Sir Arthur Conan Doyle and others have given vivid descriptions of the process of materialization of the disembodied spirits. Swami Abhedananda says that very few people understand or believe in the process of spirit-materialization. "I have seen with my own eyes and carefully examined in every possible way which I use under those circumstances. I have been called to come inside the cabinet of a seance where I felt at least twenty hands on my back, some pulling my collar, sash, and some putting hands on my back all at the same time.** I have held the materialized hand of an American Indian spirit which melted away in my hand". The Swami further says : "Some of the dying persons develop the clairvoaynce and the clairaudience. They can appear at the time of death to distant friends in the form of an apparition and they can give their messages". Further he has said : "If it (the departed soul) has strong attachments to the relatives or the friends and if it cannot get over those attachments, it hovers around them, remains close to them, tries to help them, to be loved by them, and there it is conscious of its personality.** I would be wondering while my relatives and friends and all the dearest ones do not recognise me, and there I have to suffer. Now that is what happens with certain people who do not know that they are dead.** It is just like a state of hell". "But many of the departed spirits·remain in that state of delusion for a long time. Our time does not affect the spirits. Our thousand years may be five days to them, because ours is according to our standard and theirs according to their standard. So no one can say how long a soul will remain in any particular condition, but it is important that we should remember this law that we create our future, we create our destiny, and we build our character by our thoughts and deeds". However the Swami has warned and instructed those who are eager to be mediums and who also wish to sit in the seance to communicate with the disembodied spirits that the aims and object of human life are to attain the self-realisation, and not to satisfy the cheap curiosity of communicating with the departed spirits. Because by communicating with the spirits, good or bad, a man cannot make himself free from the bondage of nescience or *maya*. The Swami says : "Supposing all the phenomena of spiritism to be true and genuine, what have the spiritualists gained by these communications except satisfaction of their idle curiosity ? Have they learned any of the higher truths ? **Vain is the hope of those spiritualists who expect to know the absolute Truth through communications from the earth-bound spirits". The Swami further says that death teaches a great lesson to all the mortal beings, and teaches that the material body as well as the material world along with its pleasures and pains, are not permanent. The permanent thing in this world is the *Atman*, which is the background or support of the body and the world. So we should go beyond the attachment of the worldly pleasures, and should attain to the highest spiritual realization of the *Atman*. The Swami afterwards concludes : "We are just playing on the surface, but the time is bound to come for each individual soul when there will be an awakening of a desire to know the real truth".

This book has been edited with care of its new edition. Various footnotes, references and some of the appendices have been added by the editor. A Preface has been added to the book.

Ramakrishna Vedanta Math   SWAMI PRAJNANANANDA
19B, Raja Rajkrishna Street,
Kolkata-700 006

CHAPTER I

MODERN SCIENCE AND HIGHER SPIRITUALISM

During the last sixty years, spiritualism has made considerable progress, convincing many scientific minds who have been earnestly seeking for the truth of man's survival after death. The experimental spiritualism began in America in 1870. In the following year, Sir William Crookes, a scientist of great reputation and a man of extraordinary genius, began his investigations with the aid of the medium, Mrs. Florence Cooke. It will be needless to go into the details of Sir Crookes' experiments which lasted for three years with that celebrated medium. During this period, he took all precautions against the possible fraud or trickery imaginable, and he employed the scientific methods of observation and experiments with delicate instruments. The seances were held in his own house with honest friends who were equally eager to discover whether there was any truth in the spirit phenomena. Many Americans became familiar with the name of Katie King, the spirit-control of Mrs. Florence Cook. She materialized herself, her pulsations were recorded, her heart-beating was heard and was photographed, and she distributed the locks of her materialized hair to those who were present there. We remembered that all these happened under strictly test conditions in his own rooms, where electric wires with bells were fixed on the walls so that the least little intrusion from outside could be instantly detected. Sir William Crookes was at first ridiculed by the scientific world, but he had the courage of his convictions which led him to publish the reports of his experiments, and he kept on experimenting ever since.

Sir W. Crookes was also aided by another celebrated medium, Mr. D. D. Home who was more powerful than Mrs. Florence Cook in withstanding antagonistic influences, and most of his seances were not in darkness, but in the bright light. For the scientific study of the phenomena of spiritualism, the Society for the Psychical Research was established in London in 1885, under the auspices of the eminent men of science in England. It is commonly known as S. P. R. The records of this Society have shown how marvellous were the scientific patience and conscientiousness of men like Edmund Gurney, Dr. F. W. H. Myers, Frank Podmore and their successors. Those who have read Myers' great work entitled *Human Personality and Its Survival after Bodily Death,* will realize the truth of this statement.

Other scientific thinkers like Alfred Russell Wallace, Robert Dale Owen, Prof. Aksakof, Richard Hodgeson, William James of Harvard, and Sir Oliver Lodge, the Principal of the University of Birmingham, England, have spared no pains to make the correct investigations under test conditions regarding the truth of the spirit manifestations. Well has it been said by Maurice Maeterlinck, referring to their laborious task :

> Not an incident is admitted that is not supported by unimpeachable testimony, by definite written records, and convincing corroboration ; in a word, it is hardly possible to contest the esstential veracity of the majority of them, unless we begin by making up our minds to deny any positive value to human evidence.[1]

We are all familiar with the fact that Prof. Myers, who was the President of S. P. R. for many years, promised his

---

[1] *Our Eternity,* pp. 82-83.

friends that he would come back after his bodily death in a decisive manner. He kept his promise, and a month after his death, he communicated with Sir Oliver Lodge through the noted medium Mrs. Thomson while she was entranced. Myers' identity was recognized by the first few words he spoke, and it was really he and no one else. He said that it was very difficult for him to convey his ideas through the mediums. He said : "They were translating as a school boy does his first line of Virgil". Referring to his present condition, Myers said that he groped his way as if through passages before he knew he was dead. He thought that he had lost his way in a strange town, and even when he saw the people who, he knew, were dead, he thought they were only visions.[2]

Dr. Hodgeson, who was the Secretary of the American branch of the S. P. R., of which William James was the Vice-President, promised to come back after his death, and a week after his departure, he came back and communicated by the automatic writing through Mrs. Piper, and William James was present at these sittings.

William James of Harvard, also in his turn, promised to come back after his death. He kept his promise by communicating with Mr. C. N. Jones, the President of the American Institute of Scientific Research, and formerly, Professor of Applied Mathematics in the University of Michigan. Mr. C. N. Jones gave the details of the communications in his article which was published in New York Papers.[3] The first communication was received on the evening of October 22nd, 1910. Five more communications followed one another and the last was on March 11th, 1911. In these, Prof. James tried his best to establish his personal identity, and Mr. Jones and others, who were present there, were all satisfied. Among other things which are interesting, Prof. James said :

---

[2]Ibid. p. 103.
[3]*Times*, Dec. 10th, 1911.

"I am thankful that there are some who are perfectly willing that I should come to them. I mean this kind man here, who is standing by my side, and who lets me use him—his body. He steps out and lets me use his body and I am thankful. I don't want to injure it or make it unfit for him in any way."

It is said that Prof. James shook hands with his friends. Sir Oliver Lodge, after making many scientific experiments with the help of Mrs. Piper and other mediums, is now convinced that there is survival of life after death. He said in his Presidential Address before the British Association, held in September, 1913 :

> "In justice to myself and to my co-workers, I must risk annoying my present hearers not only by leaving on record our conviction that occurrence now regarded as occult can be examined and reduced to order by the methods of science carefully and persistently applied, but also by going further and saying with the utmost brevity that already the facts so examined have convinced me that memory and affection are not limited to that association with matter by which alone they can manifest themselves here and now, and that personality persists beyond bodily death. The evidence, to my mind, goes to prove that the discarnate intelligence, under certain conditions, may interact with us on the material side, thus indirectly coming within our scientific ken."

The great English scientist Alfred R. Wallace also said :

> "No more evidence is needed to prove the spiritualism, for no accepted fact in science has a greater or stronger array of proof in its behalf."

Dr. Thomas Jay Hudson, author of the *Law of Psychic Phenomena,* said :

> "The man who denies spiritualism today is not entitled to be called a skeptic, he is simply ignorant."

Camille Flamarion, W. T. Stead, Prof. Hyslop and others have been equally convinced that the discarnate spirits can communicate with us. Thus we see that such great men of science, as I have mentioned, have already accepted the truth upon which the modern spiritualism is founded.

Although many of the professional mediums have been pitifully exposed as frauds, still there are genuine mediums and authentic spirit manifestations which cannot be explained by telepathy or any other theory than that of the communication of the discarnate spirits. On many occasions, the audience is deceived by the earth-bound spirits. The manifestations on the material plane, such as table-turning, rapping knocks of the spirit, etc. are ordinarily understood by spiritualism. But all such phenomena belong to the lower class of the spiritualism, or spiritism, as it is called by many. Spiritism can only satisfy our curiosity and does not explain any of our vital questions. But true spiritualism should be distinguished from that phase which is called spiritism. The higher spiritualism, therefore, is the name for that which starting from the belief in a life after death, reveals the nature of the soul and its relation to God. This higher spiritualism is at the root of all great religions of the world. The communications with so-called angels or messengers of God, or bright spirits, as they are called in India, have been the source of knowledge and inspiration of the Prophets and Seers of the Old and the New Testaments. From the time of Abraham, Jacob and Moses down to the time of Christ and his disciples, all Prophets and Seers saw the spirits, heard them speak, and followed their teachings. As is in the Christianity and the Judaism, so it is in other religions of the world. As the revelations came to the sincere and earnest souls of the past, so they have come even in this age.

Those, who have read the spirit-teachings which came through the mediumship of Stainton Moses will remember, how the higher spirits under the names of Doctor, Rector, Imperator, revealed their messages to help the mankind to bring them out of the dogmas, creeds and superstition of the existing churches.

Here we should remember that Stainton Moses was an orthodox Anglican clergyman of England. He was dogmatic and creed-bound, but still through him came the messages which were not only astounding to him, but to the Christian world at large.

CHAPTER II

DOES THE SOUL EXIST AFTER DEATH

One of the most poetical pieces of the *Upanishads*, I mean the *Katha*, which has been translated by Sir Edwin Arnold under the title of *The Secret of Death*, begins with this inquiry :

"There is this doubt ; when a man dies some say that he is gone for ever, that he does not exist, while others hold that he still lives ; which of those is true ?"[1]

Various answers have been given to this question, and metaphysics, philosophy, science, and religion have also been tried to solve this problem. At the same time, attempts have been made to suppress this question and to prevent the inquiry as to whether or not man exists after death. Hundreds of thinkers have brought forward all sorts of arguments to do away with the questions bearing upon this momentous subject.

From ancient times, there have been the atheistic and agnostic thinkers in India who denied the existence of the soul after the death of the body. They are known as the Charvakas. They believe that the body is the soul, and the soul does not exist outside of the body, and when the body dies, the soul is also dead and gone. They believe in nothing that cannot be perceived by the senses. Their motto is :

"As long as you live, do not fail to enjoy. Live comfortably and enjoy the pleasures of life. Do not

---

[1] येयं प्रेते विचिकित्सा मनुष्येऽस्तीत्येके नायमस्तीति चैके ।
एतद् विद्यामनुशिष्टस्त्वयाऽहं बराणामेष वरस्तृतीय: ॥

—कठ उपनिषद् १/१/२०

43

think of the future. Get all that you need and wish ; if you have not got money, then beg or borrow it, for when the body is burnt into ashes no one will have to be accountable for your deeds."[2]

Such Charvakas we find in almost every country. For instance, in the Old Testament we read, Solomon says :

"Go thy way, eat thy bread with joy, and drink thy wine with a merry heart, ** Live joyfully with the wife— whatsoever thy hand findeth to do, do it with thy might; for there is no work, nor device, nor knowledge, nor wisdom in the grave, whither thou goest." (*Ecclix.* 7, 9, 10)

The followers of such thinkers are spreading very rapidly, and their number is increasing every day. They are now known as the atheists, agnostics, materialists, etc. According to this class of thinkers, those who believe in the existence of the soul as separate from the body, or in a life after death, are ignorant and superstitious fools, while those who follow their ideas are the clever and intelligent beings. Most of them hold that there is no such thing as soul. No argument can convince them or change their views, because they will not admit the existence of anything which lies beyond the reach of their senses, or which cannot be perceived by the limited powers of the senses.[3] They have written volumes after volumes against the existence of the soul, and have tried to stop such useless questions of the mind, but, in spite of their efforts, have they succeeded in stopping that innate question : 'what remains after death' that rises spontaneously in almost every human heart ? No, they have not succeeded. The same question

---

[2] न स्वर्गो नापवर्गो वा नैवात्मा पारलौकिक: ।
नैव वर्णाश्रमादिनं क्रीयाश्च फलदायिका: ॥
*   *   *

[3] यावज्जीवेत् सुखम् जीवेत् ऋणं कृत्वा घृतं पिवेत् ।
भस्मीभूतस्य देहरय पुनरागमनं कुत: ॥

—सर्वदर्शनसंग्रह वृहस्पति

rises today as it arose thousands of years ago, but no one can stop it, because it is inseparably connected with our nature.

The same question was asked by the saints and the sinners, by the Prophets and the priests, by the kings and the beggars, amongst all nations in all climes. We are discussing the same question today, and it will be discussed in the future. We may forget it for the time being in the turmoil and struggles of our lives ; we may not ask it when we are deeply absorbed in comforts, luxuries and sense enjoyments, we may delude ourselves by various false argumentations. But the moment we encounter the sudden appearance of death, the moment we see that some one of our nearest and dearest ones is breathing his last, we stop for a while and ask within ourselves : What is this ? Where is he gone ? Does he still exist ? What has become of him ? Those dormant questions reappear in new forms and disturb our peace of mind. Then we begin to inquire about them again ; but at the very threshold of our inquiry, we find an adamantine wall which is almost impossible to break through. The weak intellects stop there and their feeble attempts to cross that wall produce no result. That wall is nothing but the belief that the body is the producer of the soul, and that the soul is the result of the physical form which we call the body. Those who can overcome this strong barrier, can understand whether or not the soul exists after death. The old crude way of inferring the existence of the soul after death and a future life for all men, women and children from the tradition of a single miraculous resurrection of a certain person, no longer appeals to our reason. The days of believing blindly in the authority of anyone's saying are gone by. We are no longer children, we want maturer reason, and we want to discuss that question more deeply. Those who believe in that miraculous resurrection will perhaps say that those who do not believe in it have no hope. But we no longer accept their statements. The time has come when we want to discuss the questions scientifically, psychologically, philosophically, metaphysically, and in all other possible ways.

Now let us see whether the explanation that body is the cause of the soul, is satisfactory or not. Taking it for granted that the soul, or the mass of intelligence[4], or whatever you may call it, is the outcome of the combinations of matter which make up the body, we ask : What is the cause of that body ? What force combines the matter in the form of the body ? What force is there which forms your body in one way and my body in another ? What is the cause of those distinctions ? The materialistic Charvakas will answer that this body was caused by another body of the parents. As the parents produce this body, so the body of the parents is the cause of this body. But that is not the true answer, for instead of explaining the cause of this body and this combination of matter, they show us another combination of matter, and the question remains the same. What is the cause of the combination of matter ? They answer, but they forward also another combination of matter. So, instead of answering the question and explaining the cause of the combination of matter, they say that this combination is the result of another combination, which ultimately leads to the fallacy of *regress ad infinitum*. The method of explaining the soul by the body is like the process of explaining the cause by the effect, which is putting the cart before the horse.

The modern physiologists, anatomists, pathologists, and a host of other materialistic and agnostic thinkers, however, hold that the body or the combination of matter, produces thought, intelligence, consciousness, mind or soul. They teach that thought, intelligence, or consciousness is nothing but a

---

[4] स यथा सैन्धवघनोऽनन्तरोऽवाह्य: कृत्स्नो रसघन एवै एवं वा अरेऽयमात्माऽनन्तरोऽवाह्य: कृत्स्न: प्रज्ञानघन एवैतेभ्यो भूतेभ्य: समुत्थाय तान्येवानुविनश्यति न प्रेत्य संज्ञाऽस्तीत्यरे ब्रवीमिति होवाच याज्ञव, ल्क्य: ।

—वृहदारण्यक उपनिषद् ४/५/१३

function of the brain. Moreover, they learn that every special form of thought is a result of the activity of a special portion of the brain. When we see things, or think of the seen objects, the optical convolutions of our brain are active. A certain portion of the tympanal lobes are active when we hear, and so on.

Those of the modern scientists who advocate the production of the thought by the brain, say that the mind is conterminous with the brain functions. If the brain functions stop, the mind, intelligence, consciousness and all the mental phenomena will instantly stop. The phenomena of the consciousness correspond to the element for the element, and to the operations of the special parts of the brain. They say that there is no such thing as soul ; consequently, there can be no question regarding its existence after death. They deny the existence of the soul altogether. The sensations decay, when the organic conditions change and stop, when the machinery stops. The brain brings into existence the material of consciousness of which our minds consist. Some explain the process by which thought is produced by the brain, by saying that the peculiar structure of the brain is destined to produce thought and consciousness, just as the stomach is destined to perform the function of digestion and the liver to secrete bile. As the materials of food, after falling into the stomach, change and assume new qualities, so the impressions of the brain are metamorphosed into ideas, thought, emotion, will, expressions of the face, speech, disposition, etc. through nerves. Thus thought or soul is the secretion of the brain, and when the brain is gone, the soul cannot exist. Here impressions are compared to food, as if the impressions were the gross forms of matter, or as if they could exist apart from a perceiving mind. Buchner, one of the most famous materialists, says :

> 'Thinking must be regarded as a special mode of general natural motion.'

J. Luys says :

> 'As one sees a metallic rod, placed in a glowing
> furnace, gradually heats itself and passes successively
> from the shades of bright red to dark red, to white and
> develops as its temperature rises, heat and light, so the
> living sensitive cells, in presence of the incitations that
> solicit them, exalt themselves progressively as to their
> most interior sensibility.'

Percival Lowell says :

> 'When we have, as we say, an idea, what happens
> inside of us is probably like this : the neural current of
> molecular change passes up the nerves, and through the
> ganglia reaches at last the cortical cells**. When it
> reaches the cortical cells, it finds a set of molecules
> which are not so accustomed to this special change. The
> current encounters resistance, and in overcoming this
> resistance, it causes the cells to glow. This white-
> heating of the cells we call consciousness.
> Consciousness, in short, is probably nerve-glow.'

Thus the Western materialists, who believe that the physical
forces are metamorphosed into ideas, thoughts and sensations,
describe the process by which this change takes place. Herbert
Spencer, being an agnostic, advocates the metamorphosis of
the physical forces into the states of consciousness, but he
does not describe the process. He leaves it as a mystery which
is impossible to fathom. That is, he does not know how this
metamorphosis takes place, but he is sure it does take place.
Spencer, however, identifies the soul with the brain, and
compares it to the piano. He says :

> 'Ideas are like the successive chords and cadences
> brought out, which successively die as the other ones
> are sounded, and it would be as proper to say that these
> passing chords and cadences thereafter exist in the

piano, as it is proper to say that passing ideas thereafter exist in the brain (soul).[5]

But here Mr. Spencer forgets that the piano needs a performer to produce musical sounds. Music is never brought out by the piano itself, if it does not exist in the mind of the performer. So, his analogy is imperfect and incomplete. It would have been complete if he supposed that the individual soul or mind is detached from the brain, and plays upon its nervous centres and brain cells, as a performer plays upon the keys of a piano.

Another materialistic thinker, Professor W. K. Clifford, who believes in the combination theory, says :

'Consciousness is a complex thing made up of elements, a stream of feelings. The action of the brain is also a complex thing made up of elements, a stream of nerve message. For every feeling in consciousness, there is at the same time a nerve message of the brain. Consciousness is not a simple thing, but complex ; it is the combination of feelings into a stream. Inexorable facts connect our consciousness with this body that we know ; and that not merely as a whole, but the parts of it are connected severally with parts of our brain action. If there is any similar connection with a spiritual body, it only follows that the spiritual body must die at the same time with the natural one.'

Thus the materialistic thinkers, who do not believe in a soul as separate from the brain, or independent of the physical body, try to deduce mind and intelligence from matter, or from the combinations of matter, either by applying the theory of production or the theory of combination.

In India, similar theories were advanced by the Charvakas who did not believe in the existence of a soul as separate from the gross body.[6] The Buddhists maintained that the body

---

[5] Vide *Principles of Psychology,* VII, p. 485.
[6] Vide Notes.

is the cause of the mind and intelligence, that consciousness is the result of the combination of insentient matter and unintelligent forces of physical nature. They used the illustration of the inebriating power of liquor arising from a chemical combination of certain ingredients.

But the Vedanta philosophers refuted both these materialistic theories by pointing out the fallacy of their principal arguments. Vedanta says that one half of the universe is matter or object, and the other half is mind or soul.[7] It is impossible to deduce the one from the other. In the first place, if we analyse our knowledge of matter and force, we find that we cannot know matter by itself, and also cannot know force by itself ; that what we know is nothing but a mental change. Knowledge of matter is nothing but the knowledge of that change of the mind of which we are conscious. When we say that matter exists, we are conscious of a peculiar mental change beyond which we cannot know. The mind cannot go beyond itself. Even our knowledge that the soul, or the mind, is a function of the brain presupposes the existence of another mind or knower. Whenever we say that consciousness or soul is the result of the combination of matter, that statement also requires another mind to be conscious of that idea. John Stuart Mill was right in saying that after dissecting a human brain when one does not find there any trace of the soul or mind, and denies its existence, or asserts that mind or soul is the function of the brain, he forgets that such knowledge necessarily implies the existence of his mind or soul. As the knowledge of matter, or brain, or any other kind of knowledge, depends upon the self-consciousness, it will be absurd to deny the priority of that which is the basis of consciousness, of intelligence, and of all knowledge, and with the help of which one can know the existence of matter or its combinations. G. J. Romanes says :

---

[7] Cf. Swami Abhedananda : Self-knowledge, pp. 17-18.

'We cannot think any of the facts of external nature without pre-supposing the existence of a mind which thinks them, and therefore, so far at least as we are concerned, mind is necessarily prior to everything else. It is for us the only mode of existence which is real in its own right and to it, as to a standard, all other modes of existence which may be inferred, must be referred. Therefore, if we say that mind is a function of motion, we are only saying in somewhat confused terminology that mind is a function of itself. Such then, I take to be a general refutation of materialism.'[8]

If it be a scientific truth that motion produces nothing but motion, as it has been established by modern science, how can we maintain that the molecular motion of the brain-cells produces consciousness or intelligence, which is not the same as motion, but is a knower of motion ? Therefore Vedanta philosophy teaches that the source of consciousness cannot be found in matter, but stands independent of it. What we call matter is only the medium through which consciousness manifests itself.

Dr. Schiller, an eminent thinker of the West, holding similar opinion, says :

'Matter is not that which produces consciousness, but that which limits it and confines its intensity within certain limits ; material organisation does not construct consciousness out of arrangements of atoms, but contracts its manifestation within the sphere which it permits.'

There are other agnostic thinkers who say :

'The conception of a soul as a substantive thing is a mere figment of imagination.'

---

[8] Vide Romanes : *Mind and Motion and Monism*, p. 21.

Kant says :

> 'There is no means whatever by which we can learn
> anything respecting the constitution of the soul so far as
> regards the possibility of its separate existence.'

David Hume, like some of the Buddhist philosophers, believes
that the human soul is nothing but a bundle of impressions
and ideas. Hume says :

> 'When I enter most intimately into what I call myself,
> I always stumble on some particular perception or other
> of heat or cold, light or shade, love or hatred, pain or
> pleasure. When my perceptions are removed for any
> time, as by sound sleep, so long I am insensible of
> myself and may be truly said not to exist. And were all
> my perceptions removed by death and I could neither
> think, nor feel, nor see, nor love, nor hate, after the
> dissolution of my body, I should be entirely annihilated ;
> nor do I conceive what is further requisite to make me
> a perfect non-entity.'

So, according to Hume, our souls die every night when we
sleep soundly. I think that very few of us will be ready to
accept such an explanation of the nature of the human soul.

Those, who depend on sense perceptions only, try to see
the soul by dissecting the brain, but when the senses do not
reveal it, they deny its existence. They may just as well try to
find the soul in the heart or stomach, as the ancient seekers
of the soul did. If we examine properly, we shall be able to
see logical fallacies and inconsistencies in all the materialistic
and agnostic arguments which support the theory that soul is
the result of the body, or of the combination of matter, or else
that the soul does not exist at all. From ancient times, such
materialistic conclusions have been repeatedly arrived at by
thinkers of different countries. But do our minds remain
satisfied with such ideas, and do we stop from asking again
and again : is there any life after death ? If we hear millions
of times 'there is no soul', still we cannot be entirely convinced

that we shall cease to exist after death ; we cannot believe that our individuality will be lost forever. Such solutions do not appeal to our reason. They do not satisfy our minds, nor do they bring any consolation to our souls. These statements are but that which exists eternally. If existence be a truth today, it must be true eternally.

If we deny the existence of a soul as independent of the body, we cannot explain many facts which often occur during our lifetime, nor the genuine phenomena described in the reports of the Psychical Research Society of Europe and America. We cannot ignore the facts of the agnostics who have seen their 'doubles' outside of themselves when alone in their rooms reposing on a couch or an easy chair. There are instances of such doubles talking, walking, or doing various other things. How are these facts to be explained ? There are many descriptions of the manifestation of the doubles of the Yogis in India. Various attempts have been made to explain such events by asserting that they are either optical delusions, or hallucinations of the brain. But we cannot say that they are optical delusions or hallucinations, if they can stand the test of verification. There are many properly verified instances of the appearance of the double. Suppose at night before retiring, one is sitting alone in his room, after locking the door from inside, and suppose his mind is greatly disturbed with some important business questions or some mathematical problems. He suddenly sees another exactly like himself, sitting at his desk with a pen in his hand, writing something on a piece of paper, and, after examination he finds that it is an answer to his question or the correct solution of the problem which has puzzled him for many days. What explanation will you offer ? What kind of hallucination is this ? What a varification stronger and more satisfactory than this do you want to have ? Such an occurrence cannot be explained by clairvoyance or telepathy. Some may say it is a false story, but mere assertion does not disprove the facts. Facts are facts whether we admit or deny them, whether our current theory can explain them or not. Clairvoyance, telepathy, and thought transference have failed to explain these cases. Such facts can only be explained by the theory of existence of the soul, as separable from the body. According to science, that theory is true, which can explain most facts, and we should accept it until a better theory or a better explanation comes. Those who believe in the theory of production, or that of combination, will shut their eyes to such facts. But those who believe in the transmission theory or, in other words, those who hold that the brain of the human body is the instrument through which the soul manifests its powers, will find no difficulty in explaining all the genuine phenomena connected with the 'double'. The transmission theory also puts itself in touch with a whole class of experiences that are with difficulty explained by the production theory.

Again there are authentic instances of persons appearing to their friends immediately after death.[9] There are many such instances in India, in Europe, and in every country. Such instances may occur where the persons appearing to friends ask to have their children taken care of, or bring some message. One need not go to the spiritualistic seances to experience these things. Many such experiences have come to persons in private life and in their own homes, and they have been well verified. In spiritualistic seances, ninety-nine cases, out of one hundred of spirit manifestations, are mixed with fraud, and many professional mediums have been most pitifully exposed both here and abroad. The motive power in the professional mediums is to make money, or to earn a living.

---

[9] '*** it might be possible for this departing soul to manifest itself to its friends, either in the immediate vicinity, or even at a distance, ** manifestations of the departing spirit, at the moment of death, are by no means uncommon, but are, on the contrary, very numerous'.—Carrington & Meader : *Death, Its Causes and Phenomena*, p. 382. Vide C : Flammarion : *The Unknown*, pp. 100, 108, 169-172. Cf : also the argument put forward against the atheistic theory denying the existence of soul apart from the body and after death in the *Pali Paysai Suttanta, Digha-Nikaya*, Vol. II.

In India, the Hindus do not trust in the professional mediums. On the contrary, they say it is wicked to hold public seances for money. It is more wicked to earn a living at the expense of the poor spirits. Why do you try to earn your living by making the poor spirits appear to you ? Those persons who do this are considered as the ordinary *fakirs*. Although many mediums have been exposed and many spirit manifestations have been proved to be like magic or jugglery, still those fraudulent cases cannot be the reason for denying the existence of the soul as apart from the body, or in a life after death. Now the question may arise : If the soul exists after death, does it retain its individuality ? The Vedanta philosophy says, yes, it does. The souls of the earth-bound spirits retain their personality too. Some of the Western writers who have known very little of Hindu philosophy, say that the highest ideal of the Hindu religion is the annihilation of the soul. These childish statements prove their ignorance and prejudice. We hear such things from the writers who consider themselves as great scholars after reading the descriptions of the Hindu religion given by the Christian missionaries, who do not see good in any other religion except their own, and who write simply to serve their own purposes. In the voluminous writings of the Hindus, however, you will never find a single sentence which teaches that the soul will be destroyed after death. On the contrary, you will read that the soul is eternal, immortal, deathless, and birthless. In the *Bhagavad Gita*, it is said :

> 'The soul of man is indestructible ; it cannot be pierced by sword ; fire cannot burn it ; air cannot dry it ; water cannot moisten it.'[10]

---

[10] नैनं छिन्दन्ति शस्त्राणि नैनं दहति पावकः ।
न चैनं क्लेदयन्त्यापो न शोषयति मारुतः ॥
अच्छेद्योऽयमदाह्योऽयमक्लेद्योऽशोष्य एव च ।
नित्यः सर्वगतः स्थाणुरचलोऽयं सनातनः ॥

—भगवद्गीता २/२३-२४

'If the slayer thinks that he has slain, or if the slain thinks that he is slain, both of them know not that the soul can neither slay nor be slain.'[11]

Ralph Waldo Emerson, after reading the *Bhagavad Gita*, rendered this passage in verse in his poem entitled *Brahm* :

> *If the red slayer thinks he slays,*
>   *Or if the slain thinks he is slain,*
> *They know not well the subtle ways*
>   *I keep, and pass, and turn again.*[12]

As regards the retaining of the individuality, Vedanta says that each soul after death takes with it all the experiences, impressions and ideas which it gained on earth. It takes its mind, intelligence, intellect, and powers of the senses and enjoys or reaps the fruits of its own thoughts and deeds.

If you read the funeral service of the Hindus, you will find that after the death of a person the relatives do good in the name of the departed, believing that good thoughts, prayers and good works, done in their names, will help the departed spirits. The Hindus also believe that, if we think of them constantly and invoke them asking to remain with us for our own gratification without thinking of their good, we force them to remain confined to that particular personality which was connected with their earthly bodies they left behind them. Personality is always connected with the material body. At every birth of the body, we have a certain personality according to the environments, and if we keep one soul confined in one personality or one set of environments, there will be no progress of the soul on the higher planes. Therefore it is better not to drag our departed friends to our plane of existence, but to keep helping them by sending good thoughts to them.

---

[11] य एनं वेत्ति हन्तारं यश्चैनं मन्यते हतम् ।
उभौ तौ न विजानीतो नायं हन्ति न हन्यते ॥

—भगवद्गीता २/१९

[12] Vide Notes.

The most ancient writers of the Vedic ages show that they believed in the spirit world of the *Pitars* or fathers, where the departed souls go after death.[13] The king or ruler of this place is called Yama. He was the first of the mortals to enter that world of death, and he became the ruler of those who came later.

The Hindus believe in a heaven, but not in any hell. Again the Hindu heaven is different from that of the Christian or of the Mohammedan. The Hindus believe that heaven is a realm where the departed souls go to reap the pleasant effects of their good and virtuous actions, that they remain there for sometime until the results of their good works are completely reaped, then after that period, they will return to this phenomenal world again.[14] The Christians, Mohammedans, and Zoroastrians believe in a heaven of all kinds of sense enjoyments where pleasures will come incessantly without troubles or any sort of pain. This, according to the Hindus, is not a desirable state. The Hindus say that all these celestial enjoyments are phenomenal and transitory. Supposing a spirit remains in heaven and enjoy for a million years or for one cycle, still, compared to an eternity, this is a very short time. So they say that after enjoying the results of the good works in those realms, one is bound to be born again, either here, or in some other planet according to one's tendencies and capacities. Therefore in the *Bhagavad Gita*, it is said :

'All the different worlds of spirits beginning with the highest heavens are state from where one must return.'[15]

---

[13] प्रेहि प्रेहि पथिभि: पूर्व्येभि-र्यत्रा न: पूर्वे पितर: परेयु: ।
    *   *   *
सं गच्छस्व पितृभि: सं यमेनेष्टापूर्तेन परमे व्योमन् ।

—ऋग्वेद १०/१४/७, ८

[14] ते तं भुक्त्वा स्वर्गलोकं विशालं क्षीणे पुण्ये मर्त्यलोकं विशन्ति ।
एवं त्रयीधर्ममनुप्रपन्ना गतागतं कामकामा लभन्ते ॥

—भगवद्गीता ९/२१

[15] आब्रह्मभुवनाल्लोका: पुनरावर्तिनोऽर्जुन ।
मामुपेत्य तु कौन्तेय पुनर्जन्म न विद्यते ॥

—भगवद्गीता ८/१६

Because they are within that realm of phenomena and are changeable. But he who attains to the realization of the absolute Truth, transcends all phenomena and laws which govern them.

The ancient Persians believed that the soul would rise three days after death and would go either to the heaven, or to the hell according to its thought, speech and work. This Persian idea of heaven was afterwards adopted by the Jews and the Christians. The ancient Hebrews did not trouble themselves about the life after death. They believed that God breathed life into man's nostrils, and that the breath which came from Jehovah, would go back to Him, and that the life-breath of all creatures would return to the source whence it came. That which happens to man also happens to lower animals. This life-breath was sometimes called the *Nephesh, the Ruach,* or the *Neshama.*

The ancient Egyptians believed in a 'double' which was like a shadow of the body and which remained as long as the body remained. This gave rise to the idea of mummifying the bodies of the dead. If the body was injured in any part, the double or the soul was likewise injured. So to keep the soul intact, they preserved the bodies.

The ancient Chaldeans also believed in a 'double' which would be annihiliated if the body were destroyed. They expected a resurrection of the corpse.[16] Many of the Christians have a similar idea or belief. This idea gave rise to the custom of embalming and burying the dead. Some of the Christians still believe that the body will rise after death. Others do not believe in the resurrection of the body. They believe that the soul will remain and exist through eternity although it had a beginning. The Christian idea regarding the beginning of the soul is that, at the time of birth, each soul is newly created by the almighty God. But the Hindus say that which has a

---

[16] Vide Notes.

beginning cannot live through all eternity, and it must have an end. The Hindus do not believe that the soul is created by God, or by any other supernatural being. It is eternal by its nature. It is birthless, and it cannot die. The Hindus do not mean destruction or annihilation by death.[17] They mean by it a change of the body, or the form. This kind of death is a constant attendant of Life. The phenomenal life is impossible without death, or change of forms. In fact, we are dying every day. Every seventh year the entire body changes along with its every particle and renewed atom.

Prof. Huxley says :

'Physiology writes over the portals of life, *Debmur morti nos nostraqué*, with a profounder meaning than the Roman poet ascribed to the melancholy line. And in whatever guise it takes refuge, whether fungus or oak, worm or man, the living protoplasm not only ultimately dies and is resolved into its mineral and lifeless constituents, but is always dying, and, strange as the paradox may sound, could not live unless it died.'

Although every particle of the body changes, we still continue to exist. Our continuity is not broken from babyhood to old age—we retain the same sense of 'I' and personal identity. This continuity of the conscious agent or 'I' cannot be explained by any physical or chemical law. According to the Vedanta philosophy, thought or feeling or intelligence can never be produced by any mechanical or molecular motion. 'Motion produces motion and nothing else', says modern science. As such, how can the motion of the atoms of the body produce consciousness ? That must be due to some lighter power or force. This force is ordinarily called the soul. The soul is not subject to the atomic of molecular changes in

---

[17] न जायते म्रियते वा कदाचिन्नायं भूत्वाऽभविता वा ना भूयः ।
अजो नित्यः शाश्वतोऽयं पुराणो न हन्यते हन्यमाने शरीरे ॥
—भगवद्गीता २/२०; कठ उपनिषद् १/२/१८

the body. It is rather the cause of them. It is beyond all changes, and consequently, is beyond death. It is the basis of continuity of the conscious state and also of the sense of identity in the individual. As we survive and retain our individuality after each seven years of change and renewal, so we will live as individual souls after the final dissolution of the forms of our bodies. In the *Bhagavad Gita* it is said :

> 'As during our lifetime we survive the death of the baby body, the young body, and the mature body successively and retain our individuality, so after the death of the old body we shall survive, live, retain our individuality and continue to exist through eternity.'[18]

---

[18] देहिनोऽस्मिन् यथा देहे कौमारं यौवनं जरा।
तथा देहान्तरप्राप्तिर्धीरस्तत्र न मुह्यति॥

—भगवद्गीता २/१३

CHAPTER III

THE SCIENTIFIC VIEW OF DEATH

In this age of commercialism and materialism, very few people think about death. They are rather afraid of it. They do not care to think what will happen after death. They would rather live in this world, enjoy all the pleasures of life, make the best use of everything, make a will, and insure their life, or save a little money to pay the funeral expenses and go on living. Out of the two thousand millions of people who inhabit this little planet earth, forty millions of the human bodies are disposed of every year, and a million tons of the human flesh, bones, and blood are allowed to return to their elementary state. During the last war in Europe[1], many millions of people were killed and were destroyed. Some of them were blown into atoms. But we do not think of that horrible scene. We have almost forgotten it. So we do not think for a moment that we shall die. We are not living and doing the same things as we did before. Our interest is not in solving the problem of death, although it is the greatest mystery in the world. It is as mysterious as the coming of life on this plane. But still we do not think much about it. Even the Christian churches do not take such a lively interest in this problem of death today, as they did in the last century. They would rather busy themselves with questions of social, educational and especially political problems of the day. The medicine-men of this age do not solve the problem of death, although hundreds are dying in their hands every year. They gather all the things that they can, and their ideal is to enjoy

---

[1] World War I.

the pleasures of life, and also to make the best of their opportunity.

In the *Mahabharata,* the most ancient epic of the Hindus, we read a prize question that was asked to different great men of ancient times. 'What is the most wonderful thing in the world ?' Various answers were given, but they were not satisfactory. The answer which Yudhishthira gave was accepted, and his answer was this : 'Every day, and day after day, animals and human beings are passing out of life, but we do not think of death ; We think that we shall never die. What can be more wonderful than this?'[2] This answer was given nearly thirty-five centuries ago, and the same truth prevails today. We do not think of death, although we see every day the dead bodies carried to the grave right under our eyes.

The mystery of death is not solved by mythological beliefs of the ancient peoples, which have been handed down to us through generations. The scriptures of the Jews, the Christians, the Parsees, and the Mohammedans do not explain what death is. But in some of these scriptures, we find that God commanded the first man to do certain things and not to eat the fruit of the tree of knowledge, but when the first man did eat the fruit of the tree of knowledge of good and evil, the Lord cursed him, and His curse brought death in this world. We read in the Genesis, the Lord commanded :

'Of every tree of the garden thou mayest freely eat : But of the tree of the knowledge of good and evil, thou shall not eat of it, for in the day that thou eatest thereof thou shalt surely die.'[3]

Of course, Adam did not die in the day he was tempted and he ate the fruit thereof ; but he reaped the consequences afterwards and died later. This passage shows that at first God

---

[2] अहन्याहनि भूतानि गच्छन्ति यমমन्दिरम् ।
शेषास्थिरत्वमिच्छन्ति किमाश्चर्यमतःपरम् ॥   —महाभारतम्
[3] Vide *Chapter II*, 16 and 17.

did not intend that man should die, but the death came to the world through the evil influence of Satan, the devil. It was Satan who brought death into this world. In fact, the curse was the cause, but the curse was brought about by the evil influence of the devil. Those who believe in this, that death was caused or brought about by Satan, do not care to think further about it. They leave this question as settled, and naturally they do other things, and do not try to solve the problem. They think that if it be the curse of God, it is an inevitable end of life, and let us be satisfied with it.

Scientific researches towards tracing the causes of death have brought out many truths and laws which were unknown to the writers of the Genesis and other scriptures of different nations. Orthodox science or materialistic science, as it is known to us, which denies the existence of the soul as an entity and also denies the existence of mind or life or intelligence as distinct from the results of matter, governed by physical forces and chemical actions, says that death is nothing but the cessation of life and it is an inevitable end which all being come to. The scientist do not explain it elaborately, because they do not know much about it. Still they try to explain that when the vital parts of the body wear out in this machine, then naturally the whole of the machine must stop. The vital parts are regarded as the heart, the lungs, and the brain. When any of these vital centres is worn out or injured by disease or accident, then naturally the whole machinery of the body stops.

But here a question may arise : 'Does the death of the conscious life imply death of the life of the organs ?' Or, in other words, when a person is dead, does it mean that the organs are dead also ? That is a very difficult question to answer. On the contrary, science tells us that the organs do not die immediately after the death of the body or the conscious life. For instance, if a chicken's head be cut off and its heart taken out and watched, it will continue to live for a long time after the death of the chicken. In the Rockfeller Institute, there is a heart of a chicken that has been kept for eight years, and it is still going on and doing normal action. That shows that the organs have their independent life which may continue to live even after the conscious life of the individual is dead. In the same manner, it can be shown that the cells and the tissues have their own life. They do not die, but they live for a long time after the death of the conscious life. Modern science tells us that there are two kinds of death : one is the death of the conscious life, and the other is the death of the organic and cellular life which is called the 'somatic life'. But one does not depend upon the other. In fact, the life continues to exist, depending upon the natural process of the vital force which is known as the life-force. But this materialistic science does not explain how it is that the organs, the cells, and the tissues continue to live, because it denies the existence of a vital energy, or a vital force, as distinct from all other known forces of nature. On the other hand, it considers that this vital force is a result of the chemical actions of the atoms and molecules of the organism, and, therefore, it cannot explain any further.

Professor Charles Minot of the Harvard Medical School writes in his book, *Old Age, Growth and Death* :

'Differentiation leads, as its inevitable conclusion, to death. Death is the price we are compelled to pay for our organization, and also for the differentiation which exists in us. Death of the whole comes, as we now know, whenever some essential part of the body gives way. Sometimes one, sometimes another, perhaps the brain, perhaps the heart, perhaps one of the other internal organs may be the first, in which the change of cytomorphosis goes so far that it can no longer perform its share of work, and failing, brings about the failure of the whole'.

This is the scientific view of death. It leaves death with its mystery and all its sacredness. We are not in the least able at the present time to say what life is, and still less, perhaps, what death is.

Thus by studying materialistic science, we do not gain a very clear idea of what death really means. But science goes on trying to trace the causes of death, and describes the signs of death. Science tells us that the actual signs of death are very difficult to find. The so-called popular signs of death like the stoppage of the heart-beat and pulse or respiration are not the actual signs of death, because there have been hundreds of cases where the heart-beat is stopped and the respiration is stopped and yet after sometime they are revived. The heart-beat might stop for many hours, even for days, and then it can be revived. The respiration might stop for a long time, but it can be restored. Science has recorded many cases of suspended animation where the respiration or the heart-beat is stopped for forty-eight hours in the least. But there have been other cases where men have been buried alive in a hermetically sealed box for forty days and afterwards they were taken out and revived. They lived, married, and enjoyed all the blessings of life afterwards. It is very difficult to say which would be the proper or final sign of death. Science tells us that the decomposition and putrefaction are the only final signs of death and nothing else, and that shows that people might be buried prematurely. There have been many cases of premature burial recorded in the medical journals of the world every year. And for that reason, some of the countries in Europe have passed a law that no one should be buried immediately after death until decomposition sets in. Because it is a very serious thing to bury the living beings. There have been cases of many prematurely killed by being put into the coffin and getting buried under the ground before their actual death.

As premature burial is objectionable, so premature embalming too is objectionable. The embalmers have killed many before they really died. They might have been revived and might have lived for a long time. Because it is a proved fact today that when the person is considered as dead, he might be in a trance, or in a state of catalepsy, or in a state of ecstasy.

Trance, catalepsy and ecstasy are the conditions which resemble death. The outward signs are similar. But what happens to the soul after trance or ecstasy ? Science does not know, because it denies the existence of a soul other than the mind. A person might go into a state of trance and remain in the state for hours. There are persons who can stop the heart-beat by their will. I know a Hindu Yogi who came to America a few years ago and who, in New York, went through all the medical tests to prove that he could stop his heart-beat at his will. The medical practitioners were all dumbfounded, and questioned how he could do it. It is possible, because it obeys the will of the individual, and the individual will commands and directs the organic functions. But materialistic science cannot explain how it is possible through the known laws that are accepted by these scientific thinkers.

The old Babylonian method of emblaming the body[4] and burning the dead, which has been handed down to us from pre-Christian era and which is practised today in all the civilized countries, is based upon the superstitious belief that the body will eventually rise and go to heaven. But after the decomposition sets in and the body is gone, what will rise ? Science shows that it is an absolute impossibility for the body to rise, or to go to heaven. Still some people cling to that old belief and think that their friends and relatives will eventually rise from the graves and go to heavens with their physical bodies. But the best method of disposing of the dead body is the method of cremation, because it is sanitary. It is the best method from the standpoint of health as well as from the

[4] Vide Notes.

standpoint of safety for the living beings. Why should we have so many dead bodies going through the process of decomposition around us ? It is better to get rid of them and let them go to their elementary conditions. This cremation has been practised in India from very ancient times. In the Vedas, we find that cremation was regarded as the best method.[5] But among other nations, burial or mummification was regarded as the best method. As I have already said, their idea was to keep the body intact for a long time, because the soul will eventually come back to the body. The Egyptians also had that kind of belief. They believed that if the physical body were kept intact and not mutilated, then the soul would eventually come back to dwell in that body, whereas if any part of the physical body was mutilated, that part of the 'double' (soul) would also be mutilated. They believed in a 'double',—a double exactly of the same shape and same form as the physical body. In India, we find that the Hindus have a belief in the existence of a double, but it was not dependent upon the gross physical body. They have a philosophy altogether different from that of the Egyptians and other nations of ancient times. They believe that this double might have the body and continue to live even when this gross physical body is destroyed through the process of cremation which they even now regard as the most sanitary method of disposing of the dead body.

There is another class of scientific thinkers who are a little more advanced than the orthodox scientists. They hold that the mind is a factor in cases of disease and death. They do not deny the existence of the mind, or the intelligence, or the consciousness, nor do they believe that the mind, intelligence, and consciousness are the results of the chemical actions of the atoms and the molecules of the organism. On the contrary, they hold the belief that the source of

---

[5] Vide Notes.

consciousness and mind are indestructible. So is life. Life is also indestructible. They regard that the life-force (*prana*) is not the result of the chemical actions. It is not the same as electricity or any other force that is known to orthodox science, but it is distinct and separate. They give the cases where mind can bring death through extreme emotions. Some of the functions of the mind which we call passions will create disease and death.

Dr. John Hunter, a noted psychologist, was a genius of extraordinary nature. He was a scientist, but he believed in the power of the mind, and yet he had very little control over his passions. He could not control anger. Once he had extreme anger as a result of a slight provocation, and through the extreme anger, he instantly fell dead. There is a historical record that anger kills the person instantly. The French physician, Tourtelle, witnessed two women who died of extreme anger. Extreme anger will produce stoppage of the heart-action, and poison the whole system. As extreme anger will kill persons, a slight expression of anger, or anger of a milder form, will also bring disease of the worst kind. In fact, when a mother nurses the baby while she is in that state of anger, she feeds the baby with poison, and that poison works and creates all kinds of trouble in the baby's system. It is a scientific fact today.

As anger is dangerous and is a destructive force that creates a havoc in the system, so is fear. Now, the ordinary expression that we are frightened to death has some meaning. Extreme fear will bring death, will stop the heart-action, and will stop the lungs and simultaneously other organs too. Then there are passions, hatred and grief. Grief will produce a havoc in the system. These are all the recorded facts. When there have been cases of disease and death through extreme hatred and grief, how can we deny the power of the mind ? If the mind and the mental states can produce such effects upon the physical body and bring premature death, how can we deny the existence of mind as the most powerful thing that we possess ? Therefore, the scientists, who are advanced thinkers and not bigoted like the orthodox materialists, regard mind as the most wonderful force that is working through this physical body.

There are cases of counterfeits of death, even in the lower animals. There are some of the insects which would feign death. The fox, when he is pursued by an enemy and does not know how to escape, lies flat on the ground, feigns death and remains in that state for some time. There are other animals which would even become stiff and the *rigor mortis* of death will be perceptible in the physical body of the animal. It can be produced by the mind. This counterfeit of death may be caused by different things, such as intoxication, apoplexy, heart-trouble, and so on. Thus it shows that mind can produce these things under those conditions like the sign of death, and, therefore, those advanced thinkers and scientists consider that death can be brought about by the power of the mind. They regard that this ordinary state which we call death, is caused by that self-conscious living force which is working through the organs, and when that self-conscious living force is detached, it produces death. In fact, the self-conscious living soul has vital energy or life-force (*prāṇa*) or mind with it. The mind is inseparable from the life-force or vital energy. But mind cannot work unless it has an instrument. Therefore it manufactures the instruments of the physical body. It draws from the surrounding environments like atoms, molecules or particles of matter, and charges them with the life-force, or the vibrations of the *prana*, and when the vibrations of life-force are weak and are not up to the standard of the conditions of life, then the living soul or the self-conscious mind tries to raise those vibrations of the cellular life up to the standard by making all efforts, and if it fails to raise the standard of the vibration of the cells and the tissues, then there is the death of the whole. Then the whole machinery dies.

Thus we see that there are two principal factors in the body : the one is the mind and the other is the vibration of the *prana*, or the vibratory state of the cells and tissues of the body. But the vibratory state of the cells and the tissues is governed by the mind. In fact, the mind is the creator, the manipulator and the organizer. It is the director of all the organic functions. The organs might go on vibrating in their own way, but that would not be the standard of life. There must be co-ordination. The heart-action must correspond in a certain way with the action of the lungs, and all the intricate mechanism must be adjusted in such a way that one helps the other. Otherwise, there would be no life. If one screw is loose anywhere, the screw must be tightened, otherwise the machine would not work. Now, who tightens this screw? It is the individual self-conscious life-force which is called, in ordinary terms, the living soul. The living soul means the self-conscious individualized life-force with the sense of '*I*', and that sense of '*I*' holds them together. This sense of '*I*' holds all together, unifies them, and makes the separate parts vibrate and produce a perfect harmony. That harmony is life. As in an orchestra, there might be a hundred instruments, and if each instrument goes on playing in its own way without following the direction of its conductor, it will produce no harmony ; similarly, if the organs of the body go on beating in their own way, without producing any harmony, without having any co-ordination, without being directed by their-conductor, then it is useless. Who is the conductor of the organs ? Who is the director ? The orthodox science does not see that director, but advanced science tells us that there is a director and this director has the absolute control over the whole organism. He is the living soul. At the time of death, he disconnects himself from the organs and leaves the body.

In case of trance, catalepsy and ecstasy, this living soul leaves the body, but the connection is not entirely cut off. There still remains some kind of connection. It is like the umbilical cord of a newborn babe which holds its entity as connected with the physical body. Therefore the physical body can be revived. But when the connection is entirely cut off, the body cannot be revived. Then it is called death. That is the difference. This difference very few people understand.

But this living soul which goes out of the body at the time of death, can be photographed. The most delicate and sensitive instruments have been used to weigh the body just before death and immediately after death, and making all allowances for the gases that escape, it has been found that the substance which passes out of the body at the time of death, has a definite weight of about half an ounce or three-quarters of an ounce.

This fine substance that emanates from the body at the time of death, has a luminosity. This luminous substance can be photographed, and seen by the psychic as passing out of the body. The whole body becomes enshrouded with a kind of luminous mist. I remember the case of a girl, whose brother died in Los Angeles some years ago. I heard it from her mother. At the death-bed of her brother, the young girl said : "Mamma, mamma, see, there is a mist around his body ; what is it ?" But the mother could not see it. She said that it came out of the body. The scientists have taken up that subject in Europe and are experimenting on this emanation. They call it the *ectoplasm*. It is a vapourlike substance and it has no particular form. It is like a cloud and it can take a shape or a form and can be photographed. What substance it is, they do not know, but they cannot deny its existence.

Our human bodies are emanating that substance all the time. It can be seen especially at the time when there is a medium in a trancelike condition. The materializing mediums emanate that very strongly. I have seen it in private seances, when there are no professional mediums at all. I have handled it and touched it. There is no particular feeling when we feel *ectoplasm.* It cannot be described. But when it takes a definite shape, it becomes almost like solid and like our own body. It can take any form.

At the time of death, all these vital forces that are governing the different organs, become concentrated and centralized into one point before it leaves the body, and we find the dying person's sight becomes dim, the sensations of the body become faint, and gradually the whole body goes through a transformation. And, in this transformation, there are cases, where the psychic power of the individual manifests. Some of the dying persons develop the clairvoyance and the clairaudience. They can appear at the time of death, either just before or immediately after, to the distant friends in the form of an apparition, and they can give their messages. Such cases have been recorded by the scientists. The French Astronomer, Camille Flammarion had written a book, *The Unknown,* on that subject by gathering all the authentic reports made under the test conditions in different families, which describe the experience of different people at the time of death, or immediately after death. Fifteen hundred such records were gathered, and afterwards Flammarion selected quite a few out of them, which were absolutely authentic, and published them in his book. Now these records show that there is something which is not the result of the physical body. This *ectoplasm* is a substance which contains finer matter in vibration, and this finer matter forms the under-garment of the soul, the gross physical body and the finer or etherial body existing in each one of us. We may not feel it at present, because our sight and senses are looking for the gross, material and tangible objects. But it does not become tangible until it is brought down to the planes of our senses. The plane of our senses depends upon a certain degree of vibration. We can see light when the vibration of light is within the range of our vision. From red to violet our eyes can see, but if there be less vibrations than the red, we do not see it. In order to become visible, it must vibrate in a certain way so that our organs might catch it, just as sound. Thus there are sounds which we do not hear at all, because our organs of hearing is imperfect. Similarly the etherial body cannot be seen, until it is brought within the range of our vision, by a process known as materialization. It is a process which brings the finer matter that is vibrating at a high rate into a lower rate of vibration so that we can catch it or get a glimpse of it.

The Vedanta philosophy is in perfect harmony with the conclusion of this latter kind of advanced scientists who hold that mind and the living soul are distinct factors in creating disease, also in bringing on death and in manufacturing the physical body. These ideas we find in the Vedanta philosophy which is the oldest system of philosophy in the world. The truth never grows old. The truth that was discovered five thousand years ago, is the same truth today, even if it be re-discovered by the modern scientists. So we must remember that the Vedantic truth is unique and one. There is only one condition which can be absolutely true. The others are imitations of truth. That absolute truth might have been discovered ages before, but because of the lapse of time, the truth does not change. It is the eternal truth. Therefore, we find that this finer body which I have just described, is called in Vedanta the subtle body (*sukshma-sharira*) which is the under-garment of the soul, and the gross physical is the outer garment. When the soul has performed certain functions and enjoyed certain pleasures and fulfilled certain desires, it finds that this gross physical body is no longer of any use and it does not work right. Then the living soul leaves the gross body and manufactures another. Just as you have run a motor-machine for two years, and after two years, you find that the parts are worn-out and that it has done its service, then you leave it and get another. That is exactly what the living soul does. You cannot blame the soul for doing that. Because the body is the instrument, through which the soul must manifest its powers, gain experiences, learn lessons, and gather knowledge. In this way, the living soul is progressing in the process of evolution, rising from a lower to a higher state and fulfilling its mission at every step of manifestation.

This idea of life will explain the mystery of death. Death is no longer mysterious when we know that there is an entity which has manufactured this instrument, which is dwelling in it and which leaves it when the time comes. So death does not mean the annihilation of anything, or destruction, or reduction into nothingness of anything, but it means disintegration. It means that the instrument which has served its purpose, must be thrown away and another instrument must be rebuilt out of the same material. Who can tell that the atoms and molecules which made up the body of Cleopatra thousands of years ago, are not used in the bodies of living beings today ? The same atoms and molecules that are buried with the dead bodies, have been dissolved and taken up by the vegetable life and have reappeared in the forms of plants, cereals, and we might be eating them and taking them in again. And they are forming parts of our own body. So it is a evolution. Nothing in this universe is destroyed. The atoms and the molecules go into one body, get out, and enter into another body. In this continuous process of life, its manifestations of evolution and involution are going on and the living soul is the master of it. That living soul has no death. Science tells us that which has existed once will continue to exist for ever. But the physical form of the body will be destroyed. It has no permanent existence and it is constantly changing. The form that you had when you were a little baby is gone. The form that you had yesterday, you have not got today. The form that you have this minute, you will not have it next minute. It is a continuous influx and reflux of matter. It is just like a whirlpool. The particles of matter are revolving and keeping up the shape according to the type that you have manufactured so that there would be an identity.

Now, in this vortex of the particles of the matter, which are constantly in motion, there is something that is constant and unchangeable within us. That is our consciousness. If you ever see your own hand or any part of the body through X-ray, you will find like a revelation that your body consists of the finer particles of the mist-like matter which are hanging over the outline of the bones. The gross physical body which appears as solid, is not at all solid. It is just like a cloud, and we think it is solid only under certain conditions. At the time of death, the soul leaves this material plane and enters into another plane of consciousness which may be called another dimension. We are now living in three dimensions. There is another dimension where the sense-objects do not exist at all. It is beyond the limitations of our physical body. Even the motion of the earth and the planetary system do not exist there. We cannot imagine such a state, unless we get a glimpse of that other dimension. It is called the fourth dimension.[6] Where does the human soul go ? It does not go anywhere after death, but it remains in the fourth dimension and cuts off all connections with the physical world of three dimensions. The third and the fourth dimensions are related to each other just like a wheel within a wheel. We know through the study of science that the cells of the body are constantly moving. But do we feel that motion ? When we sit still, we are enjoying the quiet. But there is a constant motion going on within our system which we are not conscious of. So the departed soul is not conscious of the changes and the conditions of the gross physical body.

Our bodies are nothing but the instruments, or the garments of the soul. Vedanta tells us that when a person dies,

---

[6] Some imagine five to seven dimensions. Dimensions are known as the layers of thought or mind, and each dimension has a special experience of its own.

he is not really dead, but he changes his old garment of the physical body and takes a new one. Vedanta says that death means a change i.e. a change from one state of consciousness to another state of consciousness, and the soul throws away the physical body at the time of death just as we throw away our old worn-out garments. This idea is beautifully expressed in the *Bhagavad Gita* :

'As we throw away our old worn-out garments and put on new ones, so the living soul, after using the body which is the gross physical garments, throws it away when it is worn-out, and manufactures a new one.'[7]

---

7 वासांसि जीर्णानि यथा विहाय
   नवानि गृह्णाति नरोऽपराणि ।
   तथा शरीराणि विहाय जीर्णा-
   न्यन्यानि संयाति नवानि देही ॥

—भगवद्गीता २/२२

CHAPTER IV

THE SOUL AFTER DEATH

The question what becomes of the human soul after death is as old as the first appearance of man on earth. Almost all nations and tribes of all climes and ages have asked this question amongst themselves and tried to solve the problem, each according to its power, capacity, understanding, and knowledge. Some tried to explain it through peculiar theories and beliefs; some through mythology, or poetry, and others through proper reasoning and scientific and logical demonstration. These various attempts of different thinkers to solve that ancient problem have ended in different conclusions which satisfy more or less the minds of various peoples in different countries. All the religions of the world are built upon the solution of this great puzzle. All the philosophies, ancient or modern, and even science of today, have spared no pains to unriddle that enigma of existence. Many have failed, and many have stopped after deep investigations and researches without finding any satisfactory explanation, and have at last cried out in despair; it is beyond our knowledge, and it is beyond the reach of human understanding. Some have become agnostics and others have denied the existence of any such thing as soul. Some said that the soul of man exists as long as the body and the combination of matter which produces the soul, exists. When the body dies, the soul is also dead and gone. Some have arrived at the conclusion that there is no such thing as an individuality. It is like the flame of a lamp.[1]

---

[1] Vide Notes.

When there is no lamp, there is no light; similarly when there is no body, there is no soul left. Everything ends with the death of the body. No sign of individuality is left after the dissolution of the physical form or the gross body. But after hearing all these various conclusions, does our mind stop to ask the same question within ourselves again and again ? No, because each individual needs an explanation which will satisfy the innate longing for the immortal or deathless life, with which each one of us is born. If we hear millions of times that there is no soul, still we cannot be convinced entirely that we shall cease to exist after death. We cannot think of such a state, and we cannot believe that our individuality will be lost after death. Such solution do not appeal to our reason, and do not satisfy our mind, nor do they bring to us consolation of any kind. In the *Katha Upanishad*, we find that Yama, the Ruler of Death says :

'Fools dwelling in the darkness of ignorance, self-conceited with vain knowledge and puffed up with the idea that they are truely wise, go round and round like the blind led by the blind.'[2] 'Hereafter never rises before the mind of an ignorant child, deluded by the desire of wealth and worldly prosperity. Such people who say : 'This is the world, there is no other,' come again and again under my sway.'[3]

These words were uttered perhaps more than a thousand years before the birth of Jesus. One of the principal features of the writings of the ancient Seers of Truth in India was the knowledge of pre-existence, continuity and immortality of the human soul. If we see the most ancient writings, I mean the

---

[2] अविद्यायामन्तरे वर्तमाना: स्वयं धीरा: पण्डितम्मन्यमाना: ।
दन्द्रम्यमाणा: परियन्ति मूढ़ा अन्धेनैव नीयमाना यथान्धा: ॥
—कठ उपनिषद्, १/२/५

[3] न साम्पराय: प्रतिभाति बालं, प्रमाद्यन्तं वित्तमोहेन मूढ़म् ।
अयं लोको नास्ति पर इति मानी पुन: पुनर्वशमापद्यते मे ॥
—कठ उपनिषद्, १/२/६

Rig Veda, there we read such prayers which show that they believed in the existence of the soul after death and immortal life. In the *Isha-Upanishad* of the *Sukla-Yayur-Veda,* we find also :

'Oh God! take me there where lies the source of everlasting light of the universe, which is indestructible, where immortality reigns supreme and make me immortal.'[4]

In a funeral hymn we read :

'Go forth, go forth on these ancient paths on which our forefathers departed, having left all sins, go home again and radiant in thy body, come together with them.'[5]

There are hundreds of such passages in the Vedas, which show clearly that the ancient Aryas believed in the existence of the soul after death. They believed in the spirit-world of the fathers or *Pitris* where the departed soul goes after death, and the king of that world of the fathers is Yama, the first of the mortals who became immortal.

The ancient Hindus believed in a heaven which they called the *brahmaloka* or the kingdom of Brahma, the Creator and the Father of the universe. Then gradually when the ethical ideas of right and wrong became very strong in the minds of the Hindus and when they understood the law of action and reaction, they believed that those who perform good and virtuous deeds in this life with the hope of getting reward, go to the realm of the fathers (*pitriloka*) and stay there as long as the results of good works will not be finished. When a departed individual has reaped fruits of all of his

---

[4] अग्ने नय सुपथा राये अस्मान्, विश्वानि देव वयुनानि विद्वान् ।
युयोध्यस्मज्जुहुराणमेनो, भूयिष्ठां ते नम-उक्तिं विधेम ॥

—ईश उपनिषद्, १८

[5] प्रेहि प्रेहि पथिभि: पूर्व्येभि:-र्यत्रा न: पूर्वे पितर: परेयु: ।
उभा राजाना स्वधया मदन्ता यमं पश्यासि वरूणं च देवम् ॥

—ऋग्वेद, १०/१४/७

good and virtuous works which brought him to that realm, he is bound to come down to the earth and to be born again, according to his desires and actions of his past birth. The spirit-world of the fathers was supposed to be in the moon. From the every ancient times the Hindus had a belief that the moon was the land of the dead, and it was the repository of all the departed souls, and all the germs of life came to this earth from the moon. It rained from the moon on this earth. The path, by which the departed souls go to the lunar region and enjoy there all the pleasures and happiness as a result of their own works and then return to the earth and are born again, was called the *pitriyana*, or the path of the forefathers.[6] All mortals are bound to go by this path and return to this earth.

But those who do good works not for getting reward, nor seeking anything on return and who live the life of purity and righteousness, will go to the *brahmaloka*, the realm of Brahma. There they will stay in all glory until the end of a cycle of evolution. In the meantime, if any one of them can attain the knowledge of the highest wisdom of oneness which is the absolute Reality, he will be free and will remain as one with the supreme Being all through eternity. Brahma, the Creator, who is the king of this realm of the gods, will in the end of one cycle be free. Then in the beginning of another cycle, another Brahma will arise from the infinite source of the absolute existence, intelligence and bliss. He will be the Creator or Projector of that cycle. This process will continue all the time. This Brahma, the Creator, is like the Governor of a state. One fills the post for sometime, does his duty, then retires. Another in the meantime becomes a candidate to be the Brahma, and so he becomes. In this way, hundreds of Brahmas have come and gone. But those who after attaining

---

[6] संवत्सरो वै प्रजापतिस्तस्यायने दक्षिणं चोत्तरं च, तद्ये ह वै तदिष्टापूर्ते । कृतमित्युपासते, ते चान्द्रमसमेव लोकं अभिजयन्ते त एव पुनरावर्तन्ते*** ।

—प्रश्न उपनिषद्, १/९

this realm of the gods do not gain the highest wisdom of oneness, come back at the beginning of the new cycle to this earth, and according to their desires and works they will be born again as the human beings of the highest order. Most righteous and virtuous will strive for the highest knowledge, or the realization of oneness. This is what they called *devayana*, the path of the *devas* or the bright ones. These two paths are described fully in the *Upanishads* in a metaphorical language, which is generally difficult to understand. They describe how the departed souls go from this earth to those regions, what stages they pass through, what experiences they gather, how they return, and how they are born, and so forth. Those who go by *pitriyana*, or the path of the departed fathers are such people who are charitable, do good to others, and perform the virtuous deeds. When such people die, they go through smoke, then to night, then to dark fifteen days, from there to the six months when the sun moves south, from there to the world of the fathers, from the world of the fathers to moon.[7]

These are the principal stages like smoke, night, and dark fifteen days, and each of these has a spirit as its ruler. These spirits take care of the departed souls and help them as guides do in a strange country. Each of these spirits introduces them to the other spirits, and thus they go very quickly to their proper destinations. There they will meet their departed relatives and friends. There they will become favourite of the gods and live there as long as their works will permit. Then when they return, 'they first take etherial invisible bodies (like minute germs of life), then they pass through ether into

[7] ‘**ते घूममभिसंभवन्ति, धुमाद्रात्रिम्, रात्रेरपक्षीयमाणपक्षम् अपक्षीयमाणपक्षाद्यान् षण्मासान् दक्षिणादित्य एति मासेभ्य: पितृलोकं पितृलोकाच्चन्द्रं ते चन्द्रं प्राप्यत्रं भवन्ति तांस्तत्र देवा यथा सोमं राजानमाप्यायस्वापक्षीयस्वेत्येवमेनांस्तत्र भक्षयन्ति **कीटा: पतङ्गा: यदिदं दन्दशूकम्।   —वृहदारण्यक उपनिषद्, ६/२/१६

Vide also *Devayana* in Rig Veda, X. 19, 1, *Pitriyana* in Rig Veda, X, 2.1, Cf. *Kausitaki Upanishad*, 1.4.

air, from air into the clouds, and then they fall with rain drops
on the earth, then they enter into human bodies through some
kinds of food; then they are born again.'[8] In this process, you
must remember that the law of what the modern evolutionists
call the natural selection, acts, and by that law they will come
through food into such bodies where they will find suitable
environments and conditions to fulfil their desires and to reap
the results of their own works. During this process of return,
their whole mental feelings and intelligence become contracted,
and they do not feel anything, nor can they remember anything.
Then they become good or bad according to their latent
tendencies which they possess and which they want to
manifest.

But those who worship God with pure heart and sincere
devotion, and those who are righteous and work for others
without any hope of getting reward and are unselfish and
believe in an extra-cosmic personal God with a certain name
and form and are dualistic or monotheistic in their ideas after
their death, will go to heaven by the *devayana*, or the path
which leads to God. It has been said in the *Upanishad* :

'They go first to light, from light to day, to the waxing
half of the moon, to six months when the sun goes
north, then to the place of bright spirits or *devas*, then
to the sun, then to the region of lightening, there a spirit
of a high order comes and takes them to the world of
Brahma, where they dwell until the end of the cycle.'[9]

---

[8](क) मासेभ्य: पितृलोकं पितृलोकादाकाशं आकाशाच्चन्द्रमसं एष सोमो राजा
तद्देवानामन्नं, तं देवा भक्षयन्ति ॥ ४ ॥ तस्मिन् यावत्सम्पातमुषित्वाऽथैतमेवाध्वानं, पुनर्निवर्तन्ते
यथेतं आकाशम् आकाशाद्वायुं वायुर्भूत्वा धूमो भवति धूमो भूत्वा अभ्रं भवति ॥ ५ ॥ अभ्रं भूत्वा
मेघो भवति मेघो भूत्वा प्रवर्षति त इह व्रीहियवा ओषधिवनस्पतयस्तिलमाषा इति जायन्ते अतो
वै खलु दुनिष्प्रपतरं यो यो ह्यन्नमत्ति यो रेत: सिञ्चति तद्भूय एव भवति ॥ ३
—छान्दोग्य उपनिषद्, ५/१०/४-६

(ख) वृहदारण्यक उपनिषद्, ३/२/१६ ।

[9](क) ते य एवमेतद्विदुः ये चामी अरण्ये श्रद्धां सत्यमुपासते तेऽर्चिरभिसं-भवन्त्
अर्चिषोऽहरह्न आपूर्यमाणपक्षं पूर्यमाणपक्षाद्यान्षण्मासानुदङ्ङादित्य एति मासेभ्यो देवलोकं

Then they may return in the next cycle, if they do not realize the highest truth of oneness. In this case, you will have to understand that all these light, day, etc. must be taken as the stages under the guidance of the spirits that are at their head or their rulers.[10]

These mythological descriptions and poetic imaginations of the ancient simple-minded thinkers of India are considered by many as childish talk, and by some as nonsense. Whatever that might be, one thing which we learn from all these descriptions is that those ancient thinkers understood that the soul cannot be destroyed after death, and that it has some purpose to fulfil, and that it must continue to manifest either on this earth or in some other planet according to its desires and works, and that all these heavens are transitory and not the unchangeable Reality. This is a great gain indeed. In very few religions you will find such an idea. All religions, such as Zoroastrianism, Christianity or Mohammedanism, end in going to heaven, and they describe heaven as the eternal and imperishable place. But the Hindu religion does not teach that. In other religions, the highest ideal is going to a heaven where we can get many things which we cannot get here, and where all enjoyments will come incessantly without any pain or trouble. But with the Hindus this is not the desirable highest state. All these heavens and places of enjoyments are

---

देवलोकादादित्यं आदित्याद्वैद्युतं वैद्युतान् पुरुषो मानस एत्य ब्रह्मलोकान् गमयति ते तेषु वह्मलोकेषु पराः परावतो वसन्ति तेषां न पुनरावृत्तिः । —वृहदारण्यक उपनिषद्, ६/२/१५

(ख) मासेभ्यः संवत्सरं, संवत्सरादादित्यं आदित्याच्चन्द्रमसं चन्द्रमसो विद्युतं तत्पुरुषोऽमानवः स एनान् ब्रह्म गमयति एष देवयानः पन्था इति । —छान्दोग्य उपनिषद्, ५/१०/२

(ग) अग्निर्ज्योतिरहः शुक्लः षण्माषा उत्तरायणम् । तत्र प्रयाता गच्छन्ति ब्रह्म ब्रह्मविदो जनाः ॥ —भगवद्गीता, ८/२४

Vide also प्रश्नोपनिषद् १/१०

[10] Cf. *Chhandogya Upanishads*, 5 : 10. 3-6; *Brihadaranyaka Upanishad*, 6. 2. 15-16, *Bhagavad Gita*, 8. 24-26.

phenomenal and transitory (even if they last for millions of years, still millions of years when compared to eternity is nothing). It is for this reason Sri Krishna, the Incarnation of the universal Spirit, says to Arjuna :

'All the different worlds of spirits, gods and others, beginning with the highest heaven of Brahma, are places from where one must return, but he who attains me, the supreme Spirit, will remain with Me for ever, will never be bound by any law of nature.[11]

Therefore in Vedanta, you do not find any special value of these heavens, nor does it deny their existence. Of course, in the heavens, the soul will stand face to face with God before His throne, and God will ask him : 'Who art thou?' The soul will answer : 'What Thou art that I am'. But along with the higher conceptions of Vedanta, all these heavens and desires for heavens gradually become quite insignificant.[12] This idea of a personal God, sitting on a throne and receiving the pious souls, we find in the ancient writings of the Hindus, I mean in the Vedas.

In the Zend Avesta, we find a similar idea of a personal God, Ahura Mazda, sitting on a throne and judging the

---

[11] आब्रह्मभुवनाल्लोकाः पुनरावर्तिनोऽर्जुन ।
मामुपेत्य तु कौन्तेय पुनर्जन्म न विद्यते ॥   —भगवद्गीता, ८/१६

[12] In the *Sankhayama-Aranyaka* (Ch. III. 1-7), we find it is described in a beautiful way. There the king Gangyayani (Gargayani?) said to Aruni and his son Svetaketu : "Those who depart from this world all go to the moon. Their breaths swell the first fortnight (of the moon); in the second it brings them to birth again. The moon is also the door of the world of heaven. ** It rains down on earth, becoming itself rain. ** Him, when he has arrived, it asks, 'Who are thou?' To it should he reply, 'From the light I came as seed, O seasons, from that produced as the fifteen-fold father-land. ** I am born and again born as the twelve-month (year) and the thirteen-month (year), from the twelve-fold, the thirteen-fold father. I know this and I recognize this. Then do ye bear me, seasons, to deathlessness. By that truth that penance, I am the season of the seasons.' 'Who art thou?' 'I am Thou.' He then sends him on." Cf : also *Kaushitaki-Brahmanyopanishad*, 1.1.6.

conduct of the departed souls and rewarding or punishing them accordingly. The Hindus did not believe at first in any hell, but the Parsees did. In the Avesta, we read what happens when a man dies.[13] The ideas of heaven and hell which we find in the Avesta influenced to a great extent the Jewish and later Mohammedan idea of heaven through the Jews. We know that the Old Testament is silent about the fate of the soul after death. In the New Testament, however, we find such ideas which perfectly coincide with the Persian descriptions. The Persians believe in the last day of judgement and a general resurrection when the victory of good over evil will be secured. The ancient Hebrews did not bother their head much about what becomes of the soul after death. They believed that as God breathed life into man that breath, which they called *Nephesh*, or *Neshama*, or *Ruach*, came from God and returned to him after the death of the body. But afterwards when the Jews came in contact with the Persians, they accepted their ideas. The Egyptians, as has been said before, had a belief that the soul of man is a 'double' like a shadow which remains as long as the body remains, but if the body be mutilated or destroyed then the soul will be mutilated or destroyed.

The Chaldeans also believed in a 'double' which will be annihilated if the bodies were destroyed. They expected a resurrection of the corpse. This belief we find amongst the Christians of today. The Greek philosophers, Pythagoras, Plato and their disciples believed in the immortality of the soul and in the theory of transmigration. Plato's ideas regarding the nature of the soul and his descriptions about what becomes after death are exactly the same as we find in the *Upanishads*. But Plato believed in a place of punishment for the evil-doers. Those who have done wicked deeds and sinful acts will go through sufferings and penalties, and when they are purified will obtain rewards for their good deeds and virtuous

---

[13] Vide Notes.

acts. Plato believed that the human soul may migrate to a human body, or to a beast and may return again to a human body.

Thus there are many speculations regarding the future existence. Now let us understand clearly what Vedanta has to say on this point. In the first place, Vedanta says that there is no such thing as death which means destruction. It admits death in the sense of a change of the forms. This kind of death is a constant attendant of life. Life is impossible without death which means the changes of the forms. It has been said before that we are dying every moment, and after every seven years it is said that our bodies completely renew all its constitutive elements. But still the form is preserved. Although every particle of the body is changed, still we continue to exist. Our continuity is not broken, and we remember things and events that happened fourteen or twentyone years ago. This continuity of the conscious agent cannot be explained by any physical or chemical laws. Then again Vedanta gives a death-blow to the materialistic theory by saying that thought or feeling or intelligence can never be produced by any mechanical or molecular motion. Motion produces motion and nothing else. Therefore motion of the atoms of the body will never produce feeling of the conscious state, but it is due to some other higher power which we call the thought-force, or the soul-power.

That power is neither yours, nor mine, but it exists in the nature. The whole universe is like an ocean of one living substance which contains the soul-power and the source of intelligence and consciousness. Our present consciousness is a reflection or manifestation of that infinite source of consciousness. In this ocean of the source of consciousness, there are rising innumerable waves of consciousness. If we study it minutely, we will see that each wave will continue to move on and on, and if the ocean be infinite, it will never stop, and it will move on from eternity to eternity and ultimately it will come back to the same place from where it started. Similarly our individual lives are nothing but so many individual waves of that infinite ocean. As each wave is moving onward to complete the infinite circle, so each one of us has a beginningless past and endless future. The socalled surface scientists of today do not admit it. They are very busy in thinking of the race, or of the species. They ignore the fact that if there were no individuals, there would not have been any race or species. The race, or the species, is an abstract concept which exists in our mind. It is the result of our generalization, while the individuals are the undeniable facts of the nature. Each of these waves start as the simple germs of the life which contain all the potentialities and will be manifested in future and try to make those potentialities into actualities by expression or manifestation through the various forms. The process, by which it expresses, is called 'evolution' which means the change of the forms. This manifestation would have been impossible, if the forms were not changed, and if the old forms were not thrown aside, the new forms were not developed. Such being the case, this change of form is what we call death. Death is death of a particular form and not of the substance, nor of the force. Death of one form reproduces, or gives birth to another form as death of the seed-form produces the tree-form, and so forth. Again that which is reproduced will die, then reproduce another, and so on.

Therefore Vedanta says that which has birth must die, and that which is dead must be born again.[14] But there is no birth or death in the soul life. The soul life is eternal and immortal. It takes that form which it wants to take. The outward form has its cause in the mental form, and the mental or thought form is the result of our desire, or craving, or

---

[14] जातस्य हि ध्रुवो मृत्युर्ध्रुवं जन्म मृतस्य च ।

—भगवद्गीता, २/२७

intense longing. So our future life will be determined by our desires, tendencies, longings, and works we do. Vedanta does not care for heaven or hell. It says that those who want to go to heaven will create a heaven, and will go there and enjoy. Those who think of hell will see hell. Those who think that they are sinners are really sinners. What thou thinkest, thou shalt become. So all these heavens and hells are the different conditions of our mind. They do not exist outside. As long as we are in the state of ignorance, we have such dreams. But when we realize oneness of our real nature with the universal Spirit, we are free from birth or death, and heaven or hell. Then our real nature returns to its pure conditions and reigns in its own glory all through eternity.

CHAPTER V

REBIRTH OF THE SOUL

Rebirth of the soul presupposes an existence of an intelligent entity, and it is separable and independent of the gross physical body. By the term *Atman*, we mean that centre of the self-conscious activity which thinks, reacts on the personal or external phenomena, and consciously performs the functions of life. How this soul comes into existence and where does it go after the dissolution of the body are questions which rise in almost every human mind. They are as old as the appearance of the first man upon this earth.

From ancient times, the philosophers and the seers of truth of all countries and all nations have made various attempts to unravel the mysteries of the birth, life and death of the individuals upon this planet. Again and again it has been asked : Why do the animals and the human beings suddenly appear into existence, live for some time, fulfil certain desires, perform marvellous deeds, display some wonderful power, and unexpectedly pass away being forced, as it were, to leave their plans and projects of their lives, half-finished and half-fulfilled ? Why is it that some come into existence to die within a few days or weeks or years without obtaining an opportunity of knowing or gaining any experience in this vast world of phenomena ? Are these events accidental, or is there a law that governs all these aimless events and phenomena that are happening everyday before our eyes ? Are these individual souls coming and going away without any purpose, or is there an aim behind all these appearances ?

The human minds cannot rest contented until these questions of vital importance are solved. The materialistic thinkers of the Western countries have thrown overboard all such questions by denying the plan and purpose of the individual life as well as existence of the soul. They explain this phenomenon by saying that intelligence is caused by the non-intelligent forces of nature, governed by the mechanical laws and some have the gross forms and some have the finer ones, and the appearance of men and animals are caused by some anatomical combination of atoms and molecules in the process of cosmic evolution. According to them, there is no soul and no life after death; consequently, it is useless to ask such questions. It is a waste of time and energy to bother our heads regarding the existence of the soul or its birth and rebirth. But the materialistic explanation does not satisfy the minds of the seekers after truth, nor does it succeed in stopping all these questions which spontaneously rise in the human minds ; on the contrary, it can be shown that the combination of atoms and molecules can never produce consciousness and intelligence, and it is an important factor and only a property of the living soul.

It has been said that motion produces nothing but motion. It is impossible for the organic functions to produce the knower or the translator of those functions into sensations, ideas, and thoughts. In the organs, the function of motion will never be that which is not motion like consciousness or intelligence. No consciousness or intelligence is an act of motion. If, however, we study the phenomena of nature with the help of modern science, we understand that the phenomenon of accident or chance has no room in the chain of phenomena, but is guided by the universal law of cause and effect, which is known as the law of causation.

Every event that has occurred in the past or will happen in future must have some definite cause behind it, and by denying this law, we not only deny the truth of nature, but we deny also the fundamental principle of modern science, which is 'something cannot come out of nothing'. Applying this truth to the facts of birth and life of the individuals, whether animal or human, we understand that they are subject to the law of cause, and they are governed by the law of cause and effect; the cause of life on this earth of all individuals is different in each; they are not accidental appearances, and they cannot be accidental. We inquire into the cause that produced the work ; we inquire into the conscious activity of the individual : Does it exist outside of the effect, as some people believe that the cause of the human being is some supernatural being, dwelling outside of the universe ? Does this cause exist outside of the effect, or does it form a part and parcel of the effect itself ? This is most puzzling, and many of the advanced thinkers have failed in their efforts to understand the proper relation that exists between a cause and its effect. Upon the proper knowledge of the relation of a cause to its effect, depends the solution of the problem.

All the scientific thinkers of the world come to the conclusion that the true cause of a thing does not lie outside of a thing, but lies in the thing itself, just as the cause of a tree does not lie outside of the tree, but in the tree itself. Cause means the unmanifested state of the effect, and effect means the manifested state of the cause. The whole tree lies in a dormant state in the seed. Nothing comes from outside of the seed, but it was in the seed, and the external conditions and environments only bring out that which existed potentially, or help in the manifestation of the latent power. The seed of an oak tree can never produce anything other than an oak tree, however powerful the environmental conditions may be. The environmental conditions cannot add to the seed one iota to that which did not exist in the seed from the very beginning. Therefore, that which we find in the effect, must have existed in the causal state from the very beginning. All the peculiarities as manifested in the effect and the tendencies that are to be found in the effect, are nothing but the expressions of the same peculiarities, the same tendencies and the same properties that existed in the germ of life from the very beginning.

Applying this truth to the phenomena of birth and life of the individuals on this earth, we can understand the process and every step of the evolution of the germ of life. Modern science tells us that a germ of life, by going through the process of evolution, can appear as a human being. If this be true, then everything that exists in human being, must have existed in a germ of life from the very beginning in a potential state. We shall have to admit that mind and all its functions, such as desires and tendencies, must have existed in that germ of life and must have remained latent until the time had come when these latent powers found favourable conditions for their expression. They have not come into existence out of nothing, because the law is what exists, must have existed from the very beginning; otherwise we would run the risk of committing the error of admitting the fallacious argument that something could have come out of nothing, and that something has come into existence from that state which had no trace of it whatsoever.

These germs of life are nothing but minute invisible centres of forces clothed with minute particles of etherial matter; and having no particular form, they can appear in any form, either human or animal, in order to manifest and express certain powers, lying dormant in those germs of life. Although these germs of life are subject to evolution, growth and progress, yet they are not destructible like the gross physical forms of the universe. These germs possess vital force as well as mental powers and intelligence. If you study the forms of the psychic powers of the microcosmic animal-tribes or micro-organisms, you will understand that the minute germs of life express power and intelligence, and even these germs of life manifest these powers through the gross forms, by manufacturing them ; but that manufacture depends upon the law which governs the gross material universe. At the time of the dissolution of the gross forms, all these manifested powers conserve and remain latent in a minute subtle germ of life by the law of persistence of force, until the time comes when the conditions become favourable for the re-manifestation of those powers that have become dormant.

These germs of life are called by various names. We may call them the vehicles of consciousness. Some call them the individual souls or egos. The Indian philosophers describe them as subtle bodies (*sukshma-sharira*) of the individuals. These subtle bodies, being governed by the law of cause and effect and subject to the law of action and reaction, appear again either on this plane or on some other to express some powers, to manifest the latent tendencies, and to gain knowledge and experience by coming in contact with these objects of sense which exist on the material plane. The reappearance of the germs of life in gross physical forms, whether animal or human, is called the 'manifestation' which is known and understood by the theory of rebirth of the soul, or doctrine of reincarnation, as it is called in the Vedanta philosophy. By rebirth of the soul, Vedanta does not mean the same thing as transmigration or metempsychosis. In Western countries, there are many thinkers and writers who do not understand the difference that exists between the theory of transmigration and that of reincarnation or rebirth, and, consequently, they write and create great confusion in the minds of the readers.

But transmigration or metempsychosis[1] has a meaning enirely different from that of reincarnation. It means the passing of the soul from one body after death into another, or, in other words, the soul after dwelling in one body for a certain length of time leaves it at the time of death and enters into another body which is ready to receive it, to gain experience and knowledge in those lives, or through those

---

[1] Vide Notes. Cf. also Swami Abhedananda : *Reincarnation.*

forms, or to reap the results of the works or deeds of the previous lives. It may enter into a human or an animal form. The doers that have performed the good deeds, will enter into the human forms or the angelic forms, but the doers that have performed the wicked deeds, will appear in animal forms, and remaining as animals for some time, will perhaps take the human forms, and then the angelic forms, and then go on and return again to this earth in the form of the higher animals. Thus transmigration means the revolution of the soul from body to body and excludes the idea of growth, progress and evolution from lower to higher states of consciousness.

The migrating substance, being of constant quantity and quality, chooses the forms and bodies according to the bent of its character or desires. It is governed by the law of causation, or by the law of action and reaction. In ancient Egypt, they believed that after the death of the body, the souls travelled for thousands of years from one body to another. Pythagoras, Plato and their followers believed in the theory of transmigration or metempsychosis of the soul.[2] Pythagoras says :

'After death, the rational mind, having been freed from the chains of the body, assumes an etherial vehicle, and passes into the region of the dead, where it remains, till it is sent back to this world, to inhabit some other body, human or animal. After undergoing successive purgations, when it is sufficiently purified, it is received among the goods, and returns to the eternal source from which it first proceeded.'

Plato also believes in this theory of transmigration. He describes in an allegorical way how and where the souls go through the progress of transmigration. He describes in the *Phoedrus* :

_____

[2] Vide Notes.

'In the heaven, Zeus, the Father and Lord of all creatures, drives his winged car, ordering all things and superintending them. **Thus when the soul is unable to follow and fails to behold the vision of Truth, she sinks beneath the double load of forgetfulness and vice, her feathers fall from her, and she drops to earth and is born again as human beings or as animals'.

Plato says that ten thousand years must elapse before the soul can return to the place from which she came, because she cannot grow her wings in less time. After the first thousand years, the good and evil souls come together to choose their lives and instead of reaping the natural consequences of their previous deeds and misdeeds, they are allowed to choose the bodies according to the experience and bent of their character. Some being disgusted with mankind, choose the animal bodies. They like to take the lives of eagles and other beings, while others desire again to take the bodies of the human beings to see what experience they can get.[3]

Through this mythological theory, you can understand what idea is conveyed by the theory of transmigration or metempsychosis. In India, from ancient times the theory of transmigration prevailed, but it was different from that of Plato. The Hindus never believed that the souls were allowed to choose their lower grades of life according to the bent of character, but they were bound to reap the natural consequences of their deed and misdeeds and enjoy or suffer by coming in the bodies, either animal or human. But even today there are many who believe in the transmigration of the souls, that the souls after death can go back to the animals and live as the animals for some time, and then go up to heaven and live there for some time. But the rational minds in India do not believe in the retrogression of the human souls into animal forms, but they believe in the doctrine of the rebirth of the souls or reincarnation.

---

[3] Vide Swami Abhedananda : *Reincarnation*, pp. 89-90.

The doctrine of reincarnation is based upon the theory of evolution and depends upon the law of cause and sequence, or that of action and reaction. These germs of life come into existence to fulfil certain powers and desires and to gain certain experience. They do not go back to the animal forms, but they live on the human plane and continue to exist on the human plane, being subject to the law of evolution. It admits the growth and progress through experience and knowledge of the phenomenal world. It is true, however, that there are passages in the writings of the *Upanishads* which apparently refer to the retrogression of the human souls into the animal nature, but they do not necessarily mean that these souls will have to take animal forms.[4] How absurd it is to think that the human souls, after manifesting human powers, will choose a dog-body to manifest those powers? How can a lower animal contain that which is greater? But there may be some people who may live like animals even when they have the human bodies, as we may find among many people cats and dogs and snakes in the human form and they are often more vicious than natural cats, dogs or snakes. That kind of retrogression to the animal nature is the result of the wicked deeds and wicked thoughts on the animal plane. These deeds and thoughts must produce their results in the manifestation of the animal nature. But this retrogression is only temporary. It helps the individual souls in gaining the experience on the animal plane only for a time, until they come out of those states, after which they will manifest the higher powers latent in those germs of life. The wicked thoughts and deeds are only our own mistakes, which we have committed on account of our ignorance. No one is born so to commit mistakes whatever. So every mistake is a great teacher in the long run. We must understand this. But as it is impossible for a human soul to gain all experiences in one short period of one hundred years or more or less, we must have to admit the doctrine of

---

[4] Vide Notes.

evolution and, consequently, the theory of rebirth or reincarnation of the souls, or of the germs of life, in order to fulfil the purpose of life and gain experiences in all the different phases of evolution.

Reincarnation of the soul does not mean the same thing as experienced by the Buddhist philosophers who deny the permanence of the soul entity, or the permanent entity of the soul. They say that an individual soul, after the death of the body, appears again in some other form, but that being is not the same being, but a being of a similar nature. That creates a difficulty. If we perform certain acts in order to reap the results of those acts, we need the same individual entity; we must admit that there is the continuation of the same being, otherwise, it would be just like one person eating food and another getting satisfaction. Then there would be no law and no harmony in this universe. Those who do not believe in the doctrine of reincarnation, believe either in the one-birth theory, or in the theory of heredity. But these two theories do not satisfy all the questions of the human minds and they do not explain the difference. Those who believe in the one-birth theory, cannot explain why the individual souls come into existence, live for a certain time, and go away. But where do they go they do not know. They do not understand the purpose of life, which is to gain knowledge and experience, and they cannot understand why little children live and die within a few days or weeks or months without any opportunity of knowing anything. What purpose of life has been served by that ? The Christian theologians, believing in the dogma of one-birth, explain that these little children who die after birth, will go to heaven and be saved by the eternal Father and enjoy the celestial bliss throughout eternity. If the Christians only believe in this dogma, they ought to pray for death of their children at the time of birth, and ought to be thankful to the merciful Father when their little babies die and go to the graves over dead bodies. But that theory does not explain the difficulties, rather it takes for granted certain dogmatic solutions which do not explain any of the difficulties. They are neither rational, nor scientific.

Three great religions of the world, Judaism, Christianity and Mohammedanism still uphold that theory of life and death. They believe that we have come into existence, remain for a short time, and pass away either going to heaven or to the place of the eternal punishment. Those who believe in such theory, cannot make their minds free from the impressions that they have received during the childhood. The followers of these three great religions believe that the souls come into existence, being created for the first time out of nothing, and continue to do certain works, being forced by the Creator, but they will have to enjoy or suffer all throughout eternity for the works performed during the short existence and which they were forced to do, not by their own free will, but by the will of the Creator who put that kind of free will, vicious or virtuous, into beings. It is as absurd as that one person who is forced to do all the acts of another person and is forced to receive the punishment or reward for the acts that are not done by himself. The only way out of this difficulty is to admit the permanence of the germ of life. If these souls exist today and continue to exist throughout eternity, they must have existed from eternity, and there must be the reappearance of that which existed in some form or other.

There is another consideration and that is this that the beginning, the ending and the continuing are the conceptions of the human minds that depend upon our conception of time, but we all know that time has no absolute existence.[5] It is only a form of knowledge of our nature, as related to the

---

[5] In the Advaitic conception, time is regarded as an appearance and as an effect (*karya*) of avidya or *maya*. It has merely an empirical reality, but is obliterated or negated in the ultimate Reality.

experience of nature outside.[6] This conception vanishes at the time of death, just as it does every night when we are in sound sleep. Can you remember, or do you have the idea of time, when your mind is absolutely resting in sound sleep? No, you cannot, because that conception vanishes for the time being, and the souls wake up after the sleep of death, just in the same way as insects wake up in the spring after sleeping through the long winter, or as a chrysalis in the bed of a cocoon, spun by itself in the month of autumn. Nature teaches us this truth of rebirth by this resemblance between sleep and death and by the rejuvenation of a chrysalis in the spring. The souls wake up after the sleep of death and put on the new bodies in order to fulfil certain purposes and gain certain experiences to reap the results of their previous action, being subject to the law of cause and effect, just in the same way as we throw away our old clothes and put on new ones. Therefore it is said in Vedanta :

'As we throw away our old garments and put on new ones, so the individual ego or germ of life, after throwing away the old body, manufactures new form for the purpose of fulfilling the aim of life.'[7]

Through this doctrine of reincarnation, the vast majority of people in India, China and Japan have found consolation in their lives and solved the extremely difficult problems that disturb the minds of the scientists and other thinkers of the world. Even in the Western countries, the philosophers like Plato, Plotinus, Proclus, Kant, Schelling, Fichte, Schopenhauer, Lessing Bruno, Goethe and others; the poets like Wordsworth, Tennyson and others, the theologians like Dr. Julius, Mueller, Dr. Dorner, Ruckert, and others have believed in the doctrine of transmigration, or rebirth of the soul. The ancient

---

[6] Immanuel Kant says in his *Critique of Pure Reason* : "Time is nothing but the form of our internal intuition. Take away the peculiar condition of our sensibility, and the idea of time vanishes, because it is not inherent in the objects, but in the subject only that perceives them" —*Max Müller's Translation.*

[7] *Bhagavad Gita*, Ch. II, 22. This *sloka* has already been quoted before.

philosophers like Origen believed in the doctrine of reincarnation, because this is the only doctrine that satisfies the human minds and answers all the questions on this subject scientifically and explains facts.

If the one-birth theory and heredity do not explain all the difficulties, we ought to try another theory which is better and more satisfactory. At one time the idea of reincarnation and rebirth of the soul spread so wonderfully amongst the Christians of ancient times that Justinian was obliged to pass a law in the Council of Constantinople in 538 A.D. to stop spread of this doctrine which would kill the Christian dogma. The law was this :

> 'Whoever shall support the mythical presentation of the pre-existence of the soul, and, consequently, the wonderful opinion of its return, let him be Anathema'.

Those who do not believe in the doctrine of reincarnation, try to explain these difficulties through the theory of heredity. But does this theory explain all the questions?

Suppose there is a young man twentyfive years old and he has inherited certain peculiarities and characteristics like talent for music, or possessing a crooked nose, or a peculiar giggle in his laugh, in which he resembles his grandfather. Now this young man, according to the supporters of this theory, has inherited all these things from his grandfather who died six years before his birth. All these peculiarities were handed down to this young man before he was born and came into a human body and when he was like a protoplasmic cell or a jelly-like substance which has neither nose nor mouth. Even at that time he inherited that queer giggle and crooked nose through his grandfather. This protoplasmic cell was smaller than a pin's head, and if you look at it through a microscope you cannot distinguish it from that of a dog, or a cat, or a bird, or a tree. Even then it had all these peculiarities. Before the brain and the nerve centres began to take forms, the musical talents and tendencies, possessed by this young man, existed in the protoplasmic cell which came down from his grandfather. Does it not seem to you absurd to think that one protoplasmic cell can contain all these tendencies, the crooked nose and giggle and talents, when there was neither brain, nor mouth, nor nose? There are many scientists who believe in the theory of heredity, but they cannot explain how one single cell can contain all the mental and physical traits and characteristics and peculiarities of father and grandfather, mother and grandmother. You have millions of cells in this human body. But what kind of cell is that which can reproduce all these powers and tendencies which are possessed by each one of us at present? This is the most difficult of all problems that the scientific minds have encountered.

There have been many theories against this theory of heredity. We must not forget that an organism can inherit only where there is predisposition to inherit, otherwise it cannot.[8] Supposing this theory of heredity a truth, but what have we learned from it? We learned that the whole of the young man existed before his birth in the protoplasmic cell and the whole character was there. Does it not seem the same thing as the pre-existence of the human being? Really it seems, as the whole human nature must have existed in that germ of life in some form or other. All the powers, intelligence and desires must have also existed there, otherwise we will have to admit that these powers have come out of nothing which would be absurd and unscientific.

Again the theory of heredity cannot explain all the causes which produce geniuses and prodigies. On the contrary, the doctrine of rebirth of the soul or reincarnation explains all these things satisfactorily. Why was it that the shephered Mangiamelo could calculate like automatism when he was five years of age? The child Zerab Cloburn, when he was under eight years old, could answer the most difficult of mathematical problems without any figures. Mozart, the great

---

[8] This has been elaborately discussed elsewhere in connection with the discussion of Weisman's theory of the 'continuity of the germ-plasm.'—Cf. Swami Abhedananda : *Reincarnation*, p. 35.

musician could repeat a sonata when he was of four years age and when he was eight years of age he wrote an opera. Hoffman could play music beautifully, before he was ten years of age. Blind Tom did not inherit his powers from his parents. He was a slave and born of slave parents on a plantation. One day he went to his master's parlour when the family was at dinner and he sat at the piano and began to play music which he had never heard. But in music he was a master. He could compose music by himself and play his own compositions for three quarters of an hour, and after once hearing music, he could repeat it note by note. He never had a lesson and could not have understood lessons. These illustrations disprove the theory of family heredity or the theory of 'cumulative heredity'.[9] Those, who believe in the theory of heredity, say that genius is the result of cumulative heredity which presents itself by gradual degree, i.e., from less germs to greater and still greater and so on. But in the whole history of the genealogy of geniuses, in all the greater examples like Shakespeare or Lincoln or Jesus or Buddha or Sankaracharya, we do not find any trace of genius in the family of these great men, on the contrary, their parents and grandparents did not show such powers.

There had been many shepherds in Galilee at that time, but Jesus the Christ was the only one who could not inherit anything from the shepherd nature of his parents and relatives. There had been many young princes and kings in India, but there was only one Buddha. Why was it? Does the theory of heredity explain all these instances? No. If we do exist now, we cannot think of our annihilation or destruction. Destruction in the sense of annihilation is impossible in this world of reality. If we exist today, we cannot think of our non-existence either before or after. Where did the soul exist before the birth of this body, no one can tell. We cannot find the beginning of the soul or its end.

---

[9] Vide Swami Abhedananda : *Reincarnation*, pp. 46-47.

There are some objections that have been raised by many who do not believe in the doctrine of reincarnation. One question had been asked very often : 'If we did exist before, why do we not remember it ?' If we examine our own lives, we do not remember many things, but still we know we did them. Do you remember what you did on the eighth of February, twenty-five years ago in the afternoon? Perhaps you will say you do not know, because you cannot remember. Our memory is only that power of the mind by which we can recall the latent impressions and ideas stored up in the mind. Memory grows, and if we develop our memory, we will remember many things which we do not know at present. In India, there are many Yogis who can remember their past experiences. In ancient Greece, it is known that ancient philosophers came to India to find out the secret of their wonderful knowledge which the Hindus possessed. Some people say that if they could remember the past, how happy they would be; but perhaps if they did, they would make a bad use of their present.

If you knew that you were going to have some great misfortunes within a few days or months, would you be equal to performing the duties on hand at present? Rather you would constantly remember those misfortunes. We should not try to satisfy the idle curiosity, by trying to know what we were in the past, but let us make our present useful, and do such acts that will help us in becoming better than what we are today. Make the best use of our present until the time comes when the higher illumination will reveal to us all the past and future like a panorama before our spiritual eyes, then we shall be able to say as Sri Krishna said to Arjuna in the *Bhagavad Gita* :

'Both you and I have passed through many births, you know them not, while I know them all.'[10]

---

[10] बहूनि मे व्यतीतानि जन्मानि तव चार्जुन ।
तान्यहं वेद सर्वाणि न त्वं वेत्थ परन्तप ॥

—भगवद्गीता, ४/५

CHAPTER VI

THE SOUL AND ITS DESTINY

The question of the soul and its destiny spontaneously arises in all minds whether cultured or uncultured. No other question touches the hearts of men and women so deeply. No other problem arouses their interest so much, or sets their minds to thinking, as this universal problem concerning the nature of the human soul and its destiny. From ancient times, the philosophers, the sages, the thinkers and the prophets have tried their best to solve this great problem to answer this momentous question. In their attempts, they arrived at various conclusions from time to time. Some of their conclusions appealed to some minds. Some say that there is no such thing as the soul which can exist independent of the body and which is separate from the body, while others deny its existence entirely. Those who believe in the existence of the soul as an independent thing from the body, say that it will continue to exist after death, i.e., it is immortal. But this question does not disturb the minds of those who deny the existence of the soul, or believe that the soul is not independent of the body, but it depends on the body as long as the body lives, or the soul lives in the body. There may be some persons among us who may be positively sure that they have no soul. But all the religions aim to lead the human mind to the belief that the soul is eternal, that it continues to exist after death, and that it enjoys the pleasure and happiness of heaven, or suffers from punishment. But such ideas are based upon the scriptural texts, or upon the writings or sayings of some great sages or seers.

The popular belief among the Christians is that immortality of the soul, or the immortal life, was brought into light by Jesus the Christ and that before the advent of Jesus this idea was unknown to the world and no one can attain the eternal life except through Jesus. But when we study the ancient pre-Christian religions and their scriptures, we find that this idea of eternal life was almost universally known and was accepted among the ancient Egyptians, Chaldeans, Hindus, Zoroastrians, Romans, Greeks, and Scandinavians. In fact, the study of the ancient religions of the world disproves the Christian dogma that Jesus the Christ alone has brought eternal light into life and that no one can attain heaven except through him. He might have enlightened the minds of certain Jewish tribes who did not believe in the scriptures, or who were in ignorance of them. But, as regards bringing this eternal light into life for the first time, we cannot accept.

Although the vast majority of the followers of different religions believe in an eternal soul which is immortal and continues to exist after death, still there is a large number of advanced thinkers who question the authority of these scriptural statements. After making independent researches, they have come to the conclusion that there is no such thing as a soul, or that the soul is one with the body, or the result of forces, or the material particles of the body. They have sufficient strong arguments to support their conclusions. In the same manner, the scientists have strong arguments to prove their theories. They have left no stone unturned to discover a satisfactory answer or result to this great problem. Fine instruments of all kinds have been invented to capture the secret, or to discover that which passes out of the brain at death. The dissected brains of the animals have been most carefully examined and minutely watched to discover what is it that passes out at the time of death from the human body. But, alas! all such attempts, or all these human efforts have failed. All these human efforts to capture that invisible something, or the existence of the visible magnetism of animals in the human form, have failed and this has driven many seekers after the soul to the conclusions of the agnostics, the atheists, and the materialists. This inability to capture the soul has made many people deny the existence of the soul altogether, or its continuance after death ; they cannot believe in anything that is beyond the perception of sense. No arguments can convince them. They try to extract intelligence from the matter. They say that intelligence, consciousness and mind are produced by the material body. They believe that consciousness and mind have no independent existence of their own and they last so long as the body lasts and after the dissolution of the body nothing is left, because they cannot see with their sense power the intelligent soul which passes out of the body. But, at the same time, no one can prove that matter and insentient forces of nature have ever produced consciousness or intelligence.

If we deny the existence of the soul as independent of the body or as something which rules over the body and regulates and directs the organic functions of the body, then we are immediately confronted with the ethical, psychological and philosophical difficulties. The denial of existence of the soul as independent of the body will destroy the ethical fitness of things as if we were nothing but machines.

If we say that our life passes out like the snuff of a candle, then why should we struggle for an existence and why worry through troubles, miseries and sufferings? What would be the use of living a virtuous life if we do not continue to exist after this gross body is dead and gone? Why should we not kill our neighbours and get everything out of them that we can in order to enrich ourselves? Posterity will take care of itself. Every individual will be extremely selfish and there will be no standard of morality. If we deny the existence of the soul which lasts after the body is dead and gone, then what is the use of building up our character and what good will it do, if all individuals are going to pass away into eternal oblivion? All the troubles in acquiring an education will be in vain. The love for wife and children, grown up through general self-sacrifice, will be cheated out of its full development. Are we then only playing a long and desperate game with worthless counters if our desires are going to be all for nothing? Is it possible? No, because if this be true, then each and every one of us ought to commit suicide and get rid of all these sufferings and miseries. We ought to throw all the scriptures into the ocean and demolish all temples and churches and live like beasts on the sense plane. If our souls are not immortal, or if we deny the existence of the soul, there would be no reason to live a virtuous life or for training our children up righteously.

This ethical difficulty will never be removed by those who do not admit the existence of the soul as independent of the body. Then again, in psychology, we will have to face the same difficulty if we deny the existence of the soul. The old materialistic theory that the soul or mind is the result of the functions of the brain, is dead and gone. It is not for sensible people any more. At the same time if we deny the existence of the soul, we shall not be able to explain this self-consciousness and ever-working functions of the brain which can be translated into sensible ideas and thoughts, and we shall not be able to explain by what force are they developed into a harmonious whole, by what force are they brought into the form of memory, and what force acts on the brain cells to produce the conscious identity of the individual ego. We have the sense of sight, the sense of hearing and the sense of touch, etc. Can the vibrations of ether produce any one of these senses? Can any mesmeric force produce the sense of seeing or hearing? It is simply impossible. No one has ever seen it. These and many other psychological difficulties will have to be removed.

The self-consciousness has never been produced by the combination of ether or matter, or by electricity. Again when we analyse this whole material psychologically, what do we gather? The psychological researches lead us to first principles, matter, knowledge, and consciousness. The whole universe can be resolved into these great principles : first, matter, then knowledge or force, and third, consciousness. Of these the matter is immutable or immortal, and psychological researches have also proved that matter has neither been created by anybody, nor are the forces. Matter is indestructible and non-creatable, and they are conserved and continue to exist. If this conservation of matter and forces be true, then we naturally ask why the third principle, through which alone the recognition of all are known, is not also conserved? If matter and knowledge are conserved and if they are uncreated and indestructible, then how do you know it? You know it by your consciousness and your intelligence. Can you know it by any other force? The recognition of matter and force depends upon your own consciousness, and if those two be conserved, then how is it that your own consciousness will not be conserved? If matter and knowledge be uncreated and indestructible, then how can we prove that your consciousness is creatable and destructible? Where did you get that knowledge from? How did you know this if you had no consciousness and no intelligence?

Here we must not forget that matter and knowledge form only one half of the universe, and the other half is the subjective world. If we were all unconscious at this minute, the existence of this room would be nothing to us. We know of it through our consciousness.

The existence of matter and the existence of knowledge must depend upon the consciousness of the individual. If one of them must be conserved, the other must be conserved also. If we analyse the phenomena of the universe and get to the principles that have manufactured these phenomena of the universe, we come to the conclusion that both matter and knowledge are conserved, and if they are conserved, your intelligence and consciousness are also conserved. In order to remove these difficulties, we are bound to admit the existence of the soul, independent of the body, which is the source of consciousness and intelligence in us, by which we know our own existence and the existence of other things of the universe. The soul cannot be produced by matter, as matter produces nothing but matter.[1] Newton discovered gravitation, but gravitation never discovered Newton. If you believe in the permanency of your own existence, you yourself are, of course, one with the body, then you think of yourself as the body.

But it is very obvious that the body is constantly changing. Then where is that permanency in our bodies? This material form or the gross physical organism will be destroyed. Then where will lie our permanency? Not in the body, but in the soul. It is the sense of 'I', which will continue to exist after this body is gone.

Having understood this solution of the problem concerning the existence of the soul, we question : if the soul continues to exist, what will become of it afterwards, and what will be its destiny? Modern science does not help us in answering the question of the destiny of the soul. It is too deep. We can only guess from the premises upon which the induction can be formed. We get the answer from the Vedanta, which is most universal and most unsectarian. It tells us that the soul, which produces the gross material form, is separable from the body and can exist independent of the body. It possesses the sense-powers, life-force, mind and intellect as well as the impressions of its physical and mental activities, and this soul manufactures the body through the mediums of parents.

---

[1] Vide Swami Abhedananda : *Self-knowledge*, pp. 17-18.

Now a question may arise : if the soul continues to exist after death, does it lose its individuality? We get the answer from the Vedanta that it retains its own individuality. It can remember where it was, who were its parents, etc.

Modern spiritualism and the result of the psychological researches have given us ample proof of the individual soul after death. Those who are highly advanced in spiritual life, do not care for their connections with earthly regions, but they rise higher above them. Souls retain their individuality, and can go to any realms. They can go to the angels, and to heaven. According to Vedanta, there are many heavens, and not only one. By heaven we understand the realm of an existence, where we go to enjoy the pleasures of life. Those who aspire after the higher spiritual life will seek higher things. They will go onward and upward, until they are one with the infinite Being.

The Christian and Mohammedan ideas of heaven and hell are the same. Their heavens are the place of eternal happiness and glory for the just, and hell a place of eternal punishment for the wicked.[2] But, in the Vedanta, you will find that it is not so.

Those souls which have desires for earthly things will have to come down to earth. Some souls will remain earth bound for a certain length of time, say one hundred, or a thousand years. The conditions will vary, and those souls, which will have earthly desires to be a king or emperor, or to have a large fortune, a large family or any other kind of ambition, will have to come down on this plane. They will be born again. So the destiny of the human soul is determined by the thoughts and desires and tendencies. We create our own destiny by our thoughts and desires and deeds. What we are today are the results of our past existence. God is not responsible for our conditions. We ourselves are responsible,

---

[2] Vide Swami Abhedananda : *Path of Realization*, pp. 173-198.

and if we understand this secret mystery of the soul, then we can mould our future in such a manner that we will never go down, but rise higher and higher, until we have reached the goal of our existence.

Those who perform good deeds and lead a virtuous life will come down on the human plane and be born again, until they rise higher in their aspirations and desires, and those that have low tendencies and died in absolute ignorance, will become idiots, subject to suffering and misery for a certain length of time, until the higher perceptions will be opened to them. So we must try our best to perform good deeds to build up our characters and to lead a virtuous life, and then we will enjoy eternal happiness and immortality even in this life.

CHAPTER VII

PRE-EXISTENCE AND REINCARNATION

Most myterious is the government concerning life and death of individuals upon this plane. From the very ancient times, the philosophers and the thinkers of all countries have tried to unravel this great mystery of nature. Again and again it has been asked why do people come into existence upon this plane for a short time. Some are born and pass out within a few weeks, or a few months, or a few years, without having any opportunity to fulfil all the desires they had, as if they are forced by some external power to leave this world unexpectedly before they have completed their desires and experiences. Why is this ? Why do some people come and live for a short time, and others live longer ? Are these all accidental ? Do the souls come here and pass out without any definite purpose and without being governed by any law ? Or is there a law behind all these appearances ? This question rises in our minds and each individual must solve this problem, otherwise he or she cannot remain contented. The mind wants solution, because our tendency is to know. So we must know, and we must solve all the problems of life and death.

When we turn towards different classes of thinkers, we find that there is a class of thinkers who are known as materialists or scientists or agnostics. They deny the existence of the soul as an intelligent self-conscious entity, but they try to explain everything through the material forces which are governed by the mechanical laws. Some of them have gone so far as to assert that appearance and disappearance of the

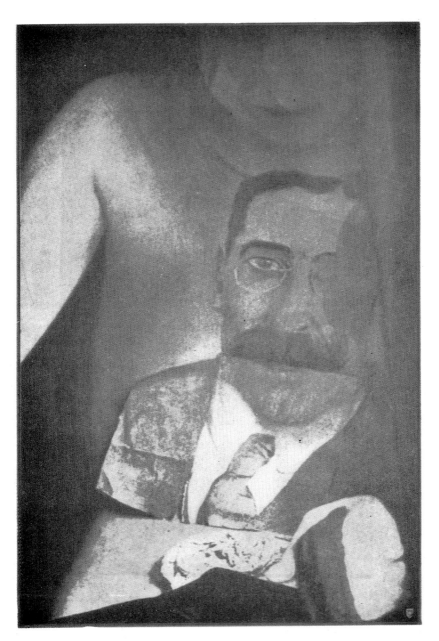

Spirit with spectacle and the Medium

The Spirit is Materialised with the help of the Medium

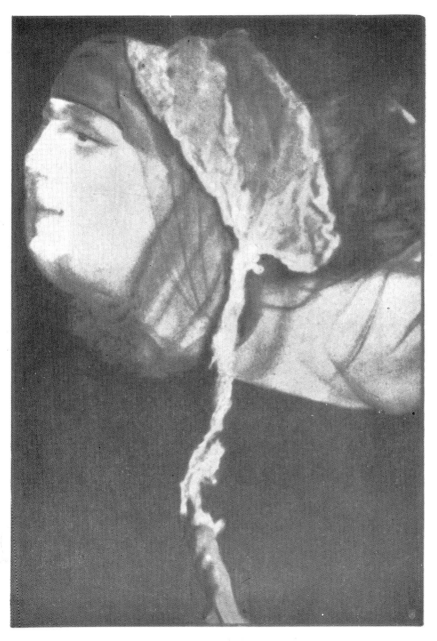

Materialised face of the Spirit with the help of Ectoplasm

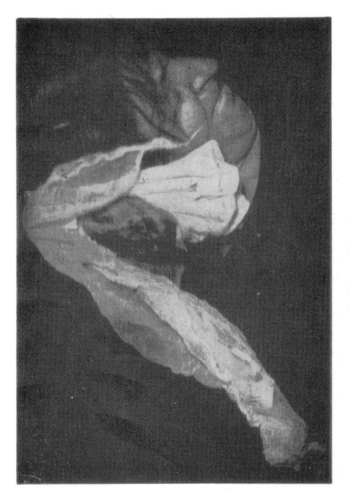

Spirit and Ectoplasm

The Portrait of Jesus the Christ, drawn
by the Spirit

Prof. Crooks is showing that Medium and Spirit are different
(Painted by S. Drizin)

The Photograph of the Spirit and the
Medium

The Figures of the Spirits coming out of the Ectoplasm.

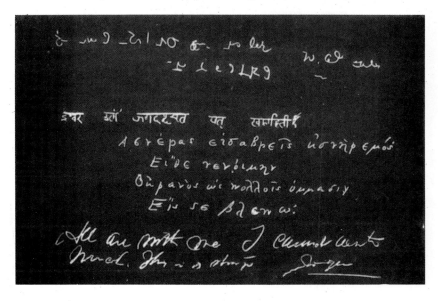

Hand-writing of the Spirit of Swami Yogananda,
in the Slate

human beings on this planet are nothing but the results of some fortuitous or accidental combination of matter or of disintegration of material particles which are caused by the natural process of the evolution of matter. There is no such thing as soul, there is no such thing as purpose of life, as all these are coming accidentally. And these appearances of human bodies or beings at the time of death cease to exist. But this explanation does not satisfy the minds of the seekers after truth. The questions are not solved. In the innermost soul of our souls, we know that it is wrong, it is not true, and matter has not produced intelligence and consciousness. We do not see matter producing intelligence and consciousness. It would be very difficult for any scientist to prove that the combination of matter, or the material particles, which are governed by mechanical laws, can produce intelligence and consciousness. On the other hand, it is a scientific truth that motion produces nothing but motion. But the intelligent soul or consciousness is not a motion; neither is it a result of motion, but it is something distinct from motion. It is the knower of motion and all the activities. Motion produces nothing but motion. It does not produce the knower who has all the power of translating the molecular activities of the brain cells into sensations, perceptions, ideas, desires and thoughts. All these are the living properties of a living soul which functions in the mind. No one has proved that brain creates the mind or intelligence, but, on the contrary, the great thinkers of the world have understood the secret of truth concerning the relation between the mind and the brain. For instance, Dr. Thomson, in his book *Brain and Personality*, explains that brain is only the instrument, but the personality or the mind, or the intelligent self-conscious entity is over-shadowing the brain. He compared the brain with a violin. Just as the violin cannot produce any music without a musician, so music is not in the violin, but is in the mind of the musician and the musician must bring it out by playing upon the strings which would touch our souls. Violin itself cannot do it. Similarly the personality is like the musician who is playing upon the strings of the nerves and the brain cells from outside, as it were, over-shadowing it and producing harmony or discord. If the musician is not well-trained, well-advanced and well-developed, instead of bringing out harmony, he creates discord just as a child who plays upon the violin instead of producing any music he would create discord, which would be a very undesirable thing.

In this way, if we analyse, we see that our soul, the self-conscious entity and thinker, is not the result of activity of the brain-cells, but is something distinct and immaterial. But yet it has the power to control and govern all the material forces that are under its dominion. If we understand that there is some entity which is our real self and possesses all the desires and·thoughts and ideas, then we wish to know : what is that something that is self-conscious ? Where does it exist? How does it produce this physical body and organism? Well, in the first place, if we study nature, we find that the law of causation is inexorable and omnipotent. The law of cause and effect governs everything in this universe. Every effect must have a cause. If we deny the law of causation, we not only deny the truth of nature, but also destroy the fundamental principle of modern science which is that something cannot come out of nothing. This theory has been well-advanced by the *Sankhya* of Kapila. In fact, non-existence cannot produce existence, or existence cannot come out of non-existence. If we exist today, we must have had a cause. That cause is something, and not non-existence. In other words, we have not come out of nothing. Applying this truth to the phenomena of life and death, we understand that all the appearances of the human beings and the animals on this plane have definite causes. Having understood thus so far, we want to trace the kind of cause that produces all these human activities or the activities of an intelligent being. What is the cause that produces all these things ? Is that cause outside of ourselves, or is it in us? This is another clear understanding of the relation of the cause to the effect which is absolutely necessary for the proper solution of any problem that we have to face.

Instead of going into the details of the methods by which the ultimate scientific truth has been established, let us take it for granted that this scientific truth that the cause of a thing is not outside of the thing itself, but is in the thing is scientific and correct. But it is a fact that the cause of a tree is not outside of the tree, but is in the tree itself ; the cause of a human being is not outside of the human being, but is in the human being. So we do not have to trace the cause outside of us. In other words, the cause is the unmanifested state of the effect and the effect is the manifested state of the cause. The whole tree remains in the seed in an invisible state or in a potential form. The environments only give the favourable conditions, under which what is latent in the seed becomes actual and real and manifested. The environments do not give any of the powers to the seed which were not already there. The environments simply give the proper conditions. If we understand this clearly, then we find that the environments do not create, but the creative power is in the seed itself, and that seed does not manifest the causal state, until it has taken the form of the tree. Now apply this truth to the human being, or to its manifestation. If the cause is in us, then what is that cause? That cause must be something which contains all the peculiarities which a human being can manifest in his lifetime. The cause retains all the potentialities of the forces or powers of the mind, of the thought, of the desire, and of the intelligence just as the seed of an oak tree contains all the peculiarities of an oak tree. Those conditions or powers which are latent in the seed of an oak tree, cannot be changed by the environments, but they will become manifested into an oak tree and not in a chestnut tree. This is a real fact. This has been scientifically proved. Therefore the causal state of a human being will manifest in the future and that causal state is invisible just as we do not see in a seed all the latent tree that is already there. The seed of a banyan tree, for instance, is as small as a mustard seed, and if it is given to you, you would not know what it is, but it contains a gigantic banyan tree which will cover the area of a mile in circumference and will produce, perhaps, seventy five or a hundred trunks of one tree. There is such a tree in the Botanical Garden near Calcutta. One tree covers an area of a mile and has seventy five trunks. It shoots the roots which afterwards grow into the trunks of the tree. That gigantic tree which would last for thousands of years like one of the big trees here in Mariposa Grove, is contained in that seed. No other seed will produce that. All the peculiarities of a banyan tree are in that seed. Similarly, the invisible germ which you may call an amœba or bioplasm or protoplasm and which will afterwards appear as a human being, contains all the potentialities of that human being in the invisible state. If we deny this, then we run the risk of committing that blunder that something has come out of nothing. But the scientific truth is that whatever exists in the end, existed also in the beginning. If in the end we find a human being like Abraham Lincoln or Shakespeare or Plato, then the germ, or the seed form which has manufactured that particular manifestation, contained all those powers in an invisible state. You may call it a germ, or you may call it by any other name. Names do not make much difference. Leibnitz called it Monad.[1] Scientists call it the germ of life. The Vedanta philosophy calls it the subtle body. The subtle bodies are the invisible germs or nucleii which contain the mind, the intelligence, the reasoning, the power of thinking, the will power, and all the senses i.e., the powers of seeing, hearing, smelling, tasting, touching, and so forth. All these powers are there in the germ of life. It also contains the impressions of the previous manifestation, and those impressions are

---

[1] Leibnitz's conscious Monad is somewhat similar to *Anu* of Kanada.

embedded in that substance. That substance is etherial or electric i.e., the minute particles of the matter which are held together by that force which is called the life-force, or the vital energy.

Now this subtle being is the real man. It appears in the form of a human body which it manufactures and lives in. Just as an oyster or a crab would manufacture a shell as a dwelling-house, so this germ of life or the subtle body of the individual, whether it is human or animal, takes only the form according to its desires, or according to its tendencies. The human germ of life will manufacture a human body, and, if it desires to be of any particular animal form, it manufactures that form. It has no particular form, but it can take any form. This subtle body contains everything. So we do not gain anything from outside. It is already there. It has infinite potentialities and infinite possibilities.

At the time of death, the individual germ of life contracts all its forces and powers, and all these are centralized into a nucleus and that nucleus retains the life, the mind, the powers of the senses, and all the impressions and experiences that the individual has gathered. Then, in course of time, when the favourable conditions come, it manufactures another form. Parents are nothing but the principal channels through which these germs of life, or the subtle bodies find proper conditions of manufacturing human being by obeying the laws of nature. Parents do not create the soul. In fact, the parents cannot give birth to a child according to their will. It would be an absolute impossibility. Unless the soul comes to them and nourishes the germ, it would be an absolute impossibility. These subtle bodies are like water globules. As a water globule may remain in the form of water in the ocean, so it may go up and become invisible in a vapoury state in a cloud and then come down again in the form of a drop of rain. Then it may remain again in the mud, or it may be frozen into a solid substance when you can handle the form of a solid substance, or you can handle the form of a piece of ice. But it is never destroyed. It may become invisible or visible. These conditions do not change the globule of water. It is there and this globule of water of the subtle body arises in the beginningless past in the ocean of the eternal life, and retains the reflection of the supreme Spirit in the form of intelligence. It may appear on this earth, or it may go to another planet. It has the power to travel with the speed of light. It can follow the way of light from one planet to another with vibrations or waves of the ether. It can shoot out instantaneously. It has such a power. And this subtle body may remain on this plane in the human form. Then after death, it might go to heaven or to some other planet, or remain in an invisible state until the proper conditions and suitable environments are found. Then it gravitates according to their desires. This whole process is governed by a law and this law is called the law of reincarnation or remanifestation of the subtle form in the gross physical form. This law is inexorable. No matter what we want to do, or whether we admit its existence or not, it is working just the same. The same forces which have brought us here this time will bring us here again. Who can stop it? Your will or my will would not stop it until we understand this law, outgrow it, and go beyond it. So we may think that we deny it or we do not want to believe such stuff. Well, the ignorant fool may say that we do not believe in gravitation and deny its existence, but still his whole being is held up by the force of gravity. He could not live without it. The molecules of his body would fly asunder if there were no force of gravity to hold them together. He could not live on the surface of the earth if he were not held down by the force of the gravity. Still he can deny it. But his denial amounts to nothing and simply betrays his own ignorance that he does not understand the law. In the same way, anyone who denies reincarnation, betrays his own ignorance, because he does not know the law.

Those who do not believe in reincarnation, believe in the one-birth theory. Two great religions, Judaism, with its off-shoots Christianity and Mohammedanism, and Zoroastrianism, rather believe in the theory of one birth, and try to explain all the inequalities and diversities which we find among us. But they do not succeed. They believe that the souls of the individuals have been created out of nothing for the first time, and some of them tell us that they will continue to exist for ever. Now, how is it possible that anything that has a beginning at one end, will continue to exist forever at the other? It is absurd. It is an absolute impossibility. Anything that has a beginning must have an end. If you believe that the individual souls that have been created out of nothing for the first time, will continue to live forever, then you have to admit that these souls were not created out of nothing, but they existed before. In Genesis, you read in the first chapter that God created man after His own image. In the second chapter, you read that He made man out of the dust of the earth, and blew the breath of life into his nostrils. There are the two statements. There were two stories, which were prevalent amongst the Phoenicians of ancient times and the ancient Jews. The writer of Genesis accepted those two stories and put them together in the chapters. But the two ideas are radically opposed. Which will you accept ? But if God created man after His own image, how did He create him ? Well, the second said that God created him out of the dust of the earth. But it should be remembered that earth is the material insentient matter and so it does not explain how the breath of life came into existence. All these difficulties that arise in our minds after studying these statements cannot be solved in any other way unless we accept the idea that the spirit or intelligence or consciousness was never created, but the body was created or manufactured through the process of evolution. As the breath of life was never created, so the mind and soul were never created, but the soul retains the image of the Lord, or the supreme Spirit.

In other words, as Vedanta explains, the breath of life contains the reflection of the supreme Spirit that is all-intelligence. We cannot explain anything by the theory of one-birth, or by that of creation of the soul out of nothing because if God creates the soul out of nothing, why does He make so many varieties of characters? Some are born to enjoy and to show their genius and wonderful talents. Others are kept to manifest nothing but ignorance and other weaknesses. How can you explain those things ? A person may have five children. One might be a murderer, another might be a genius, another might be an artist, and so on. What makes all these inequalities and diversities ? If God creates each one separately at the time of the birth of the body, then who is to be held responsible ? Not the parents, but God Himself. Why could not He do better ? That question must rise in our minds and we must try to find the solution.

Then another question rises : why do children come into life to live only for a short time, for a day, or for a few weeks? Why do they pass away without gaining any opportunity to earn anything, or gain experience in this vast world of phenomena ? Who is responsible and what becomes of those children ? Well, there might be a theory—they would go to heaven and enjoy eternal life. For those who could believe that story, it is better to pray for death of their children before they commit any more harm, and thank the Lord that their little bodies are covered by the grave. I would do that if I had little children and believed in such a thing. Why should they go through all these miseries and troubles? If we could go to heaven straight by dying in childhood, we would rather die than live. So this theory does not explain anything, but makes it appear to us as absurd and irrational. Then if you admit the theory of predestination and grace, that also does not help us very much. If we are predestined and pre-ordained to do these things, and if a murderer is pre-ordained to murder somebody and before he had any will it was all arranged by the Creator, then why should we hang the murderer ? We should hang the Creator, because He is responsible. Therefore we cannot find any solution.

Then there is another creed of heredity. Does heredity explain all these inequalities and diversities? No, it cannot. How can heredity explain the cases of prodigies and geniuses? Take the case of the young Polish boy who is a great chess player. He is only eight years old. He is now in New York, I think. He began to play chess when he was five years old and has beaten all the great experts and champions of London and Paris after playing thirty-three games at a time and defeating them all.[2] What mental power does he possess? He has brothers and sisters. They are not uncommon. Neither are the parents in any way uncommon. He is the only one. How can heredity explain that ? Take the case of Goethe, the great German poet. He was an octogenarian poet and philosopher. When he was ten, he was a master of Greek and sixteen other languages. There is a Frenchman now[3] in Columbia who knows more than a dozen languages. He knows more than his teacher can teach him. The theory of heredity cannot explain these cases of prodigies and geniuses. But there is another theory that would explain them. Whatever a person has manifested in this life, he had it at the time of his birth from the very beginning, i.e., he gained the power in his previous life. So any talent or genius is only the expression of all that was developed in the particular soul. I saw a girl who was six years old in New York city. She could play on the piano Bach and Bethoven and all the difficult music with such an ease and such a perfection that you would be surprised. She could hardly span the octave and yet she was playing this rapid music with most wonderful expression. Her mother was with her and she was not a musician. Her father was never a musician. How do you explain that ? Heredity cannot explain.

[2 & 3] As to the lecture delivered in America, sometime between 1901 and 1905.

But we can explain that theory easily. Because this child was a musician and the soul of this child was a musician in her previous incarnation, and now she has manufactured another form with a little brain. Her brain is not developed enough to understand such music, but the musician is overshadowing the brain and manipulating all these strings of the brain and the nerve-cells and producing all this wonderful music. That is the only rational explanation.

If we deny pre-existence of the soul, we cannot explain immortality. Immortality does not mean that it has a beginning at one end and endless existence on the other. Pre-existence explains the continuity of life in the past, and immortality explains the continuity of life in the future. Immortality means an eternal life. You cannot accept one half and deny the other half, because each would be incomplete. So the complete soul-life means eternal past and eternal future. The soul was never born and was never created out of nothing. It is the grandest theory and it is satisfying. It is comforting that we have not come into existence out of nothing, but we have everything in the beginning. If we are the images of God, then we possess all the powers. God was not a substance that came into existence suddenly like a mushroom, but He is eternal, and naturally our soul-life must be as eternal as God's life. In fact, we are parts and parcels of God. In this way, if we understand how great and grand and beautiful we are, we do not have to accept any such idea that after death we will discontinue to live. But, on the contrary, we can say that so long as we have desires and those desires are to be fulfilled on the human plane under our present conditions, we will come back to this plane. If our desires change, we will go to other planes. For instance, if I have a desire to become an artist like Michael Angelo and if I in this life cannot become a Michael Angelo and still possess the desire in my soul, do you think that desire will have no fulfilment or manifestation? Nothing will stop the fulfilment of that desire, because that desire will bring me back to the proper environments and other conditions where I will gravitate and then start from my childhood with a tendency to become an artist. Nothing can stop me and I will continue so long as that desire is strong. I will continue until I become a master artist. And that is the law of nature. So whatever desire we possess, if that desire be strong, then that desire will mould our future, create our destiny, and make us accordingly. This idea has been given in the *Bhagavad Gita* :

> 'Whatsoever desire is very strong during the lifetime, becomes predominant at the time of death, and that desire moulds the creation of the subtle body of the individual and that determines the future of the individual.'[4]

So, that gives us an opportunity to find out what we shall be in future. We will make our future by our thoughts and desires. If you desire to be a great politician, you will be a great politician. If you desire to be a great saviour, you will be a great saviour. If you desire to be a great artist, you will be a great artist. In fact, you live in the eternity. Do not despair. If you cannot be a great artist in this life, there are hundreds of lives coming to you, till you get that desire. And when one set of desires is fulfilled, another will spring up. As each individual soul possesses infinite potentialities and possibilities, so it can express an infinite variety of manifestation. Because we are all eternal and are parts of the Infinite.

The idea of pre-existence of soul and reincarnation has settled the questions and solved the problems of life and death amongst the ancient philosophers like Plato, Pythagoras and the Neo-Platonists and also amongst the poets like Wordsworth, Tennyson, Walt Whitman and others. Walt Whitman said :

---

[4] यं यं वापि स्मरन् भावं त्यजत्यन्ते कलेवरम्।
तं तमेवैति कौन्तेय सदा तद्भावभावितः ॥

—भगवद्गीता, ८/६

'As to you, Life, I reckon your are the leavings of many
death. No doubt I have died myself ten thousand times
before.'

He learned this truth through the study of Vedanta, just as
Emerson learned the belief in reincarnation from the study of
Vedanta. It is also true that there is no other philosophy which
manifests this idea so strongly as Vedanta does. Of course,
Plato and Pythagoras got their ideas from India through
Persia and Egypt. The Hindus understood the secret of this
law of pre-existence and reincarnation even at the dawn of
human civilization on the earth. That idea spread among the
early Christians until the time of Justinian, who anathematized
all those that believed in this idea, in the Council of
Constantinople in 538 A.D. He said :

'Whoever believes in this wonderful doctrine of pre-
existence of the soul, let him be anathema'.

The churches from that time have not accepted it although it
is in the Old Testament as well as in the New Testament. It
does not preserve their scheme of salvation. But outside of
the orthodox people, there are millions of people in the world
who find comfort in this idea like the Buddhists, Japanese,
Hindus, and poets and thinkers of all countries. Therefore it
is the rational solution and it explains all the causes of
inequalities and diversities and the appearance of the prodigies.
Heredity or the theory of one-birth as explained by the
orthodox theologians, does not explain or solve the problem
of life. Now you may have noticed that there are persons who
cannot accept this theory of pre-existence and reincarnation,
because they cannot remember. They say, well, if we existed
before, why do we not remember what we did ourselves? Do
you remember what you did in your childhood? Would you
say you did not exist then, because you cannot remember?
Certainly not. What you did when you were a child? All the

existence you have gone through and the details have passed out of your memory, but the knowledge you have gathered through those experiences, is the part and parcel of your being and that has shaped you as you are. Memory is of short duration, and it is sometimes powerful and sometimes very weak.

But modern spiritualism has thrown a different light on this subject. It says that the souls that have passed out remember their relatives, remember the conditions under which they passed. So the memory continues. Take the case of Raymond, the son of Sir Oliver Lodge. He remembered everything how he died and so on, and he communicated to his father and mother and told them. So, that shows that we retain our memory even. But the instruments, the brain and the nervous system are destroyed. Therefore the memory is not the product of the function of the brain, but it is a power of the mind which we retain so long as there would be the mind. However, the memory is not so important. If we do remember our past, we might make bad use of our present. Therefore it is not desirable. Suppose somebody knows or understands his past, and knows that he had committed wicked deeds, and he is going to suffer for it, and he would be constantly thinking of that. He would lose all these opportunities and make a bad use of his present. He would not be able to do any work properly. He would be worrying about how to avoid the misfortune that is coming. He would not be able to sleep even, or eat a good meal. Therefore the Vedanta philosophy tells us not to think of the past but to mould our future and present, so that we can make our future better. Of course, there is a method by which we can remember our past, because all the experiences that we have gained during our lifetime, are stored up in our subliminal or subconscious mind where all these impressions are pigeon-holed. We can bring them out, if we focus our intelligence upon any particular branch of the experience which we like to remember. There are cases again like two lovers who fall in love at the first sight. There we can explain that these souls loved before, and naturally they remember that and feel as if they had met each other. And what is love? Love does not mean any passion. It means the attraction of two souls. It is not on the physical plane, but must be on the soul-plane, because love is God. It is the divine force; it is the divine attraction of two souls. It there be pure love between any man and woman, that pure love will continue to hold them together even after death of the body, because the body cannot interfere. But at the same time we must remember that love must be mutual. If the husband loves the wife and the wife loves the husband truly and unselfishly, then that love is mutual. But if you love somebody and that somebody loves somebody else, then there would be no meeting again, until both were attracted to each other. Therefore it is necessary to develop that kind of love which would be mutual and then that love will hold the lover and the beloved together throughout eternity. There is no separation in it. So you need not be afraid of being separated from your beloved, and if your beloved be born again, after you go from this plane, you will be born again and you will come together unexpectedly and enjoy the beautiful effects of pure and divine love.

Therefore, if we study this carefully, we see that pre-existence and reincarnation go hand in hand and they explain all the difficulties and problems of life and death as well as of existence and also that we are the creators of our own destiny. Our present life is the resultant of our past and our future will be the resultant of our present. Whether we remember or not, that does not make any difference. We are subject to this eternal law. But there are souls who can remember. If we rise on the height of our spiritual consciousness, we can see our past and future just as if it were eternally present. Therefore Sri Krishna said to Arjuna :

'Oh Arjuna, both you and I have passed through many births. You know them not, but I remember them all.'[5]

So anyone, who reaches that state of superconsciousness, develops a sight. By developing that sight one can see the past and the future and remember all the experiences that one has gone through and all the experiences that one will go through. And when he understands that life is eternal, he does not worry about the conditions of the failures and successes or diseases or sufferings of this earthly plane. This life on this plane is only for a short time, but from the standpoint of eternal life we are never born and we are never going to die, because we are birthless, deathless, eternal, immortal, and also part and parcel of the infinite Spirit which is worshipped under different names among different races.

---

[5] Vide *Bhagavad-Gita*, Ch. IV. 5.

CHAPTER VIII

PRE-EXISTENCE AND IMMORTALITY

One of the fundamental principles of philosophy and religion of Vedanta is immortality of the human soul. According to the teachings of Vedanta, each individual soul is immortal by nature. However sinful it may appear to be from the moral standpoint, it will continue to exist after death of the body. It cannot be annihilated or destroyed into nothingness. It can never cease to exist.

On this point the religion of Vedanta differs from the dogmas of those dualistic religions, which maintain that immortal life can be obtained only by a few chosen ones as a special gift of God, while others will perish. Many of the orthodox Christian theologians hold that the continued life after death in the eternal future is not a natural gift, but a special one, being conditioned upon the proper use of this life. They think that immortality is a reward of merit, or of good works, or of an ethical life, or of faith in the Christ. Here we may ask, who will decide how many degrees above zero one must be moral in order to obtain the gift of immortality ?

If we examine minutely we shall find that this dogma of conditional immortality is not based upon a rational foundation. It makes God, the merciful Father, partial and unjust. How can we imagine that a just, impartial and merciful Father will grant immortality to some of His children and allow the rest to perish simply on account of their immoral acts or mistakes?

The religion of Vedanta does not teach this dogma of conditional immortality ; but, on the contrary, it says that immortal life cannot be a reward or a gift of any superior being, because that reward or punishment is nothing but the result or reaction of our own actions. Since every human action is finite or limited by time and space, and consequently non-eternal, it cannot produce an eternal effect in the form of immortal life. No human action, either of the mind or of the body, however good or virtuous it may be called, can produce an eternal effect which is unlimited by time or space. It will then be against the law of cause and sequence which makes every effect or result similar to its cause, both in nature and in quality.

There is another important point on which the conception of immortality in Vedanta differs from that of Christianity. Christianity, believing in the theory of special creation of the individual soul at the time of birth, denies pre-existence of the human soul previous to the birth of the body, yet it admits the continuity of the soul after death in an eternal future. This doctrine again is not based upon a rational foundation, nor is it supported by any fact of nature, because it is impossible for a thing which has a beginning in time to last for ever. No one has ever seen or heard of any substance which began to exist at a certain time, but continued forever in future. Can we imagine a stick, the one end of which is in our hand and the other end is endless and unlimited ? No, it is impossible. We cannot think of a thing which has a beginning or a limit, either in time or in space on one side and, on the other side, is unlimited by either time or space. As we cannot imagine any earthly object or material thing of such a nature, how can we imagine that the soul which had its birth in time and space, will continue to exist forever ? We cannot conceive that a soul which came into existence at the time of birth will remain forever after death in eternal future, or in endless time. Therefore immortality which means the eternal continuity of existence, pre-supposes the existence of the soul previous to the birth of the body. If we believe in immortality of the human soul, we shall have to admit its pre-existence also, because that which is born, must die, and everything that has a beginning, must have an end. This is the law of nature; we cannot go against it.

The laws of nature are always uniform and universal. There is no such thing as an exception. All exceptions are governed by other laws which we may or may not know. They are only the expressions of different laws. Anything that is born must be subject to death, and that which has a beginning must have an end. If we wish to be endless or immortal in future, we must have to admit that we were beginningless or immortal in the past. Here some people may think, how is it possible that we existed in the past? If we apply the law that because we exist today, we cannot come into existence out of nothing, then we will get a glimpse of the idea of pre-existence. And, for this reason, Vedanta teaches both immortality and pre-existence. No theory of immortality can be perfect or complete without admitting the pre-existence of the soul. No theory has successfully proved the necessity of an eternal future life in the case of one whose existence in the past has been proved to be unnecessary. If you say that your pre-existence was unnecessary, so your immortal life will be equally unnecessary. If the world could get along without you before, why should it not get along without you hereafter? What necessity will there be for an immortal life in future, if you did not exist before? If you have come into existence all on a sudden, you can go out of existence all on a sudden. Who will prevent us from becoming such an ephemeral substance?

In Vedanta, true immortality means eternal existence in the past as well as in the future. Pre-existence and immortality are so closely related to each other that if we deny one, we cannot accept the other. For logically we shall be incorrect; we shall go against the laws of nature, and our statement will be founded, not upon rational ground, but upon some dogma or doctrine which has no foundation. In Vedanta, therefore, we learn that each individual soul existed before the birth of the body. If we believe that we shall continue to exist after death, we shall have to admit that we existed in the past, otherwise, we cannot have immortal life in future. We have not come into existence for the first time out of nothing, but our present is a connecting link in the chain of our past and future existences. We may not know it, we may not possess the memory of our past lives, but still we existed just the same.

Here it may be asked, if we existed before our birth, why do we not remember? This is one of the strongest objections often raised against the belief in pre-existence. Some people deny the existence of the soul in the past, simply because they cannot remember the events of the past. Others again who hold memory as the standard of existence, say, if our memory of the present ceases to exist at the time of death, with it we shall also cease to be and we cannot be immortal, because they hold that memory is the standard of life, and if we do not remember, why, we are not the same beings!

Vedanta answers these questions by saying that it is possible for us to remember our previous existences. Those who have read Raja Yoga, will recall the aphorism :

'By perceiving the *samskaras* one acquires the knowledge of past lives.'[1]

Here the *samskaras* mean the impressions of past experiences which lie dormant in our subliminal self and are never lost. Memory is nothing but the awakening and rising of latent impressions about the threshold of consciousness. A Raja

---

[1] Vide *Patanjala-darsana*, 3-18.

Yogi, through powerful concentration upon these dormant impressions of the subconscious mind, can remember all the events of his past lives. There have been many instances of the Indian Yogis who could know not only their own past lives, but correctly tell those of others. It is said that Buddha remembered five hundred of his previous births. Sri Krishna says in the *Bhagavad Gita* :

> 'Both thou and I, Arjuna, have gone through many births; thou knowest them not; but I know them all.'[2]

This shows that Sri Krishna remembered them, because he was a Yogi and Arjuna could not remember, because he had not the power to do so.

Our subliminal self or the subconscious mind is the store-house of all the impressions that we gather through our experiences during our life-time. They are stored up or pigeon-holed there in the *chitta*, as it is called in Vedanta. The *chitta* means the same subconscious mind or subliminal self which is the store-house of all impressions and experiences.[3] These impressions remain latent, until favourable conditions rouse them and bring them out in the plane of consciousness. Here let us take an illustration. In a dark room, pictures are thrown on a screen by lantern-slides. The room is absolutely dark. We are looking at the picture. Suppose we open a window and allow the rays of the midday sun to fall upon the screen. Would we be able to see those pictures? No, because the more powerful flood of light of the sun will subdue the light of the lantern and the pictures. But although they are invisible to our eyes, yet we cannot deny their existence on the screen. Similarly the pictures of the events of our previous lives upon the screen of the subliminal self may be invisible to us at present, but they exist there. Why are they invisible

---

[2] तान्यहं वेद सर्वाणि न त्वं वेत्थ परन्तप ।   —भगवद्गीता, ४/५
[3] Here the *chitta* means the mind or the *manas*.

to us now? Because the powerful light of the sense-consciousness has subdued them. If we close the windows and the door of our senses from outside contact and darken the inner chamber of our self, then by focussing the light of consciousness and concentrating the mental rays we shall be able to know and remember our past lives as well as the events and experiences thereof. Those who wish to develop their memory and remember their past should practise Raja Yoga and learn the method of acquiring the power of concentration by shutting the doors and the windows of their senses. That power of concentration must be helped by the power of self-control, i.e., by controlling the windows and the doors of our own senses.

These dormant impressions, whether we remember them or not, are the chief factors in moulding our individual characters with which we are born ; they are the causes of the inequalities and diversities which we find around us. When we study the characters and the powers of the geniuses and the prodigies, we cannot deny the pre-existence of the soul. Whatever the soul has mastered in a previous life, it manifests in the present. If we possess wisdom and knowledge which we gathered in our previous lives, then it matters very little, whether or not we remember the particular events or the struggles which we went through in order to gain that knowledge. Those particular things may not come to us in our memory, but we have not lost the wisdom. Now study your own present life and you will see that in this life you have gained some experience. The particular events and struggles which you went through are passing out of your memory, but the knowledge which you have gained through that experience, has moulded your character and has shaped you in a different manner. You will not have to go through those different events again to remember how you acquired that experience ; that is not necessary and the wisdom gained is quite enough.

Then again we find among ourselves persons who are born with some wonderful powers. Take, for instance, the power of self-control. One is born with the power of self-control highly developed and that self-control may not be acquired by another after years of hard struggle. Why is there this difference? Bhagavan Sri Ramakrishna was born with the God-consciousness and he went into the highest state of *samadhi* when he was four years old. But this state is very difficult for other Yogis to acquire. There was a Yogi who came to see Sri Ramakrishna. He was an old man and possessed of wonderful powers, and he said : 'I have struggled for forty years to acquire that state which is natural with you'. Sankaracharya, the great commentator of the Vedanta philosophy, wrote his commentary when he was twelve years of age. There are very few thinkers and philosophers in the world who can understand the spirit of his writings. They are so deep and sublime that ordinary minds cannot grasp them. There are many such instances which show that pre-existence is a fact and that these latent or dormant impressions of previous lives are the chief factors in moulding the individual character without depending upon the memory of the past. Because we cannot remember our past. But because of the loss of memory of the particular events, the soul's progress is not arrested. The soul will continue to progress further even though the memory may be weak.

Each individual soul possesses the store-house of his previous experiences in the background in the subconscious mind. Take the instance of two lovers. Now what is love ? It has already been explained that it is the attraction between two souls. This love does not die with the death of the body. True love survives after death and continues to grow, and becomes stronger and stronger. Eventually it brings the two souls together and makes them one. The theory of pre-existence alone can explain why the two souls at the first sight know each other and become attached to each other by the tie of friendship. This mutual love will continue to grow and will become stronger and in the end will bring these lovers together no matter where they go. Therefore Vedanta does not say that death of the body will end the attraction of the attachment of the two souls, but as the souls are immortal, their relation will continue forever. But we must not forget that relation and love must be mutual. If you love some one and that person does not love you, it will be one-sided. It will not bring the two souls together. So there must be a mutual attraction. In Vedanta, we learn that as immortality means the continued existence in the eternal future, so pre-existence means the continued existence in the eternal past. One cannot exist without the other. Each of these only expresses the one half of our soul-life which is eternal and both of these together make a complete whole, and that is the eternal soul-life. It existed before and it was always unborn, and, therefore, it will continue to exist in the future forever. Our present life is the resultant of the past and our future will be the resultant of the present. Nothing will be lost.

Modern spiritualism has thrown a little light upon the future that even the departed spirits do remember their past relations. This shows that memory does not depend entirely upon the physical organism, but goes with the soul wherever the soul goes. That is the real memory. The physical organism may be destroyed, but memory lives. It is the body through which the subliminal self is reproducing powers which are latent in it. So our present life is the resultant of the past. It contains all the previous impressions and experiences of past lives and only under certain conditions they can be remembered. But here we must remember that immortality does not necessarily imply that we should go to heaven to eternally enjoy the celestial pleasures, or go to eternal hell of our evil deeds. These ideas are not necessarily included in the meaning of immortality. According to Vedanta, immortality includes the meaning of progress, i.e. progress of growth and evolution of the soul from lower to the higher stages of development. It also includes the idea that each individual soul will manifest the powers which are already latent in the soul by going through different stages of growth and development until perfection and omniscience and omnipresence are acquired. In order to attain to this and to accomplish this highest end, the soul must manifest itself in various stages of life and gain experience. That cause which brought us on the plane of existence, will continue to bring us here again in future. If the same cause remains in us even after the death of the body, then nothing can prevent us from coming back to this plane of existence in order to fulfil our desires and purposes. This idea leads to the theories of rebirth and reincarnation of the individual soul. The rebirth and reincarnation of the individual soul is based upon the truth of the eternality of the soul-life which is expressed by pre-existence and immortality. The exodus of the soul after death into heaven or into some realm of punishment or lower realm depends entirely upon the thoughts and deeds of the individual soul, and the soul's stay in these realms is temporary and dependent upon the condition of reaping the results of those thoughts and deeds. That is, the soul will remain there as long as it has not thoroughly reaped the fruits of its thoughts and deeds. At the expiration of that time, the inmates of heavens and other realms will come back on this plane, in order to gain further experience and more powers and knowledge until perfection is reached. Vedanta does not say that heaven is eternal, but it is temporary and non-eternal, and the soul has the power to transcend heaven or to go beyond all celestial realms. Why should we be limited to one particular spot? If we do not care to return to this realm of phenomena, we shall be dissatisfied even when we have gone to heaven. Then will come the time when we shall try to go further beyond until we have become absolutely perfect and divine. Therefore it is said in Vedanta :

'Even the highest heaven is temporary and non-eternal. The realms that exist between the earth and the highest heaven mark only the phenomenal growth and progress of the individual souls. Those who go there and remain there are subject to birth and rebirth. They will come back again. But those who have attained to perfection transcend all heavens, understand eternal life and remain perfect for ever and ever.'[4]

---

[4] Cf. *Bhagavad Gita,* VIII, 16-27.

CHAPTER IX
SCIENCE AND IMMORTALITY

The popular belief in Christendom is that Jesus the Christ brought the eternal life and immortality to light and that immortality cannot be obtained except through him, as if this conception of eternal life, or eternal life after death, which is understood by immortality, did not exist before the advent of the illustrious Son of Man. But the students of comparative religions find that in ancient times, long before the Christian era, this same conception of eternal or immortal life existed among the ancient nations like the Egyptians, Chaldeans, Hindus, and other different branches of the Aryan nation, such as Zoroastrians, the ancient Greeks, Romans, Scandinavians, and so on.

If we study the most ancient records in Egypt, which go back between 12000 and 8000 B.C., we shall find in those earliest records that the ancient Egyptians had a belief in the resurrection of the body as well as in eternal life for those who were righteous. The crude idea of resurrection of the body was afterwards rejected by the priests and the speculators in Egypt when the idea of a 'double' or soul as independent of the gross material body developed. But the ignorant masses kept up the belief in the resurrection of the material or corruptible body, just as we find today it is upheld by the majority of believers in orthodox Christianity. The ignorant classes cannot believe that the soul can be separated from the body and can live without the body. They believe that the soul clings to the body. Attachment to the gross material form is so great that we cannot think for a moment that we can do without the body, or can exist without this material form which we have clothed with so much care and which we have kept up with beautiful things and nice dishes, and so on.

Among the writings of the old Egyptians who lived in the time of the fifth dynasty, that is, in 400 B.C., we find such expressions as,

The soul to heaven, the body to earth,

The heaven hath thy soul, the earth thy body.

You will have to remember that 3500 years before the birth of Christ such expressions were uttered and written down by the thinkers of Egypt. These ancient Egyptians believed that the souls of the righteous would go to heaven, enjoy celestial pleasures, and would eat and drink because they would have a light, active and etherial body, and, therefore, they needed food and drink. That was their conception and it was for that reason the relatives and the friends of the deceased used to put food in the grave and sometimes they would place amulets and other charms in the graves, believing that the departed ones might need such things to protect themselves against evil influences. And again in some other writings, we find that the souls of the deceased would go to heaven and they were apparently in white linen, they wore white sandals on their feet, and they walked in the fields of peace, sat with gods, and ate the food of light. There were canals, water courses, roads, boats, chariots, horses, and the duplicates of all these things which we find on this plane, in heaven. The enjoyment of all these pleasures and comforts, lasting throughout eternity, was the meaning of immortality according to these ancient Egyptians.[1] They believed that the souls of these departed ones would go to heaven and enjoy all these celestial pleasures, the highest ideals of pleasures we can enjoy on this plane which became eternal. The enjoyment of

[1] Cf. Swami Abhedananda : *Path of Realization.*

these pleasures throughout eternity was the meaning they gave to immortality. We must remember that by 'eternity' we do not mean a million or a thousand million years, but a time without end. Can you grasp the meaning of eternity, a time without end, enjoying these pleasures? A similar belief we find among the ancient Greeks in the Elysium Fields. The Greeks believed that the righteous ones who went to the Elysium Field, would continue to enjoy the celestial pleasures throughout eternity. Each of the deceased ones would resume the pleasures and occupations in which they delighted during their earthly career. Such a belief prevails among the Swedenborgians and other churches even to this day. Not long ago a clergyman of the city of New York wrote an article in a newspaper in which he said :

'The activities of our beings on this earth will be the activities of our beings in heaven. We cannot change this ; it cannot be changed, but we must find and look for such occupations. In whatever form of existence we can conceive of the occupations of life, must shadow and type the occupations of heaven, and in nobler and in higher forms, we must go on doing what we are doing today on this earth.'

If this remark be true, I would like to know how many of our cooks, waitresses, lawyers, bell-boys, and street cleaners would like to continue the same work throughout eternity and without having an end of time. I would like to know how many would like to go on doing them.

Among the pious Christians, we find the belief that the enjoyments of heaven and the conception of the eternal life are connected with a belief that the everlasting playing upon a harp would be the principal occupation in heaven. There is a hymn which used to be sung in the churches and it gives a description of the heavenly enjoyments, where the Sabbaths never end.

So we see that before the time of Christ there was a belief in the eternal life among the Chaldeans, Egyptians and Greeks. Among the Chinese, the Hindus and the Zoroastrians, we find a similar belief in the eternal life and the celestial pleasures in heaven. So when we examine the dogma of the Christian theologians that Jesus the Christ brought to light for the first time an immortal life, we stop and ask the question whether it is true or not. Jesus the Christ might have enlightened certain tribes among the Jews who did not believe in a life hereafter or the life after death, but he did not bring that idea to the world for the first time; and even the crude idea of resurrection after death which prevailed among the Jews at the time of Christ was taken from the Parsees during the Babylonian Captivity (586-538 B.C.). If we read the Zend Avesta, we shall find that each individual, howsoever good or wicked he may be, must resurrect on the third day after death and then must go to heaven or to some place of punishment. That idea prevailed among the Jews. The Pharisees accepted it ; the Sadducees rejected it, and the other class of orthodox Jews repudiated it.

So we find by studying the other religions of the world that this belief was not introduced for the first time, but has come to mean the eternal life in heaven. Yet the question of immortality is a very difficult problem. Most of the thinkers and the metaphysicians of the world have tried to solve this problem of immortality. Some of them have arrived at certain conclusions which are either for or against the existence of the eternal life after death. But if we analyse the meaning of the word immortality, we know that it means deathlessness or the state which is not subject to death. Then comes the question, what is death ? If by death we mean destruction, annihilation and absolute dissolution of universe into nothingness, then there is no one in this world who is subject to such a death or annihilation. Science has proved that matter as well as force is indestructible. So every particle of matter, however minute or gross it may be, is not subject to absolute destruction or death ; and in that sense, we must say that matter is immortal, force is immortal, and energy is immortal, because they are not subject to either destruction or annihilation. The old gross conception of death is that it is a kind of sleep. The spirit or the soul goes into unconsciousness at the time of death ; in that slumber of unconsciousness, the soul remains until the morning of resurrection when it is again combined with the body. Both the body and the soul go to heaven or to hell, awaiting the judgement of the merciful Father. Death was regarded by the Christian theologians as the greatest enemy of the mortals and it meant the doom of the soul throughout all eternity. The good soul remained good forever and the wicked suffered throughout all eternity. That dreary conception of death still prevails among a certain class of the Christian believers, and the horror and despair also permeate the atmosphere of the sacred shrines under the vaults of holy places and the people tremble with fear when they think of the approach of death. Because it stamps, fixes the doom of the individual soul, and stereotypes the individual so that it lasts forever. Again the wicked man who has no religion will have to suffer throughout eternity. Now science has opened our eyes to the fact that death is not such an evil. Science says that death is not an enemy attacking life and we cannot live without dying, and death is also a constant continuation of life. In fact, growth would be impossible if there were no death. So there is no reason to fear death.

A scientific thinker does not fear death, but regards it as a necessity for change or growth. By death, science means a change, i.e., change from one form into another. In our lifetime, we see that naturally every seventh year we have almost a new body and every molecule of our body is constantly changing. Every microscopic cell in our organism is producing the new forms. The old forms are dying and different new forms are coming up. When you plant a tree, you will see how the seed dies before the plant begins to grow. So death is the beginning of a new stage of life, and, therefore, we must not cling to that old belief, thinking that we must regard death as the constant enemy of life, but we must regard it as a friend of life. Now if by death we understand a change, then the word 'immortality' will receive a new meaning ; that is, it will take that state which does not die and is not subject to death. Or, in other words, immortality means a state which is absolute, unchangeable, deathless or absolutely unchangeable. So the real meaning of immortality is persisting in existence, without being subject to any change whatever. Now if that be the meaning of immortality, is there any state which is absolutely free from changes of all kinds ? This is a great question. The answer to this question is very deep. We shall have to analyse the whole phenomenal world to find out if such a thing as unchangeability exists. For science tells us that everything is subject to change and everywhere we see the signs of change and decay. You all know how the solar system has come into existence from one mass of nebulous matter. Gradually it becomes congealed from that gaseous form and becomes solid. Then again it goes back to that gaseous state. Our physical bodies are subject to change. In fact, our bodies are for ever changing. If you can imagine yourself as a whirlpool in ether, or if you have seen your hand through the X-rays, then you will know what your body is like. All around yourself there are the same etherial particles of matter in a homogeneous mass which is an impenetrable, thick solid substance. There is no space between the particles and you cannot separate them. In that mass, there is a little eddy here and there and that we call our bodies. Every minute cell of the body is constantly under change. We understand by sensation that something comes from the external world, either in the form of light vibration or in the form of air vibration and that affects our nervous systems, produces certain changes in the optical nerves and different nerves of the brain cells, and there a certain vibration is produced and that vibration is interpreted by consciousness as change. So we see at every step that there is a change, and without change we cannot hear any sound and cannot see any colour and cannot smell anything. All the feelings and thoughts are certain kinds of vibrations. They grow and disappear. One range of vibration shifts us on a certain region of consciousness and other range produces other vibrations of emotions.

So all the vibrations mean change. Our whole being also is subject to change. Then where is that immortal existence, we ask this question to science. But science does not answer. There is no such thing in the world as the absolute unchangeability. The phenomena of the world must change. Anything that exists in time and space is subject to change, and so with any form we can imagine. The form may be of matter or ether, but in either case, it is subject to change. Now by 'immortality' can we mean that the soul will be clothed with a new form and will go to heaven and enjoy celestial pleasures during eternity, clothed in etherial form and without any change throughout eternity ? Can we imagine an etherial form which will last like a statue, because any emotion or feeling presupposes some kind of change so that it will have a body which would not be subject to any kind of change ? No, we cannot conceive of such a thing. So immortality cannot be applied to the celestial bodies, no matter how fine or etherial they may be.

If we analyse the conception of pleasure, we find that we cannot have any feeling of pleasure if we have no conception of pain. Similarly if we have no conception of pain, we could have no conception of pleasure. We can only know what one feeling is, by comparing it with the other feeling we had before and also knowing the difference. And then if we are going to enjoy pleasure throughtout eternity, we must have some sort of conception of pain, otherwise we cannot enjoy pleasure throughout eternity. It is for that reason that those who believe in an eternity, will have to believe in eternal hell fire. The underlying truth of it is that we cannot enjoy the one without experiencing the other.

In the gross descriptions of hell and heaven, we find that here is a glass wall, separating hell from heaven, through which the souls, enjoying celestial pleasures, can see the others suffering and can compare and enjoy their pleasures ; otherwise there is no enjoyment. It would be truly impossible for us to enjoy that pleasure if we enjoy that all the time and have no break. Now if we like music and hear music day and night without doing anything else, music would be a pleasure no more to us and within six hours we would be tired of it. If we see one colour all the time, it would no longer be a colour. If we can go to heaven and remain there throughout eternity, it would be no pleasure at all. Now under all these conditions we cannot find that eternal life in heaven with a finer body is the meaning of immortality, nor the enjoyment of celestial pleasures of the same kind without having any conditions for comparison, is the meaning of immortality. Those who believe that immortality means a personal immortality, do not understand the meaning of the word 'personality'. Now what is the meaning of personality ? It is a kind of mask, it is a garment of the mind. We have read of double, triple and quadruple personalities. There was a girl in England who had ten personalities, each of which was distinct. So by personality we must not understand a certain state of consciousness. It is like an assumed character on the stage. When the individual soul assumes a certain character and plays a certain part in the drama of life, then that particular character is the particular personality for the time being.[2] When different ideas develop and different tendencies and desires appear, then different personalities come up. Then we forget our old personality. So, if we analyse our personality,

---

[2] Cf. 'Individuality and personality' in the Swami's book, *True Psychology*.

we will find that it is subject to disease, decay and death. Therefore, personality does not mean the absolute unchangeable state either on this plane or in heaven.

Some persons believe that immortality is a conditional one which is not a natural gift, but is a certain gift of God to certain individuals. Then comes the question as to what kind of gift it is and under what conditons it is received. Who will decide how many degrees above error one must be in order to obtain that gift from God ? Some people may say certain modes of living and work and the devotional exercise are sufficient for receiving the gift. Still if we analyse these devotional exercises and mental and physical works, we will find that all our actions are governed by the law of action and reaction, or by the law of cause and sequence. Every cause must produce an effect. Now if the result be eternal or everlasting, the cause must be eternal or everlasting, because a finite cause can never produce an infinite result. It is against the law of nature. Now call our actions either good or evil. If we add all our good and evil deeds or actions during a lifetime, even of a hundred years, they cannot be unlimited. The effect, therefore, cannot be unlimited. Realize then that cause must be unlimited too. God cannot even change that law, because, no matter how powerful He may be, it is His own law. Can we imagine the law of cause and sequence stopping for a second ? No ; otherwise the whole universe would fall to pieces. So those who believe that God changes the law of nature, are simply making some statements which have no ground whatsoever. We cannot take any stock in those statements. So God cannot give a free gift to any individual indiscriminately, because the theologians say that there must be some kind of devotional exercise to bring that gift. Now if we depend upon some devotional exercise, then that is also a limited cause and must produce a limited effect. Then everlasting life as the reward of all our good acts is an impossibility. We cannot get it, because it would be contrary to the laws of nature. Therefore the philosophers in India do not believe in such a statement. They believe in many heavens. By the law of action and reaction, they try to explain that the earthly life is subject to change like the heavenly pleasures. Therefore eternal life is not eternal, it is temporary. Millions and millions of years, when compared to eternity, would appear to us like a flash of light, as it is temporary. Therefore all the great philosophers in India have said :

> 'From the highest heaven to the limit of the universe all these different places of existence are subject to growth and change.'[3]

Those who do good deeds, go to heaven, may remain there till their time expires, and then they go to some other realms. They may return to this earth, or if they go to heaven, they enjoy celestial pleasures there for thousands of years. But it must end. Even if we get the celestial bodies, those bodies are subject to change. Then all those higher beings, the angles and the archangels who dwell in those celestial regions are limited. They may have the psychic perception, but still there is limitation. And that conception we find in no other religion or philosophy, except in the writings of the great thinkers of the Vedic age. Because the thinkers and the seers of the ancient Vedic age went deeper and so they would not accept anything on hearsay. A revelation of God, which does not appeal to reason, does not touch our own senses, does not conform to all the laws of nature, and cannot be the truth. If Christ was possessed of immortal life, then each one of us must have it by birthright, otherwise Christ had not got it. There is one universal law just as the law of light, or the law of action and reaction, or the law of cause and sequence. They are all alike, and we find at every step this law prevails. As Christian science says :

---

[3] *Bhagavad Gita,* VIII, 16.

'Discover the laws of nature ; if you cannot harmonize the truths of Christ with the laws of nature, you have not discovered any truth.'

Your going to heaven does not mean the attainment of immortality, and having a celestial body does not also mean that. Then what is the true meaning of immortality ? Is it possible to have anything unchangeable in this world of changes ? This question disturbed also the mind of the thinkers long ago, and today Kant, Huxley and Ernst Haeckel have tried to discover something which is the unchangeable Reality and the absolute Truth. But have they really discovered it ? I think that they are not successful.

Those who have searched this truth, can be divided into two classes. The one may be classed as the materialists who deny the existence of the soul as separate from the material body, and according to them, all such questions of immortality, God, and souls are mere waste of time and energy. Of course, they try to find out everything from the matter and the force. They say that force is immortal, and energy is immortal, and that is all. But can we remain contented with those conclusions of the great materialistic thinkers of the world ? The materialistic thinkers are not the product of the twentieth century alone. In olden times and even in the Vedic age, there were those who denied the existence of anything that existed beyond the range of sense perception. They denied anything that is abstract. They did not find that soul exists independently of the body. They rather mixed up the soul with the material body.

Among modern scientists too you will find that there is such a class and so their arguments do not satisfy our minds. Even if they tell us that there is no soul, yet a voice within tells us 'go and search again, and you will find something better'. So if we go on searching, at every step we hear a voice speaking from within that there is something immortal.

Otherwise this question of immortality would never arise. Because our longing for immortality is too strong, we cannot resist it. Try to think of yourself as dead, but you cannot. You may think of your body as lying dead, but you are standing beside it and watching over it. You cannot think of yourself as non-existent, because the very idea that you are dead or have ceased to exist presupposes that you are conscious of that idea, and, therefore, you cannot be this. Why is it that if our whole nature was not meant to last throughout eternity, we have such an idea ? It is a part and parcel of our being and we must go on searching until we find it. Those who imagine that the body and the soul last throughout eternity are mistaken. The atoms will arise, because they are indestructible. But like the material body, the astral body is destructible. The finer etherial form which may manifest itself through cells is also destructible, it is earthly. Then, where is the immortal spark of our own being ? After searching within the body as well as in the realms of mind and intellect, the great thinkers and inspired sages of the Vedic age declared that our soul is immortal. The soul is like a receptacle of a finer substance which is like the source of our conscious existence and that source is immortal. It is not subject to change and they called it the *Atman*. It is not the same as ego, but is the Knower of the ego. It is not same as '*I*', but that, by which we know ourselves it is I am standing here, I am hearing, and that is our true Self ; that is the *Atman*. You may say : 'How can we know the existence of such a thing' ? You do not have to search outside, as it is already within. But tell me, are you ever conscious of your brain ? You will say, no, you do not know that you are the interpreter of the brain. Similarly it may be asked that if the source of consciousness is the source of matter, then who knows matter ? Matter does not know itself, and, therefore there must be someone other than matter, who knows matter.

Modern science has resolved the whole phenomenal universe into three states and has explained that those states are matter, energy and consciousness. These three states or things are the fundamental principles of the universe. If you have studied science or any of the philosophies of the world, you will find these three things. But, in truth, matter and energy are inseparable. They are different states of the same substance. Then there comes the third thing, consciousness. Most of the materialistic thinkers try to separate or divorce this consciousness from matter and force, and the idealists try to divorce matter and force from mind or consciousness. A modern Christian scientist says that there is no matter, it is all mind and all consciousness. Now ask them what they mean by mind, and what they mean by matter. They will say that they do not know. In fact, all these three, matter, force and consciousness are indestructible, incorruptible and eternal. The question comes up : what is the nature of the third substance ? If matter is indestructible, force is indestructible, then what becomes of consciousness ? Shall we believe it to be the result of matter and force, as the materialists declare ? When you have the conception of matter, it is a state of consciousness, i.e., knowingness. When you have conception of force or energy, it is a material state. They are incorruptible and indestructible. If two states of consciousness be indestructible, then what will be the nature of consciousness itself ? Will it be indestructible ? If the fruit of the tree is indestructible and eternal, can you believe that the tree is destructible and non-eternal ? These are the fruits of the tree of consciousness, and if the two states of consciousness be indestructible and eternal, then the tree of consciousness is also indestructible and eternal. Really we cannot know the existence of matter, if we are unconscious. Put a scientist into the chloroform state and ask him if he is conscious of the existence of matter. Surely he will say that he does not know, as he is unconscious. You may look through a microscope at an atom and divide it into subdivisions i.e. into an electron or an ion. If these be incorruptible and indestructible, then the two states are also indestructible. It is always the knower which knows. Matter does not know and energy does not know, and this knower is our true Self. It is not far from us, but it is the innermost being within us.

Your mental conditon may change, you may be in anger, you may have another passion, you may have certain desire, you may think of the body, and you may think of yourself as wicked or spiritual, but all the time you know that these feelings are nothing but different states of your consciousness. It is the background of the spirit or of your personality like the background of the canvas, upon which your personality is painted by the divine hand. You may change the picture, but the canvas will remain always the same. We can realize our true Self which will be more lasting than the celestial pleasure, and which will be as eternal as Divinity itself.

The books will not reveal this Truth. By reading books and scriptures and their commentaries, we cannot know the absolute Truth. We can neither understand our immortal nature by thought, nor by works, nor by devotional exercises, but if we search it within our heart, we can understand our immortal nature. Separate the source of consciousness from its attachment to the material things, analyse your own nature and discriminate, and then see what part is in you that is unchanging like the witness which is the knower of the body and of the sense perceptions, intellect, apprehensions and feeling. Enter into the cave of your heart and you will be able to realize the *Atman*. Through the practices of concentration and meditation you enter into the state of the superconsciousness and there you will be free. There you will realize that you are beyond the body, beyond the mind and beyond the intellect and death. Death cannot touch you then, and the fear of death will vanish from you for ever. Then you will know that fire cannot burn you, water cannot moisten you, air cannot dry you, and swords cannot pierce you, but you are immortal, unchanging, eternal, everlasting, and divine.[4] Then no fear of death exists. Because all fear proceeds from ignorance and selfishness and when you have eliminated all ignorance, the Divine illumination will come, the sun of wisdom will shine above the horizon of your mental plane, and there you will see the light of the eternal Truth, and then you will see what is real and immortal. If you study the scriptures of the Hindus, you will find that the divine thought of immortality is the highest ideal of the Hindu scriptures. But how is it to be obtained ? It will be obtained by being conscious of your immortal nature. Because knowing is being. When you know yourself as immortal, you are immortal. But if you know yourself as a limited physical thing, you are going to die. All our knowledge is a state of consciousness. So if you change this state of consciousness, you will never die. Because you are yourself the changeless principle, and so change of any kind will not affect you. Change is fleeting and unreal, but you are immortal. When you know God, you have attained everything. To know God means to be God ; *'brahmavid brahmaiva bhavati.'* So if you wish to know God, you must know your true self which is immortal, divine, eternal, everlasting and one.

---

[4] *Bhagavad Gita*, II, 23-24.

CHAPTER X

THE SPIRITUALISM

The question often rises in our minds as to what exists after death. This question rises today and it will rise always in the minds of all. The same question was asked by the kings and the beggars, by the sages and the saints, and by the philosophers, the thinkers and the religionists of all countries all over the world. We are discussing it today, and tomorrow the same question will rise again in other minds. For the moment we might forget, and we might not take heed of the condition after death of the physical body, but the time is sure to come when we shall wake up and would ask the same question. We might be absorbed in our daily occupations, in the struggles for existence, and in troubles and tribulations which we have to encounter every day. We may forget that we will live after death or what will happen after death. But as soon as we see someone passes away, see our relatives, the dearest and the nearest friends pass out of the body, we stop and think where have they gone. What has become of the body ? The body is going to decompose. What was there to keep it alive and where has it gone now ? The same question will arise again and again and disturb the peace of our minds. Until we find the proper solution of that question, we can never have peace in our minds.

But before we find the solution of that problem, we discover at the very threshold of our inquiry an adamantine wall standing before us which is almost impossible to break through. The weak intellects stop here. The feeble minds with feeble efforts fail to go beyond that wall, which is nothing but a belief that the body is the producer of the soul and that the soul is the result of the functions of the organism of this gross material body. The popular belief that every soul will rise after death, because of the miraculous resurrection of one particular individual at a certain time does not appeal to our minds any more. We have outgrown those states of foolish belief and blind faith. We wish to get positive proofs. We want to discuss the subject psychologically, metaphysically, and scientifically. Now let us see whether this theory that the body produces the soul is correct.

There are three theories given in the attempts to prove the existence of the soul : the one is the production theory, the second is the combination theory, and the third is the transmission theory. The production theory is the theory described by the atheists, agnostics, materialists and evolutionists. They believe that the body produces the soul ; but they do not answer the question how the body can produce the soul which is a mass of thought, or a mass of intelligence, or whatever they may call it. These materialistic thinkers might tell you that a body is produced of other bodies i.e. the bodies of the parents. But what force is there that holds all the molecules and the particles of matter together and combines them, and produces your body in one particular form and my body in another form ? What makes these distinctions, they do not answer those questions. They say that it is unknown to us and it is a mystery, but the bodies of the parents produce the bodies of the children and this is true. But what produces the bodies of the parents ? They say that their parents produce the bodies. But that is not the true answer. In trying to explain this theory, they produce another combination of matter without explaining the forces which combine and preproduce these conditions. They simply make an assertion and that assertion leads to a fallacy that the body produces a body, but that is not the real cause that produces the human body. It is like explaining the cause by the effect ; it is like putting the cart before the horse. So the explanation does not appeal to our minds. At the same time we notice that among the hosts of the physiologists, medical practitioners and pathologists, there is a belief that the body produces the soul of thought, intelligence, consciousness, and whatever you may call the mind, and some have gone so far as to locate the particular functions of the mind in some particular parts of the brain. For instance, when we see the objects before our presence, particular convolutions of the brain are stimulated, and when we hear a sound, our tympanal lobes are stimulated, and so on. Those who believe in the production theory, tell that the mind is conterminous with the functions of the brain as well as with the nervous states, and they try to explain that so long as the brain is active, the mind exists; but when the brain stops its functions, the mind is dead, because the mind cannot live independent of the functions of the brain. Their theory is that certain impressions come through our nerves and they are poured into the brain by the peculiar functions of the brain. They are metamorphosed into ideas, thoughts, emotions, feelings, sensations, expressions of the face, speech, and so on. Just as foodstuff, after falling into the stomach, is metamorphosed and changed into different elements by digestion, and as the stomach is functioning to produce digestion and the liver is to secret bile, so the brain secretes thoughts, intelligence and consciousness. And that is their argument. According to them, the impressions are like the material bodies or the body-stuffs that go into our nerves and fall into the pot of the brain and are instantly changed into thought, intelligence, ideas, and so on.

But when we examine the brain properly, we find that a man can live and perform his functions even when half of his brain is diseased and decayed. Such cases have been experimented upon and recorded. There is a great medical surgeon and physician in New York city, Doctor Thompson, who is an authority in the Roosevelt Hospital. He has written a book in which he describes the records and statistics that have been taken after post-mortem examinations. A man had lost half of his brain. It was absolutely gone and in his whole lifetime, he did not know at what time he had lost the half of his brain and it made no change in his mode of life, in his thoughts, and in his occupation. He could utilize the one half of the brain that was in good condition and make it perform the functions of both the halves.

A man who uses his right hand, has his centre of speech on the left side of the brain. Now this is one of the most important proofs that has been brought out by scientific men of this age. Our speech-centre depends upon the action of our arms to a great extent. A left-handed man has his speech-centre developed on the right side of the brain and the right-handed man has his speech-centre on the left side of the brain. If one half of the brain is decayed or diseased and if that man be right-handed and the left side of the brain is diseased, he becomes absolutely mute and dumb and he cannot speak. But if he uses the left hand, after a few days or a few weeks he will be able to develop a speech-centre on the right side of the brain and then he will be able to speak his language fluently. These are experimented, and are proved facts.

What do these prove ? They prove that mind is something distinct from the brain and the brain is the instrument which is utilized by the soul, or the mind, or whatever you may call it. You may call it personality. But personality is not the result of the function of the brain. On the contrary, it is one who uses the instrument of the brain as if from outside. We may compare the brain with a piano. A piano can produce music when there is music in the soul of the musician. But there is no music in the piano. It must be in the conscious mind of the musician who must be outside of the piano and must play upon the keys. So there is music of all the harmonious activities of our body and mind and that harmony is in the mind of the soul and that soul is playing upon the cells of the nerve-centres in the brain from outside. As if the brain is over-shadowed by some invisible entity who is playing upon the brain and producing its harmony, or if there be no harmony of music in the soul, there is discord which is manifested in ourselves. So the production theory has become almost absurd today. No scientific thinkers who have studied all these experiments, made by the great scientists of the world, can believe any more in the theory that the brain secretes the consciousness, as the liver secretes bile. It is an absolutely irrational statement.

The combination theory explains that the neural current is a stream which produces a stream of feelings. There is no connection between them, they are running simultaneously. Some of the psychologies that are taught in the schools and colleges, teach the idea that consciousness is a stream and a complex thing, made up of a stream of feelings and when these currents pass through the nerves ganglia and cortical walls, the cortical walls make a resistance. This resistance produces a kind of nerve-glow of white heat-glow, and that glow is their consciousness. That is a very absurd idea.

We have another explanation better than this, given by the transmission theory which is more satisfactory. According to this theory, the soul or the mind is outside of the brain. It is not the result of the brain, but is something like a self-conscious entity which is using the brain, just as a musician uses the piano and plays on the keys. Now that theory is generally accepted by all the spiritualists and the religionists and all the metaphysicians and the philosophers, and they understand the true language of the soul and its relation to the body. Those who do not believe in the transmission theory, cannot explain how these instances of phenomena which are recorded by the Psychical Research Society of America as well as those of Europe and elsewhere such as the appearance of the 'double', happen. For instance, suppose you are sitting in your room and you are absolutely in repose while conscious, reclining in a rocking chair or on a coach, you are alone and your mind is greatly disturbed by some business problem. You do not know how to answer it. Suppose there is no one to distrub you or to interfere you in any way in the room, or in the house. Your door is locked. Now suddenly you see your 'double'. This something is like yourself, coming out of you, going to the desk, taking a piece of paper and a pencil in hand, and solving your problem and leaving the written answer on the paper. Then you are dreaming, as it were, and suddenly you wake up, go to your desk and you find the solution. You remember that you saw your double, but you do not know what it is. It is like an apparition. There have been many such instances. How do you explain this ? Who has done it ? Did somebody else go into the etherial form which is similar to your own form from outside ? Even if you believe that you admit the existence of intelligence or an intelligent entity which can exist without the material and gross physical body, that can satisfy your mind, but these cases cannot be explained by any theory other than the transmission theory. This transmission theory tells us that the double is the astral self of the individual and this astral self is something which can live independent of the gross material body ; and this astral self can pass out and can appear in etherial form and perform many acts which our ordinary waking self cannot do. The astral doubles are sometimes perceived by the relatives and friends of the dying persons.

It is found that the dying persons may have a very strong attachment to their children. If their children are going to be orphans, if there is no one to take care of them, and if their relatives are at a distance, their great desire to help their children would make them project their astral body or double, and appear before the relatives, and give a sudden message. Sometimes it happens after the death of the individual, and, in most cases, it is at the time of death, just at the moment when the individual is passing out of the body or the minute before. There have been records of both kinds. Now how do you explain these if you do not believe in the transmission theory ? If the soul is the result of the functions of the brain, then everything would be at an end. But it is not the fact. These experiments have proved that there is such a thing as a soul or a personality or an entity which is self-conscious and which continues to live even when the gross physical body is left behind. Vedanta accepts the transmission theory. It tells us that matter is one half of the universe which is the object, and the mind is the other half of the universe, which is the subject. The one half of the universe cannot produce the other half and so they remain simultaneously. They are in existence from the very beginning. That is the existence of the mind and the matter. Matter is the object of perception, and mind is the perceiver. So you cannot have any sensation of perception of matter if there be no subject in you who perceives. Our knowledge of matter is nothing but a state of our mind. It is the state of consciousness. This consciousness must be prior to any condition of matter, or any experience of sensation or of feelings that are produced by the contact of matter with our senses. No one can deny the priority of consciousness, or of the self-consciousness. If you are unconscious, you cannot have any perception. So you see that every experience that we have is more or less subjective. We call our knowledge of matter is only a personal knowledge of the object, but a great deal of that knowledge is subjective, that is, we are conscious of our own minds. We cannot get out of our own minds anywhere. We cannot go into the chair or the table, and find out what is going on there and how the table affects our senses, and produces sensation ; if such sensations are the states of consciousness of our own mind, then we know that there is such a thing as a table or a chair ; otherwise we can never do it. Now, one of the scientific facts is that motion produces nothing but motion. But our consciousness or intelligence is not motion. Can you refute this ? No, it is something beyond motion. It is what understands and knows motion. So how can motion produce the activity of the brain, or the activity of the molecules, of the nerves and of the brain cells ? How can that motion produce something which does know itself ? That is a proof against all the materialistc theories. Therefore to say that the soul is the result of the function of the brain which is the intelligent entity, is an impossibility.

Referring to that priority of the mind, when you dissect a brain, for instance, and you do not find any such thing as the self-existing or the self-conscious entity, you deny the existence of a soul. This very denial of that particular case presupposes the existence of another mind which must think that way—the mind of the dissector. So in every instance there is the priority of the mind before any conception that you can make. If you say that you have no soul, it would be just as absurd, as if I say at this moment that I have no tongue. I am using the tongue while I am talking, and if I deny the existence of tongue, I would be a fool. Similarly, if you deny the existence of your own self as a self-conscious entity, you are using that self-conscious entity as a foundation while you are denying it, which would be absurd and ridiculous. Now, after realizing this condition that the soul is that self-conscious entity which is prior to all the material conditions and is not the result of the motion, we ask the question whether that soul can retain its individuality. Now here you will notice little distinction between individuality and personality. Again many people get these mixed up.

Some people take personality as individuality and individuality as personality. But we will go to the root of these two words, and will keep the original meaning before our minds, and then we will have no more confusion. The word *personality* comes from the Latin *persona*, the mask.

The personality is that particular consciousness which is related to the physical body. Thus you are Mr. or Mrs. or Miss So and so. That is your personality. You are an active man ; you are a businessman ; you have hunger and thirst and all the limitations of the body. That is the mask which the individual is wearing at the present moment. But individuality is something which is beyond the body and is indivisible. That which is indivisible, you cannot cut or disturb like your sense of 'I'. It is like an indivisible current. It is the continuity of one thought, the thought of 'I'. I was a school-boy, and I played with my school-mates. The same 'I' have gone through all these other experiences. Now I am standing or sitting here and that is identity or foundation or individuality which is indivisible. It is the property of your spiritual self, or the spiritual consciousness. It has no relation to your personality at all. Now that personality might be left here and might change ; but your individuality, the sense of 'I', can never change, because that sense of 'I' will continue to exist with you, no matter where you go. You are an unit of force, and that unit is a self-conscious unit, and when you leave this body, you take that sense of 'I' with you, whether you have a gross physical, or an astral, or a causal body. You have always the sense of 'I' with you. When you dream, you have the sense of 'I' within ; when you are in sound sleep, you have this sense ; otherwise you would not remember that you slept and had no dreams. You can never get rid of this sense of 'I' unless you attain to the highest liberation or the freedom of the soul and become one with God. Then your individuality is infinite. Just as the individuality of Christ was not lost when he realized that he and his Father were one, but it became infinitely expanded. Therefore we can never lose our individuality. Sometimes some of the souls, after passing out of the body at the time of death, contract all the forces that are scattered all over the body and come to a nucleus like an atom, and there it may lose its personality for the time being.

This personality is subject to change and might be held in an earth-bound condition. If it has strong attachments to the relatives or the friends and if it cannot get over those attachments, it hovers around them, remains close to them, tries to help them, to be loved by them, and there it is conscious of its personality. For instance, if I build a beautiful house and that beautiful house abounds in beautiful furniture and such things, and if I have devoted most of my time in decorating that house, I become so attached to it that after death I would dislike to leave that spot and I would remain right there, invisible. I might not be seen by others, but my strong attachment will hold me there in that place. I would be wondering while my relatives and friends and all the dearest ones do not recognize me and there I have to suffer. Now that is what happens with certain people who do not know that they are dead. They retain their personality.

At the time of the war in Europe,[1] there were soldiers who died with the feelings of revenge, hatred and anger in their hearts. It is a fact that after death they found that they were continuously fighting. They projected the forms of their enemies and tried to fight against them. It is a state of unrest. It is just like a state of hell. There is a worse hellish condition after the death of the soldiers who fight in the battlefield in the spirit world than they have here. Sometimes a soul passes out suddenly when his body is blown into atoms through an explosion. The shock of that explosion is so great that the soul remains unconscious for a long time. There happens no further progress of this soul. Those who understand the spiritual laws, never advocate war, because we have no right to take the lives of the individuals, especially of our own brethren who have come to this world to develop their conditions. Instead of helping them, we are taking their lives, cutting it short suddenly by swords and by all kinds of instruments of war. It is a terrible state of affairs, and the

---

[1] World War I.

souls, after passing out of this body, are in a state of the unconsciousness. They do not know where they are. Then they are in an utter confusion. They need help of someone to guide them and to make them realize that they have left their bodies. They need help for restoring their lost consciousness.

A story now comes to my mind, of what was supposed to have been a communication from one of the residents of that city, Los Angeles, who passed away in 1913. He was a Supreme Court Judge and he was supposed to communicate with this world through some friends. It was a very terrible condition for the particular woman whom he met in the other world and whom he knew in this material world. She was living in a boarding house and after she passed out, she was still living in a boarding house, and she was eating beef steak, meat and potatoes, but she did not like coffee. The coffee was very poor and she grumbled. She said : "It is terrible. I cannot sit at the table with the same friends. And potatoes are not very good." But still she was hungry and she ate. Now that gives the idea of what we can do, when we are in an earth-bound condition. She did not realize that she had passed away, but she thought that she was still living. She thought that it was funny that she did not have the same or better friends than she had here in this world. That shows that we take all our desires with us after death and we manufacture these objects of enjoyment by our thoughts. The realm beyond death is the realm of the realized ideals, or of the realized thoughts. If we think of a piece of bread, the bread is there and we will eat. If we feel hungry, we are eating. If we think of coffee, we are drinking coffee. Thus we see how important it is for us to understand this that if we die with the attachment to any particular kind of food, or any particular kind of clothes or jewels, or anything in this life, we carry that attachment with us, and with our desire we manufacture those things out of the finer material in the spirit world. Instead of progressing and casting off these first conditions which are narrow and which limit the progress of the souls, we take them with us and continue to enjoy them until we go to sleep and wake up. If our good thoughts and good deeds would help us, then we could go on progressing. But many of the departed spirits remain in that state of delusion for a long time. Our time does not affect the spirits. Our thousand years may be five days to them, because ours is according to our standard and theirs according to their standard. So no one can say how long a soul will remain in any particular condition, but it is important that we should remember this law that we create our future, we create our destiny, and we build our character by our thoughts and deeds.

It is not that we suddenly get transformed and grow wings, but it is the continuity of this present life. Life after death means the continuity of this life only on another plane. But it is not a place. There is no space relation. It is like a wheel within a wheel. Just as you can hear the vibrations of different musical instruments, one can be of low vibration and another of high and both can exist without interfering with each other. At the same time you can hear both. Similarly around this earth there is a spirit world. It is like the fourth dimension. It is on another plane. All that exist here in this material plane, do not exist there, because the space-relations do not exist there.

Those who have firm faith and belief in a heaven, where the angels sing the praises of the Lord, where there would be peace like the peace on Sunday in a city, where everything is closed, or is in a peaceful church and those who believe in things like these, will find them there. Because all the human beings are attracted to those dream-like states which we call heaven. And there are many such heavens. The Mohammedan who believes in the *houris* and the drinking of wine and having fine air and plenty of shade, and if he holds that as an ideal, will go to a plane of consciousness where he will project all these ideas and make his own heaven.

But these conditions are not eternal. They are like dream states. There are many such heavens. Each nation and each particular tribe among different nation had held a certain belief of what they would enjoy after death in a celestial realm. For instance the Red Indian who has his belief in a hunting ground, goes to heaven like the hunting ground. He believes in that like the old Scandinavian going to Valhalla, where he would sit in front of Odin and he would fight with his other friends, and during the fight he would be wounded and then miraculously healed of his wounds. Then they would run and chase a wild boar and have a big feast and this will continue everyday throughout eternity. Some will find peace that way, but not throughout eternity. I have mentioned already that eternity is a long time, and even millions of years are not to be considered as eternity. Eternity means time without end and without beginning. It is just like a circle. Eternity forms always a circle. All progress must go up to a certain point and then it will come back again. Some go to heaven suddenly. At the time of the expiration of their celestial happiness, their other desires will wake up which are dormant for the time being and those will bring them down to this plane again. They will be born again as the human beings. Now you need not get frightened about it, for they had such desires. There is no one who forces them, but it is their desires. They are creating their own conditions. That is the law. No one punishes the wicked, no one rewards the virtuous, but the soul rewards and punishes itself as the result of its own thoughts and deeds. We gravitate. You are here, because you have the desire to come to this world and enjoy certain pleasures and gain certain experiences which you would not get anywhere else. The same conditions prevail after you have gone to heaven. You will come back here again, and will gain some new experiences. And this is a great blessing that it is so, otherwise, it would be a very monotonous state of affairs to play on the same harp. I would not enjoy that. You might enjoy, because you have been trained to believe that is a high state. So the condition is this that after death we continue to live and go through different realms where we develop certain powers and each of them contains the potentialities and the possibilities. You must not think, three scores of years and ten in one plane have finished your manifestation. It could not be. The Christians have been taught that the Lord created them at the time of their births and they came suddenly out of nothing and they will continue to live forever. That is not possible, because the eternal life does not mean that it has a beginning at one end and at the other end it is endless. It has already been said that you can not imagine of a stick which you are holding at one end, and the other end would go to eternity and be endless. No, because what has a beginning, must have an end. That is the law of nature. No one can imagine a thing having a beginning but no end. Some think that this physical body can be kept throughout eternity, but that is impossible, because that which has birth must die. Of course, it may go through a transformation, but it would not be the same body, just as we do not possess the same body which we had when we were babies. The baby-body is changed into the young body and that into the mature body, because every seven years every molecule of our body is renewed.

You have not the same brain, same sense of sight, and same sense of hearing ; it is constantly changing. But, in the midst of these changes, there is something unchangeable, and unless you realize that something, you cannot expect to have permanent peace and happiness, because in the midst of all changes, you remain as the centre, around which all the changes are going on like a whirlpool. You are the self-conscious entity, which can never die. So have faith in yourself that you are immortal. By immortality is meant eternal life, both beginningless and endless. No one has created you, and no one could create you out of nothing. God

Himself could not also create, but He projects everything from within. So you existed first as a part of God and you have come here in this world through experience, and manifested your powers, and again you are going back to God. Thus you complete the circle. It is the play of the divine forces of nature, and you are only their manifestations. Each individual unit of the self-conscious entity will realize its infinite nature by going through a great many manifestations either in this cycle, or in a cycle that will come.

You must understand that the soul can come down from the heavenly plane to this plane of consciousness and be born again with more developed powers, either to gain new experiences, or to help others to gain knowledge. There are certain souls who are perfected and who come down consciously, remembering all that they have gone through. They remember it all, and they have come down through sheer joy, as it were, to help humanity and set an example like Christ or Buddha or other saviours. But we do not have that power. We gravitate, being forced by our past deeds. For instance, I have the desire to be one of the best artists and before I realize my ideal, if I suddenly pass away, I think that my desires will have gone for nothing. But that is not true, because they will bring me back again, and put me in the proper environment through the proper channel, so that I could realize my ideal of the artist once more. That is a great comfort that it is so. One plane of life is not enough. We have been told that everything was fixed before we came to this plane ; but how can one individual understand or know everything of this world of infinite phenomena unless they have infinite lives ?

For that reason the teachings of Vedanta are in perfect harmony with nature. It does not condemn any such ideas, but it puts them in their proper places. Some people have dreams of heavens, and they will go there. But if we are told that this heaven is an eternal state, we are hearing a statement which cannot be true. We must realize that the life after death is the continuation of the present life and we make our future according to our thoughts and deeds. We are the creators of our destiny, of our character, and of our future, and we will continue to live and come back and be born again on this earth or on some other planet. We may go to some other planet where there are different conditions and we may develop up the infinite realm of this universal Spirit. There is no end of experiences, but a perfected soul reaches that state where there is no more birth, no more death, and no more disease, sorrow, or suffering. There reigns the absolute peace and happiness, perfect knowledge and wisdom which are the highest goal of human life.[2]

---

[2] In the *Brihadaranyaka Upanishad* (4.4.6), we find :

तदेव सक्तः सह कर्मणैति लिङ्गं मनो यत्र निषक्तमस्य ।
प्राप्यान्तं कर्मणस्तस्य यत् किञ्चेह करोत्ययम् ।
तस्माल्लोकात् पुनरैत्यस्मै लोकाय कर्मणे ॥
इति नु कामयमानोऽथाकामयमानो योऽकामो निष्काम आप्तकाम आत्मकामो न तस्य प्राणा उत्क्रामन्ति ब्रह्मैव सन् ब्रह्माप्येति ।

That is, being attached, he together with the work attains that result to which his subtle body (*sukshma-sariram* or *lingam*) or mind is attached. Exhausting the results of whatever work he did in this life, he returns from that world to this for (fresh) work. Thus does the man who desires (transmigrates). But the man who does not desire (never transmigrates). Of him who is without desires, who is free from desire, the objects of whose desire have been attained, and to whom all objects of desire are but the self, the organs do not depart. Being but Brahman, he is merged in Brahman— Vide also the *Manduka Upanishad*, 3.2.2.

CHAPTER XI

SPIRITUALISM AND VEDANTA

The *Gita* says :

यान्ति देवव्रता देवान् पितॄन् यान्ति पितृव्रता: ।

भूतानि यान्ति भूतेज्या यान्ति मद्याजिनोऽपि माम् ॥ ९/२५

The supreme Lord says : "The votaries of the gods or angels go to the gods : to the ancestors go the ancestor-worshippers. The spirit-worshippers go to the spirits ; but those who are devoted to Me, attain to Me and reach perfection."

Modern spiritualism claims to have a supernatural origin like all other great religions of the world which have been founded upon the supernatural revelations. It has played its most important part in toning down the dogmas of the Christian theology in reforming the religious belief of the vast majority of the American people and in starting fresh inquiries and investigations in the realm beyond the grave. Within the last fifty years modern spiritualism have given wonderful demonstrations regarding the existence of disembodied spirits who continue to live even after the dissolution of their gross material forms. It has brought comfort and consolation to the hearts of many people who were suffering from the evil effects of scepticism and unbelief concerning a future life, caused by the dry theories of the atheistic, agnostic and materialistic thinkers of the last century.

Through the help of modern spiritualism, many of the educated and uneducated people of this country have now arrived at the conviction that there is such a thing as the human soul or a conscious entity which continues to exist after the death of the physical body. Modern spiritualism has taught that the souls of the dead are not destined to suffer eternally, but that they are comfortably situated, and do not forget their earthly friends and relatives. On the contrary, like the guardian angels, they watch over their beloved ones and are always anxious to help them and protect them from the dangers and misfortunes that surround their earthly lives. Modern spiritualism has taken away the horror of the post-mortem condition of life and has enabled the human minds to look upon death as the threshold of that wonderland, the inhabitants of which enjoy new lives, new experiences, and renewed pleasures and happiness. Thus having establilshed a belief in the life after death, modern spiritualism has claimed to lay the foundation of a religion under the direction of those spirits who have control over the mediums, or of those wise spirits, who visit the spiritualistic seances, whether private or professional, with a desire to enlighten the minds of the sitters by imparting the knowledge of supernatural things.

The attempts of modern spiritualism for establishing a religion upon the experiences gathered through the communications of the departed spirits, remind us of those ancient times when the primitive races were groping in the darkness of ignorance and their minds were struggling hard to see a ray of light in that thick mist which veiled the realm beyond the threshold of death. In fact, the study of modern spiritualism leads us back to that age when the religion of the primitive tribes consisted in keeping up the memory of their dead relatives and friends ; when after seeing the ghost-like apparitions of the deceased, they came to believe that their ancestors were alive even when their bodies were mouldering in the grave. It also takes us back to that age when the principal form of worship was to please the departed spirits by doing such acts as they had liked most during their earthly career. This kind of ancestor-worship was the ancient form of spiritualism ; and many scholars of modern times maintain that it was the beginning of all religions that are supposed to have a supernatural origin.

The ancestor-worship, of course, as we all know, means a belief in the spirits of the departed ancestors and the supernatural powers which they possess, as well as our constant remembrance of them and our services in their memory, either by following their directions or by seeking to rouse their sympathy and kindly feelings so that they may help us during the distress and misfortunes of our earthly lives. This ancestor-worship is to be found in almost all religions of the world. After studying the ancient religions of different countries, we find clear traces of this old form of spiritualism among the ancient Egyptians, Babylonians, Chaldeans, Assyrians, Chinese, Parsees, Hindus and other races inhabiting different parts of the world.

The ancient Egyptians, like the modern spiritualists, believed in the departed spirits. Their idea was that within the physical body of man there was a soul, having the shape of the gross body in every respect and with smaller hands, feet, and other limbs. It was like the 'double' or the counterpart of the physical man. When the physical man died, his counterpart or 'double' went out of the body and lived. The life of the 'double', according to the Egyptian belief, depended upon the condition of the material body i.e. so long as the gross form remained intact, the form of the 'double' would remain perfect. But if any part of the dead body was mutilated or injured, then the similar part of the 'double' would also be mutilated or injured. It was for this reason that they cared so much to preserve the dead bodies by making mummies and building pyramids. This belief was the fundamental principle of spiritualism and the ancestor-worship of the ancient Egyptians.

The Babylonians and the Chaldeans also believed in the departed spirits, but not exactly in the same manner as the Egyptians did. They believed in the wandering shade of the dead which was called 'ekimmu' i.e. a spectre. It was like the shape of the physical man with similar form, but they thought that it would meet with great misfortunes if the dead body were not buried with proper ceremonies, and so they observed a great many ceremonies in order to make the departed souls free from all misfortunes. The Babylonians believed that the souls of those dead bodies, which were not buried with proper ceremonies, could not enter the house of the dead, called 'arallu' i.e. the underground abode of the dead. It was like the 'sheol' of the Hebrews. Therefore, the Babylonians, Chaldeans and Assyrians took special care in burying the dead. The embalming of the dead body, the building of monuments and tombstones and decorating of them with flowers, wreaths, flags, and other grave-offerings, which are practised today by the Christian nations in Europe and America, are but the remnants of the ancestor-worship of the ancient Babylonians and Chaldeans. These customs have been handed down to us and we now blindly follow them without knowing their original meaning.

In the same manner, it can be shown that the religion of the ancient Chinese was purely the ancestor-worship. The Chinese have always believed in the spirits of their departed ancestors and relatives. They invoke them seeking their help in time of need, and pray to them for welfare and prosperity. Even today the departed ancestors in China are honoured with titles and praises for the meritorious acts performed by their descendants.

The ancient Parsees believed in the spirits of their dead forefathers and called them 'fravashis' or fathers. According to their belief, the spirits of the righteous were raised to the rank of the angels, the archangels and the gods. The Parsees used to invoke them, praise them, pray to them, and ask help and blessing of them. They used to offer them food and other offerings in memory of the 'fravashis' or fathers. Thus we see that the ancestor-worship or the ancient form of spiritualism gave foundation to the religion of the Parsees as well as of the Egyptians, Babylonians, Chaldeans and Chinese.

In Judaism, Christianity and Mohammedanism traces of ancestor-worship have been discovered by modern scholars and higher critics of the scriptures. In the 28th chapter of the first Samuel· in the Old Testament, we read that Saul went to consult with the witch of Endor who had familiar spirits. At the request of Saul, the witch invoked the spirit of Samuel who appeared and gave him good counsels. The witches and wizards of the Old Testament were nothing more than the mediums of modern spiritualism. If the spiritualistic mediums of the present day had lived about four centuries ago, they would have been condemned by the Church as witches and perhaps would have been hanged or burned at the stake.

The Hebrew word 'Elohim', which has often been translated as God in the English Bible, was applied also to disembodied spirits. It is said that the witch of Endor saw Elohim ascending out of the earth ; here Elohim was used in the sense of disembodied spirit of the dead. It was a kind of materialization of the departed spirits, such as is to be seen in the seances today. Do we not find a clear trace of the ancestor-worship in Judaism when we read :

'And Saul perceived that it was Samuel, and he bowed with his face to the ground and did obeisance.'[1]

The saint-worship among the Roman Catholics is another form of ancestor-worship or a remnant of ancient spiritualism. If we go to Rome or to any other part of Italy, we see the status of canonized saints over their tombs which are decorated with flowers and lighted candles, and the spirits of those saints are invoked with prayers and offerings. In fact, the beginning of the altars of churches and temples can be traced back to the graves of the ancestors who lived righteous lives.[2] The offerings and the sacrifices in the name of God likewise originated in the belief that the departed ancestors had hunger and thirst just as they had when they were in flesh and blood.

---

[1] *Samuel I.* Ch. XXVIII, 14.
[2] *Vide Notes.*

That which was at first the food and drink for the dead, developed into the form of sacrifices. The Holy Communion, the offering of thanks, and the Eucharist of the Christians are only the relics of the ceremonies connected with the ancestor-worship or the spirit-worship of the primitive people. Similar ceremonies still prevail among the heathen races who have never heard of Christ or of his crucification. They were the spontaneous expressions of the human minds which revered and honoured the memory of their departed ancestors. The chants and the praises which were used by the primitive people to describe virtues and heroic qualities and the deeds of their dead ancestors, have gradually taken the forms of the hymns of praise which are sung in churches and temples. Both Christ and Mohammad had believed in the departed spirits, and saw the angels ascending and descending over their heads, and received revelations through those who were but the spirits of the righteous.

In India, from the very ancient times the belief in departed spirits has played an important part in shaping the religious ideals of the Hindus. This belief found expressions in the oldest scriptural writings of the Vedic period. As early as the time of the Rig Veda which goes back at least five thousand years before the birth of Christ, the idea was very common and there we read many hymns with invocations, addressed to the *Pitris*, or the departed Fathers.[3] They were

---

[3] In the 10th Mandala of the Rig Veda, there are 72 *mantras* between the 14th and 18th *Suktas*. Those *mantras* or hymns have been addressed to Pitriloka, Yama, Pitriloka-Devata, Agni, Sarayu. Pusia; Sarasvati, Water; Soma, Mrityu, Dhata and Tastha in connection with the burial, cremation and partial cremation. In the 2nd hymn of the 16th *Sukta* we find also the seed of reincarnation of the soul :

श्रृतं यदा करसि जातवेदोऽथेमनं परि दत्तात् पितृभ्य: ।
यदा गच्छात्यसुनीतिमेता-मथा देवानां वशनीर्भवाति ॥

That is, "O Agni, when you will born his body satisfactorily, send him then to the inhabitants of the *pitriloka*. When he will be born again (*yada gacchatyasunimetamatha*), he will be devoted to the *devatas*". This hymn proves also the existence of the soul in the world beyond death.

invoked, praised, and invited to accept the offerings made to them at the time of the 'Shraddha'. The Sanskrit word 'Shraddha' means anything done in the memory of the departed ancestors. It includes the prayers, the praises, and the offerings. One of the daily duties of the Hindu house-holders is to spend a few minutes in thinking of their departed ancestors and in doing some good works in their name. They will feed the poor and the hungry, or give clothes to the needy, or make pilgrimages in the name of their dead relatives. The Hindu belief is that the fruits of such good works, when performed in the name of the departed spirits, will go to them and help them in their onward progress. All virtuous deeds, performed by the relatives and friends of the departed ones in the name of their ancestors, will surely bring good results to them.

According to the religion of Vedanta, the souls of the ordinary mortals remain earth-bound for some time after their death, and expect help from their relatives and friends who are left behind. The good thoughts and the good deeds of the living help the departed spirits in obtaining release from the earth-bound condition, and thus they are enabled to rise higher and enter into the realm of the *Pitris*, Manes, or Fathers, in order to reap the fruits of the virtuous deeds, done either by themselves, or performed for them or in their name by their descendants, friends and relatives.

The realm of the ancestors is called the *Pitriloka*,[4] where the departed spirits of the ancestors, it is believed, enjoy the

---

[4] We give here the following references of the *pitriloka* from the Vedas, Brahmanas, Upanishads and others :

(1) "Pitaro Yamarajye" etc.—*Vajasaneyi-samhita* (Madhyandina-sakha) 19.45; *Narayani-samhita*, 3.11.10; 156.11; *Kathaka-samhita*, 38.2 ; *Taittiriya-brahmana*, 2.6.34; *Apastamba-shrauta-sutra*, 1.9.12; *Sankhayana-grihya-sutra*, 5.9.4 ;

(2) "Pitrisadanam tva lokam avastrinami" etc.—*Maitrayani-samhita, Manava-shrauta-sutra*, 1.8.2.9 ;

(3) "Pitrisadane tava loka a sadayami" etc.—*Atharva-veda-samhita*, 18.4.67;

heavenly life and the celestial pleasures. This realm is ruled by the first of the mortals, who, through good works, raised himself to that state of consciousness. He is called in Sanskrit 'Yama'. Those, who have read the *Katha Upanishad* and Sir Edwin Arnold's *Secret of Death,* are familiar with this word, Yama, the Ruler of the realm of the *Pitris* or Manes or Fathers, who bestow all comforts and happiness according to the desires of those who reach that plane of existence. The realm of the Fathers or the ancestors corresponds to the heaven of the modern spiritualists. To go there is the highest ideal of the ancient ancestor-worship and also of modern spiritualism. Spiritualism, whether ancient or modern, cannot describe any stage beyond the realm of the Fathers. The religion which the modern spiritualists preach and claim as the true religion, does not take us further than this belief that we shall meet our departed ancestors, friends, and relatives, and rejoice in their company after death, and enjoy all the pleasures of life. The same ideal has been maintained by the ancestor-worshippers of all countries. The heaven of the ancestor-worshippers of ancient times is the heaven of modern spiritualists. It is the realm of the Fathers. Many people may doubt its existence, but there is no reason for such doubts. Spiritualism leads human minds only a step beyond the grave in the world of phenomena, and opens the way to the belief in this realm of the departed spirits. Where the ideal of the ancestor-worship or the heaven of modern spiritualism ends, there is the beginning of the higher religion of Vedanta which points out the path that directs the individual souls to the

---

(4) "Pitrinam lokam api gacchantu ye mritah" etc.—*Atharva-veda-samhita.* 12.2.45; Vide also AV., 18.3.73; 12.2.9; 3.29.4; RV., 10.2.7.10; 15.1-4; 10.16.1-14; 10.17.3.9.

(5) "Pitrilokam gamayan jatavedah" etc.—*Atharva-veda-samhita,* 18.4.64;

(6) "Pitrilokat patim yatih" etc.—AV., 14.2.52;

(7) "Pitrin imani lokam" etc.—*Asvalayana-grihya-sutra,* 47.11 : Vide also *Sankhyayana-grihya-sutra,* 4.10.5.

eternal Truth which is beyond all phenomena, beyond heaven, and above the realm of the Fathers, and even far beyond the reach of the angels, or the bright spirits, or the gods. After ages of investigations into the nature of life, one can possibly lead in the *Pitriloka*. The Vedantic sages and seers of Truth have discovered that the heaven of the Fathers is not the highest abode of the eternal Truth, but it is phenomenal and is subject to the laws which govern the phenomenal universe. They say that the inhabitants thereof are bound by the law of *karma*, or by the laws of cause and effect or of action and reaction, and their stay on that plane is temporary although it may last for thousands of years. The Vedantic seers of Truth say that the ancestors or the Fathers do not know the highest Truth, or the absolute Reality of the universe, and being bound by desires, they cannot reach the plane of Divinity, and, consequently, they cannot teach the divine Truth which they do not know themselves. ·

These ancient seers of the absolute Truth have realized through their own experience that the inhabitants of the spirit world, or of the heaven of the ancestors, or the realm of the *Pitris*, do not and cannot know the highest Truth on the plane of Divinity. Therefore, they cannot teach others, and so they have warned their disciples, followers, and seekers after Truth in general not to waste their time and energy in seeking spiritual help from those departed spirits who have no knowledge of truths that exist beyond the world of psychic phenomena and who do not possess the power of helping any seeker after divine realization.

Disregarding such wise warnings, the American spiritualists of modern times have been spending their time and energy and wasting their money in the vain hope of gaining the favour of those departed spirits, of learning the mysteries of life and death from them, and of solving the problems which trouble most human minds. The modern spiritualists claim to establish the foundation of a true religion upon imperfect knowledge, derived from the communications of the foolish, deceitful, idiotic and ignorant earth-bound spirits who control the mediums and pretend to know everything regarding the realms beyond death. The students of Vedanta often wonder how sensible men and women can sit in public seances night after night and listen with great admiration and rapturous attention to the senseless prattle of ignorant spirits who are supposed to control the weak minds of the mediums.

Having spent some time with the mediums of all kinds that exist in America, I wish to say a few words regarding my experience. I have been invited by the spiritualists to speak for them and to attend their seances. I had accepted their invitations with great pleasure in order to make some investigations for my own satisfaction. I have seen many materialized spirits and have spoken with them. I have had long conversations with some who spoke through tin trumpets and have asked them many questions, but I have not found a single spirit in any seance and not a single medium who could answer my questions satisfactorily. I have asked them about the life after death, the origin of the soul, the true nature of the soul, its relation to the universal Spirit, etc., but such questions, however, have never been answered by them ; on the contrary, on many occasions they have confessed their ignorance and have said : 'We do not know ; you know better than what we can tell you'. Some spirits have often referred to me for my approval of their answers to the questions which they were asked by other sitters. A few years ago, I was amused to hear from a materializing spirit in a public seance : 'Oh, here is a thinking-box ; what can we say before him ?' This exclamation came from an American Indian spirit. I was sitting next to the husband of the medium and as he was a friend of mine, I asked him the meaning of such a remark. He said : 'She refers to you'. I inquired : 'Why ?' He replied 'She thinks you are very wise, and she cannot show her power'. I am sorry to say that the seance was not successful that evening.

On another occasion, I had a long talk with a spirit, and asked her many questions regarding the mode of living in the spirit world, and her answers to my questions were perfectly idiotic. The spirit said that she went to schools and studied books. I asked : 'What books do you read ? Can you mention the name of any book you read ?' 'No', she said. 'I do not know the names.'

Sometimes, however, I have noticed that telepathically my own thoughts and my own ideas and very expressions were reproduced as perfectly as if I was answering my own questions. I was also pleased to hear the remarks which the spiritualistic medium made after hearing my discourse on *Reincarnation*. Some of them congratulated me and said : 'My spirit-guides have taught me exactly what you have explained.' But other mediums did not like the idea of reincarnation at all, because they had not learned it from their spirit-controls.

Supposing all the phenomena of spiritism to be true and genuine, what have the spiritualists gained by these communications outside the satisfaction of their idle curiosity ? Have they learned any of the higher truths ? Have they understood any of the laws that govern the spiritual nature of man ? Have they known why human beings come to this earth and why they go away suddenly ? I have asked many of the mediums as well as their spirit-guides, and have found that they do not know anything regarding the origin of the soul. Their answers are always based upon the dogmas of Christian theology, which they learned in their childhood in Sunday schools. They say : 'God creates the soul at the time of birth, and the soul continues to exist forever.' If one asks : 'How do you know that the soul did not exist before the birth of the body ?' They do not answer.

Although many of the spirit manifestations and spirit communications have been exposed as fraudulent and many of them can be explained by telepathy and thought-transference, still there are some genuine phenomena which cannot be explained by any other theory than that of the communication of the disembodied spirits. On many occasions, the audience is fooled by the spirits, some of whom are neither wise nor truthful. In some cases, they take the appearance of some other spirits and deceive the sitters. The poor and innocent mediums may not know that such tricks are played upon them by their dishonest spirit-guides, so they are not to be held responsible for the fraud in many cases. But the spirits are to be blamed. Therefore how can we expect to learn the absolute Truth from these spiritualists whose controls and guides themselves are ignorant, deceitful, and not wiser than the mediums ? Vain is the hope of those spiritualists who expect to know the absolute Truth through communications from the earth-bound spirits. In India, the seekers after the absolute Truth do not go to any spiritualistic medium to obtain the knowledge of the soul or of God, because they are taught from their childhood that the spirits who do communicate with the ordinary mortals through mediums are ignorant and earth-bound. They need our help more than they can help us in any way.

These seekers after truth do not seek wisdom from the Fathers, or the departed ancestors, because they know that the inhabitants of the spirit-world or heaven, or the *Pitriloka*, the realm of the Fathers, are not perfect, but that they go there being bound by desires to enjoy the fruits of their good works for sometime. At the expiration of that period, They are forced to come down from that plane to the world,[5] that eventually they are bound to reincarnate as human being in

---

[5] Vadarayana in his *Brahmasutra* (3.1.1-27) has mentioned how the soul, accompanied by the *mukhya-prana* (chief vital air or spirit), the sense-organs and the mind and taking with itself nescience (*avidya*), moral good or ill-*karma*, and the impressions left by its precious existence, leaves its body

order to fulfil other human desires which are latent in them and to reap such results of works as are to be obtained on the human plane alone. No individual, remaining in the plane of human desires, can escape this wheel of birth and rebirth which covers all the stages between the highest heaven on one side and the earthly existence on the other. So long as desires remain in us, we are bound to go through the changeful conditions and existences, and meet such environments as are subject to changes. Those who enter into the heaven of the modern spiritualists are similarly subject to the law of *karma*, or that of cause and sequence. Being bound by that law, they must remain there until they have reaped the results of their good deeds and good thoughts. They will then come down to this phenomenal earth and will be reincarnated again as human beings, in order to satisfy their human desires and human tendencies on the human plane. Cycle after cycle, the individual souls remanifest themselves on different planes of existence, in accordance with their thoughts, desires, and works. They may go to the heaven of the Pitris, or the ancestors, or any other higher realm of the spirits.

Having understood this grand law of *karma*, the Vedanta philosophers and the seekers after absolute Truth in India

---

(after death) and obtains a new body. In the 3.1.8 *sutra*, he says particularly :

कृतात्ययेऽनुशयवान् दृष्टस्मृतिभ्यां यथेतमनेवं च ।

Acharya Sankara in his commentary explains it, "the souls of those who perform sacrifices and the like, rise on the road, leading through smoke and so on, to the sphere of the moon, and when they have done with enjoyment (of the fruits of their works), again descend, having dwelt there, "*yavatsampatam** punaravartante yathetam,*"—they return again that way as they came" etc. Again in connection with the *sutra* :

तत्साभाव्यापत्तिरुपपत्ते: (३/१/२२)

Sankara has explained the method of descending of the souls, after quoting the text of the *Upanishad* : "They return again by the way they came, to the ether, from ether to the air. Then the sacrificer, having become air he becomes smoke, having become smoke he becomes mist, having become mist he becomes a cloud, having become a cloud he rains down. Vide all Max Müller : *The Six Systems of Indian Philosophy*, pp. 175-180.

searched for that subtle path, by which the individual soul can escape the wheel of rebirth in this world and transcend all laws and all stages of the phenomenal universe from the heaven of the spiritualists and the ancestor-worshippers up to the highest realm of the *Devas,* or the gods. In the *Bhagavad Gita,* the Lord says :

'Even the inhabitants of the highest heavens are subject to the laws of rebirth and reincarnation. He alone is free from birth and rebirth and transcends all phenomena, who, after knowing the absolute Truth and after realizing the supreme Spirit, becomes one with the Divinity.[6]

The path which leads to the realization of the absolute Truth, or to the abode of the eternal and unchangeable Reality of the universe is different from that which leads to the realm of the fathers, or to the heaven of the spiritualists or the dualistic religions. The entrance into the heaven of the ancestor-worshippers depends upon good and righteous works. It comes as the effect of good thoughts and good deeds. But the performance of good deeds and good thoughts cannot produce as its result of the attainment of God-consciousness, or Divine realization or absolute Truth, which is the highest ideal of all religions. No amount of good thoughts and deeds can produce as their effect which is beyond thoughts and mind, and consequently, beyond the reach of their effects, because the Divine realization is not within the realm of the psychic phenomena, nor can it be reached by mind, intellect, and the sense powers. The path which leads the individual soul to the realization of the Absolute, is neither through the righteous works, nor through the belief in the departed spirits, nor by the worship of the spirits of the ancestors, but through

---

[6] *Bhagavad Gita*, VIII, 19.

the Self-knowledge or the knowledge of the relation which the individual soul bears to the universal Spirit. That path is called in Vedanta, the *devayana,* the divine path or the path which leads to Divinity.[7] The travellers on this path are those who are the most sincere and earnest seekers after the Absolute. They do not care for the phenomena, whether physical or psychic, their souls soar high above the clouds of desires that cover the light of the spiritual sun in the ordinary mortals ; but their highest aim, loftiest aspiration and deepest longing of the soul are to realize that unchangeable Truth which is beyond mind and intellect and which the fathers in the heavens of the spiritualists cannot reach. We must go there in order to find the correct solution of all the problems concerning life and death. True religion does not depend upon any of the physical phenomena that are to be seen in the seances, nor is it based upon the ancestor-worship. Therefore the religion of Vedanta tells us not to seek divine wisdom from the departed spirits, and not to waste our time and energy by going after them, because the result will not be successful. The spiritualists who seek the highest wisdom from the communications with the departed spirits are deluded, and they do not know the limitations of those earth-bound souls.

---

[7] *Chhandogya Upanishad,* 5.10.3-4, and *Brihadaranyaka Upanishad,* 6.2.15. In the 18th verse of the *Isha Upanishad* we find also : *"Agne nayasupatha raye asmana"* etc. The word *supatha* means the *devayana* which is opposed to *dakshina-marga* of the workers (*karmis*), who perform sacrifices with the desire of going to heaven or to some other higher *lokas*. In the *Bhagavad Gita* (8.24-25), there is also mention of the paths, *uttarayana* and *dakshinayana* :

अग्निर्ज्योतिरह: शुक्ल: षण्मासा उत्तरायणम् ।
तत्र प्रयाता गच्छन्ति ब्रह्म ब्रह्मविदो जना: ॥ २४
धूमो रात्रिस्तथा कृष्ण: षण्मासा दक्षिणायनम् ।
तत्र चान्द्रमसं ज्योतिर्योगी प्राप्य निवर्तते ॥ २५

Such earth-bound souls may take the form of a great wise man or a sage and may appear in a seance and pretend to give the highest truths, but the sensible persons will easily find out how deceitful some of them are. We must be very careful in dealing with the spirits. I have seen people who, after investigating spiritualism and seeing all these phenomena, have lost all faith, and have become atheistic in their ideas. The modern spiritualists are like babies in this line of thought. The seekers after the absolute Truth in India have searched, and gained experience for thousands of years in studying the characters of the earth-bound and also of the higher spirits. The Hindus do not allow anyone to become mediumistic. They say that those who go into that condition are committing a great psychological crime, by making their own minds and bodies which they have got for their own development, subject to the influences of other spirits for the fulfilment of their desires.

We know that the mediums get more or less moral and physical wrecks in the end. If spiritualism can enlighten the minds of the peoples as they claim, why do we see that many of these mediums are ignorant and idiotic ? They do not understand the moral and spiritual laws that govern our souls. They have lost the power of self-control. They cannot control the trance-like condition when their animation is suspended, and their mind, brain and the whole body are at the mercy of another power outside of themselves.

The will-power of the mediums is generally weak. Their vital energy, life-force and intellectual powers are used by other spirits which have control over them. Once I asked a good materializing medium how she felt after coming out of the mediumistic condition. She replied : 'I feel as though there were nothing in me, as if all vitality and life had been taken out of me. I cannot think or do anything for sometime'. Is not this a pitiable condition ? It is for this reason in India, the earth-bound souls who are trying to get possession of the weak-minded mortals are delighted to find anyone who seeks their help.

The genuine phenomena of spiritism may do some good in the way of satisfying the curiosity of certain people, or of bringing the assurance that there is a life after death. They may foretell some petty trivial events in connection with our business or daily life, but they cannot bring to us the highest wisdom and happiness which come to the soul through Divine communion. These spirits are not the angels, as the spiritualists claim, but they are, in reality, the earth-bound spirits. The modern spiritualism may encourage the hope of meeting the departed spirits of our friends and relatives, and may bring consolation in the minds of those who doubt their existence, but it cannot give us the realization of the absolute Truth, or the attainment of God-consciousness. It cannot lift us above the realm of the fathers or the ancestors who are dwelling in the *pitriloka*. The aim of religion of Vedanta, on the contrary, is to make the individual soul realize its own true nature and to bring its reunion with the universal spirit and to transform it into the divine Being which transcends all the limitations of time and space and all the laws which bind us to this earthly plane. The aim of the religion of Vedanta is to make us realize the eternal Truth in this life and to be perfect as the Father in Heaven is perfect.

The attainment of God-consciousness is the highest ideal of Vedanta. It shows the way, by which we can reach the ultimate goal of all religions, manifest Divinity in the deeds or actions of our daily life, and becoming free from selfishness and independent of physical and mental conditions, as to how

we may live as a living God. For this reason, it is said in
Vedanta :

> 'You may read the scriptures, or repeat scriptural
> passages day after day ; you may offer sacrifices, prayers
> and invocations to the spirits or angels for help, or
> worship the spirits of departed ancestors for wisdom
> and knowledge ; but so long as you do not realize the
> true nature of your Self, so long as you do not feel that
> reunion of the individual soul with the universal Spirit,
> you shall not attain to spiritual freedom and perfection.'[8]

---

[8] कुरुते गङ्गासागरगमनं
   व्रतपरिपालनं अथवा दानम्।
   ज्ञानविहीने सर्वमनेन
   मुक्तिर्नभवति जन्मशतेन ॥

CHAPTER XII

SPIRITUALISM AND ANCESTOR-WORSHIP

Many scholars maintain that the ancestor-worship was the beginning of all great religions that claim a supernatural origin. The ancestor-worship, as we all know, means a kind of belief in the spirits of the departed ones and in the supernatural powers which they possess and also constant remembrance of those spirits in our minds. Resignation of the will under their direction will rouse the sympathy and kind feelings for those who are left behind them. It has been said before that among the ancient religions of the world we find traces of this ancestor-worship among the Egyptians, Chaldeans, Chinese and Hindus and other races that inhabit different parts of the world[1]. Among the ancient Egyptians we find a belief similar to that of the modern spiritualists. They believed that within the body of the human beings there was a kind of being, similar in form to human beings with similar hands, feet, and all other parts of the body, and it was something like the 'double' of the physical man. This counterpart or 'double' went out of the body and lived, and, according to their belief, the life of this double or counterpart, depended upon the physical form of the human beings.

---

[1] There was a common belief among the tribes of the Bantu stock of Africa, among the Zulus, the Thonga and other Caffre tribes of South Africa, the Ngoni of British Central Africa, the Abondel, the Masai, the Suk, the Nandi, the Akikuyu of German and British East Africa, the Dinkas of the Upper Nile, the Betsilee and other tribes of Madagascar, the Iban or Sea Dyakas of Borneo, and even among the Romans and Greeks that "the dead come to life and revisit their old homes in the shape of serpents and other animal forms".—Vide J. G. Frazer : *The Golden Bough* (3rd ed.), pt. IV, Adonis, Attis, Osiris, Vol. I, pp. 82-107.

If any part of this physical form was injured, the similar part of the double or counterpart would also be injured. It is for this reason the Egyptians cared so much for the dead bodies of their ancestors, and preserved them by making them into mummies. The pyramids were built for the purpose of preserving the mummies or the dead bodies[2]. The Egyptians had the belief that so long as these physical forms would remain perfect, this double would remain perfect and intact. The ancient Babylonians had a belief a little different from that of the Egyptians. They preserved the dead bodies,

---

[2] A. W. Benn mentions in this connection : "What we have now to examine is the general condition of popular belief, as evinced by the character of the funeral monuments, erected in the time of the empire. Our authorities are agreed in stating that the majority of these bear witness to a widespread and ever-growing faith in immortality, sometimes conveyed under the form of inscriptions, sometimes under that of figured reliefs, sometimes more naively signified by articles placed in the tomb for use in another world. 'I am waiting for my husband,' is the inscription placed over his dead wife by one who was, like her, an enfranchised slave. Elsewhere a widow 'commends her departed husband to the gods of the underworld, and prays that they will allow his spirit to revisit her in the hours of the night.' 'In death thou art not dead,' are the words deciphered on one mouldering stone. 'No,' says a father to a son whom he had lost in Numidia, 'thou hast not gone down to the abode of the Manes but risen to the stars of heaven.' At Doxato, near Philippi in Macedonia, a mother has graven on the tomb of her child : 'We are crushed by a cruel blow, but thou hast renewed thy being and art dwelling in the Elysiam fields'. This conception of the future world as a heavenly and happy abode where human souls are received into the society of the gods, recurred with especial frequency in the Greek epitaphs, but is also met with a Latin-worship countries.

Originally, peculiar to Greece, where it still exists under a slightly altered form, this superstition penetrated into the West at a comparatively early period. Thus in the tombs of Companion alone many hundred skeletons have been found with bronze coins in their mouths, placed there to pay them passage across Styx ; and explorations at present show that this custom reaches back to the middle of the fourth century B.C. We also learn from Lucian that, in his time, the old animistic beliefs were other appurtenances of deceased persons along with their bodies, under the idea that the owners required them for use in the other world ; and it is to such deposits that our museums of classical antiquity owe the greater part of their contents."—Vide *The Greek Philosophers* (1914), pp. 503-504.

embalmed them, and built tombs over them, putting flowers, wreaths and flags over the graves. This is practised in these days in Europe and America, and is a remnant of the ancestor-worship of the Babylonians. The main religion of the Chinese is the ancestor-worship. The Parsees of the ancient days believed also in the departed spirits and called them the *fravashis*, or the fathers. They invoked these spirits, prayed to them, and asked help and blessings of them.

According to the belief of the Parsees, the spirits of the righteous people had been raised to the ranks of the arch-angels and the guardian angels. The Parsees used to offer food and sacrifices in the names of the departed fathers and called upon them whenever they wished anything of a supernatural nature. Thus we see that this ancestor-worship gave a foundation to the religions of the Parsees as well as to the Babylonians, the Chinese and the Egyptians. In Judaism and Mohammedanism, traces of this worship are discovered by modern scholars.

The Hebrew word 'elohim', which is translated as God, is used with the meaning of departed spirit. The Witch of Endor saw 'elohim' come out of the earth. Do we not find a trace of the ancestor-worship when we read in the Samuel :

'And Saul perceived that it was Samuel, and he bowed with his face to the ground and did obeisance'[3] ?

---

[3] Vide *Samuel I,* Ch. XXVIII, 14.

Rev. A. W. Oxford also says : 'Since we find the graves of the ancestors of Israel situated on mountains (Numb. XX, 28 ; Josh. XXIV, 30) or connected with places where there stood either a tree or a stone (Gen. XXIII, 17; XXXV, 8-20; Numb. XX, I ; Josh. XXIV, 32), it is impossible to avoid the conclusion to which we are led by many other considerations that the pre-Jehovistic worship was that of ancestors.'—*Religious Systems of the World* (1901), pp. 56-57.

He further mentions : 'From the worship of holy stones and trees arose the *messeba*, or holy pillars, and the *aschera*, or holy poles 4.4. The *teraphim*, used apparently, like the ephod, as oracles (Ezek. XXI, 21; Hos. III, 4), may have been images of ancestors as they were of the size and shape of a man (Sam. XIX, 13). The theory that they were images of ancestors is supported by Gdn. XXXI, 19.'—Ibid., pp. 56-57.

The sacrifices that are made in the name of God, originated from the belief that the departed spirits have hunger and thirst just as much as when they were in flesh and blood. This offering of food and drink gradually developed into sacrifices. The communion and the offering of thanks and the Eucharist of the Christians are only the relics of the ceremonies in connection with the ancestor-worship. The chants and praises that were offered by the primitive people to commemorate their ancestors and to describe the heroic deeds and virtues of the departed spirits, gradually developed into the hymns of praise which we have today[4].

Both Christ and Mohammad believed in the departed spirits and angels, good and evil. They received revelations through these angels who were righteous and holy. Amongst the Mohammedans we find that they erect mosques and tombs. These graves are regarded as holy places, and are visited by pilgrims from time to time. In India, this belief in the departed spirits played an important part in shaping the religious ideals of the Hindus ; and that belief found its expression in the most ancient scriptural writings. In the Vedas, we read that these spirits of the fathers were invited to accept the offerings of food and drink at the time of the *shraddha* ceremony[5]. When a person dies, after a fortnight or a month all the relatives gather to do good works, and perform sacrifices in the name of that departed spirit. They feed the poor, and give wealth and make charity, etc. The word *shraddha* means doing good in the memory of someone. One of the daily duties of the Hindu householder is to spend a few minutes in thinking of the departed ancestors and in

[4] Prof. Sayace similarly found ancestor-worship and Shamanism (a low form of ghost propitiation) at the root of the religion of the ancient Accadians. Similar customs have been traced among the Greeks and Amazulu, among the Hebrews and the Nicaraguans, among ancient English people (Britons), Digger Indians, and the primitive people of the Andaman Islands.—Vide Menzies : *History of Religion*, pp. 111-113.

[5] Vide Notes.

doing certain good acts in their name, giving something to the poor and feeding the hungry or giving clothes to the needy. The Hindus believe that these good acts, when done in the name of the departed spirits, are a help to the spirits in their onward progress.

According to the Hindu belief, every mortal after death remains earth-bound for sometime, and those spirits who are in that condition, seek help of the living ones, the descendants, relatives and friends to free them from the earth-bound condition. The good deeds and the good thoughts, performed in the memory of the departed ones, help them, giving them chances of getting out of that earth-bound condition, and gradually they rise in the realm of the fathers where they stay and reap the results of the good works, either done by themselves or performed in their name by the descendants, friends and relatives. The realm of the fathers was discovered by the first mortal who by good works succeeded in finding the path to that realm, and afterwards became the ruling god of those who came later. (This is called the *pitriloka.* Those who have read the *Katha* and other *Upanishads,* are familiar with this name. This realm extended all the comforts of life to those who reached there. This realm of the fathers is heaven, the ideal place of the ancestor-worshippers as well as heaven of the modern spiritualists, even though they do not call it by that name.

The religion of the spiritualists, whether ancient or modern, cannot describe that state in which their ancestors live. That religion cannot take us beyond that realm and cannot give us anything beyond the belief that after our death, we shall meet our departed friends and live and rejoice with them for ever and enjoy happiness in that heavenly condition. But this heaven of the ancestor-worshippers and also of the modern spiritualists is not the highest heaven. Where the heaven of the ancestor-worshippers and modern spiritualists ends, there begins the foundation of the true religion which leads to the abode of the eternal Truth which is beyond all laws, all psychic conditions, all pleasures, and all comforts of life.

After ages of investigation the Hindu sages and the seers of Truth have discovered that this realm of the fathers is not the eternal abode of Truth. It is phenomenal, and the inhabitants of this realm are not free, but bound by desires for pleasures and comforts of life. They are subject to the law of *karma*, of cause and effect, of action and reaction, and their stay on this plane is temporary although it may last for thousands of years. They went deeper than the modern spiritualists, and by investigating the conditions of life in that realm, they saw what conditions are connected with their stay in that realm.

The ancient seers amongst the Hindus saw that these fathers cannot get beyond that realm, cannot rise on the plane of Divinity, do not understand the divine Truth, and, consequently, cannot be the teachers of divine Truth. Having realized this, the seers of Truth amongst the Hindus warned their disciples, followers and seekers after Truth in general not to waste their energies and time asking help of those who cannot know truths beyond the psychic plane and who are within the phenomenal world and cannot rise on the plane of Divinity.

Disregarding the remarks and the warnings of these ancient seers of Truth, modern spiritualists seek wisdom and knowledge of Divine things from the disembodied spirits, and try their best to gain favour of the departed ones, with the hope that they will learn something about God and the true nature of the soul and the relation of the individual soul to the universal Spirit. They try to lay the foundation of true religion, depending entirely upon knowledge gathered from the communications of some foolish, idiotic and earth-bound spirits of the dead. The Hindus wonder how sensible persons can sit night after night in the public seances, and listen to the senseless prattle of those ignorant spirits who do not know anything, and cannot understand or teach us anything about the higher truths of our life.

I have already said before that having spent sometime with the mediums of all kinds that exist in America, I have not met a single medium or departed spirit who could answer satisfactorily any of the questions which I asked them regarding the life after death, or regarding the true nature of the individual soul or its relation to the universal Spirit. On the contrary, I heard many spirits say, when asked these questions : 'You yourself can answer these questions better than we can'. Sometimes I heard many spirits refer to me, when some questions were asked by other sitters. I was amused to hear some spirit say in a materializing seance last summer, and it was the spirit-control of the medium who appeared and the first thing the spirit offered was this : 'Oh, here is a thinking-box, how can we talk before him ?' I did not understand what was meant, and afterwards I found this expression was used in reference to me.

The spirits would come and talk about certain things, but on some occasions, I noticed that some of the answers were nothing but the reproductions of my thoughts, my ideas, and my familiar expressions, and they were telepathically reproduced as perfectly as though I was answering my own questions. I have already said that, on other occasions, when I was lecturing on the theory of reincarnation, the mediums who came to hear me, spoke their opinions after lecture. Some came, and said to me : 'My guide teaches exactly what you have explained this afternoon'. This guide had taught them reincarnation, but other mediums disliked it very much. They came and said : 'This is a horrible idea. I heard so many conflicting opinions that I cannot describe them now. Some would say : 'reincarnation is the only solution of life', and other spirits would say differently. If they know everything, why should they not teach it ? Why should their opinions be so conflicting ? So how can you expect to know the ultimate Truth and reality of the universe and the nature of our true self and its relation to God from these spirits, who are no better than the mediums themselves ? As the mediums can be controlled by anyone, so their spirit-controls are simple beings that cannot explain anything of a higher order. I have already said before that supposing that these spiritualistic seances had been proved to be true, what have the spiritualists learned from these communications beyond a kind of satisfaction of curiosity and beyond the means of earning a livelihood ?

In India, of course, we do not allow our friends to become mediums, rather we think it is a disease. If one becomes mediumistic, it is very hard to get out of that condition. We do not allow public seances, because we have more respect for our ancestors and departed friends, and we do not wish to make money at the expense of these spirits. We would rather die of privations than bring down those spirits and ask them for help in the way of living and making money. The Hindus, of course, do not care so much for these kinds of seekers after truth. They do not go to the spiritualistic mediums and to public seances, because they know that the spirits who do communicate are ignorant and earth-bound. They rather pray and send good thoughts to them and try to do good acts in their names, so that they would be released from their earth-bound condition.

The wheel of birth and death covers all the stages that exist between the highest heaven of the gods and the plane of the human beings. We are going up and down according to our desires. But having discovered this grand law, the seekers after the absolute Truth searched for that path by which the individuals may escape this wheel of rebirth or reincarnation and reach that state from which there is no return. They transcend all phenomena and go beyond the realm of the Fathers. It is said in the *Bhagavad Gita* :

'All the realms, beginning with the highest, heaven, are phenomenal. Inhabitants, therefore, are subject to the laws of cause and effect, or of action and reaction ; no one is free from those laws. He alone is free who has transcended phenomena, and who, after knowing Truth, has become Truth, and who, realizing the supreme Spirit, has become one with that Spirit'.[6]

The path that leads to heaven of the ancestor-worshippers is called the *pitriyana* i.e. the path of the ancestors, or that of the fathers.[7] But the other path which leads to the realization of Truth is different from this path. The entrance into the heaven depends entirely upon the good thoughts and deeds of the individual, but no amount of good thoughts and deeds can produce that which is beyond all thoughts and is beyond the effects of thoughts and deeds. The path, which leads to the realization of the absolute Truth through the knowledge of the true Self as well as of our relation to the universal Spirit, is called in Sanskrit the *devayana*[8], the divine path. The teachers of this path are those who are most sincere and earnest seekers after truth, who care nothing for phenomena, whether on the physical or psychic plane, and whose souls soar high

---

[6] The *Bhagavad Gita*, Ch. VIII, 16.

[7] *Pitriyana* is known as the *dhuma-marga*, the dark way of the fathers. In the *Chhandogya, Brihadaranyaka, Katha, Prashna* and other *Upanishads,* and in the *Bhagavad Gita*, it has been described nicely. But its seed we find often in hymns of the Rig Veda used with a sacrificial instead of a funeral connotation :

पन्थामनु प्रविद्वात् पितृयाणं (१०/२/७)

(RV. X, 2.7), i.e., 'O Agni, you are born of earth and sky (*dvava-prithivi*), 4.4. You know that definite path to the *pitriloka*, there, be thou so bright as to illumine that path'.

[8] Its nucleus we find in Rig Veda, the oldest writings of the Hindus. There we get the hymn :

परं मृत्यो अनु परेहि पन्थां यस्ते, स इतरो देवयानात् । (१०/१८/१)

(RV. X, 18 : 1). i.e., 'O Mrityu, go back through a different path : Give up the path that leads to the *devas* ('*archir-marga*') and go through the way other than this (*pitriyana* ?)'.

above the clouds of desires that cover the light of the spirit-sun in ordinary mortals. The most genuine phenomena of the modern spirits may help some in satisfying the curiosity or in bringing a kind of hope of meeting the departed relatives and friends, and a kind of consolation in the hearts of those who are longing to meet their friends and relatives, but beyond that it cannot give the realization of Truth or the attainment of God-consciousness. The aim of true religion is to bring the individual soul into union with the divine Spirit and to make each soul realize that reunion with the Spirit, making that soul free from the bondages and desires and longings for pleasures and happiness. He who has attained to that realization is free from ignorance and selfishness and from all other imperfections. He does not go to a spirit for knowledge, but finds all knowledge within himself. He goes to the fountainhead of all knowledge and draws the water of knowledge from that source. Spirits cannot teach such things, and fathers or ancestors cannot teach him who has realized his oneness with the supreme Being. Such a soul is emancipated and is perfect as the Father of the universe is perfect. He is a living God upon this earth.

CHAPTER XIII

THE SPIRITUALISTIC MEDIUMSHIP

The phenomena of the modern spiritualism have opened a new field for scientific investigation and have inspired earnest men and women of Europe and America with a desire to communicate with their departed friends and relatives. The sceptics and the agnostics, who had no faith in a life after death, have discovered some truths about future life through the genuine communications of the disembodied spirits. They have learnt that death of the body is not the end of the soul-life, but, on the contrary, it is only the threshold of that wonderland where the spirits of the dead continue to exist and enjoy new experience and new pleasure.

Modern spiritualism, as has been said before, has given a death-blow to the hell-fire doctrines and other dogmas of Christian theology as well as to the theory that the souls of men are detained to suffer eternally. It has demonstrated the fact that the spirits of our dead friends and relatives are anxious to inform us that they are comfortable, and that they take great interest in our mundane affairs, and are always ready to direct us in the right path and help us by giving good counsels, and protect us from dangers and misfortunes which often threaten us from distance. These and many other beliefs of similar nature have been maintained by majority of the spiritualists who try to communicate with their departed friends by the developing mediumistic conditions. We are all familiar with the process of developing mediumship. Those who wish to become mediums, seek the company of other friends who have the same desire. They form themselves into a circle which is known as the *developing circle*. They are told by other mediums, or by their spirit-guides, to select a definite room where they should sit as often as possible at least once a week, but the sittings must be at the same hour and in the same evening of the week. They must begin each sitting promptly at the hour agreed upon, because the spirits are just as busy as we are here constantly discharging our duties and obligations. So they must make previous appointments and come exactly at the appointed moment to help in the *developing process*. It requires at least five or six sittings to magnetize the atmosphere of the room, and when it is thoroughly magnetized, the *developing process* of mediumship will begin. The sittings must be held in absolute darkness. As a dark room is indispensable to a photographer who wishes to develop a negative, so it is absolutely necessary for one who wishes to be a medium. Here we should remember that mediumship is a negative condition of the mind and the body which can be easily brought about if the sitters do not think of anything, but remain passive and simply hold a receptive attitude as if waiting to get something. The darkness which cuts off physical vision, being the negative pole of light, will naturally help in quietening the sense activities and in bringing them into an absolutely negative state. The soft sweet music is very helpful in the *developing process,* but the sitters themselves should not be the performers of music, because the very efforts to sing requires a positive will and an activity of the mind. Among the sitters those who are of the negative type, should alternate with those of the positive tendency. During this time, the sitters must not think of anything and must not ask any question, but surrender themselves to the will of their invisible controls, and calmly wait for the wonderful results of the *developing process*.

The best results of mediumship will come to those among the sitters who have been able to surrender absolutely their body, mind and will to the will of the spirit-controls. Gradually the spiritual intelligence will control the will, the volitionary powers, and the sensory organism of the medium.

This control may be partial or complete. The partial control may be over a certain part of the brain, or any particular organ, or any nerve centre, or any limb or muscle of the body. The partial control can be divided into two general classes : the nose, conscious, and the other, unconscious. Each of them can again be subdivided into various other classes in accordance with the phenomena. There are many men and women throughout the country who have some of their mental functions partially under the control of some outside spiritual intelligences, from whom they occasionally receive messages in the form of certain impressions and of which they are not conscious, but they do not lose consciousness of their bodies, or of their surroundings. In this conscious impressional mediumship, one may speak or write about things which one does not know or understand. Some of these classes are known as the inspirational speakers and writers. But the other class includes those mediums who are not conscious of any outside spiritual control which partially influences their minds. They will speak and write not knowing under whose control they are speaking and writing. There are some who partially become unconscious of their bodies and surroundings at the time of speaking or writing. Partial control of the muscles and the nerve centres leads to a variety of mediumship. Planchette writing, Ouija Board manipulating automatic writing, clairvoyance and clairaudience are but some of the different phenomena of muscular and neurotic mediumship. When a spirit controls the muscles of the arms, the medium can move heavy weights. When the optic nerves and the retina are controlled, the medium is able to see pictures or images which are presented to their consciousness by their spirit controls. Similarly, when the nervous organism of ear and the auditory nerves are controlled by the spirit, the mediums can hear such sounds which their controls desire them to hear. In the same manner, the partial control can be made over other senses like smell, taste, or touch. Some are conscious, while others are unconscious of this control. This partial control generally leads to fuller and more complete control, if the sitters continue the *developing process*. Complete control over the mind and the body of the medium is manifested in trance mediumship. Its phenomena are varied and extremely attractive, because this kind of mediumship is of a myterious character. The medium is generally thrown in a state of deep sleep which resembles the hypnotic sleep. Whatever happens in this state, the medium is unconscious of. The controlling agents have absolute domination over the physical instrument of the medium. The spirits can use the vocal organs of the mediums, or another organ at their will. The will and the volitional powers of the medium are thrown into absolute suspension. Through the body of the medium the spirits can speak or perform any phenomenon without producing any impression upon the conscious being of the medium. Just as a patient in a hypnotic sleep may talk or walk or eat or dance or do any other act, being under the perfect control of the will-power and the suggestion of the operator, but not remembering any of those acts or words after coming back to normal consciousness, so a trance medium does not remember what transpired during the state of trance.

There are many such trance mediums among the spiritualists in every country. This trance mediumship may gradually develop into what is called the 'materializing mediumship'. The medium goes into a state of profound trance. The spirit-controls who are experts in the art of materializing, understand the process. They can draw the vital and magnetic energies out of the medium's physical & mental organisms and combine them with the external non-composite elements and attenuated matter (*ectoplasm*)[1] and produce phenomena which can be perceived by the sitters.

---

[1] Sri Arthur Conan Doyle says : "** the witnesses averred that certain people, whom they called 'materializing mediums', had the strange physical gift that they could put forth from their bodies a viscous gelatinous substance which appeared to differ from every known form of matter ; pen that it could

Of course, there are many fraudulent materializations which have been exposed again and again in America as also in Europe. But there are also genuine materializations, some of which I have seen with my own eyes and have carefully examined in every possible way which I could use under those circumstances. I have been called to come inside the cabinet of a seance where I felt at least twenty hands on my back, some pulling my collar, sash and some putting hands on my back all at the same time. Then one of the spirits spoke : 'Do you think that the medium has been doing all these?' It was absolutely dark in the cabinet, although there was a dim light shaded by a wooden box in a corner of the room. The same voice then said : 'Put your hands on the medium', and pulling my hands placed them on the medium. And I felt the stiff limbs of the medium whose hands were tied across tightly with a thick cord, seated on a rocking chair in an inclined position in a dead trance. I have held the materialized hand of an American Indian spirit which melted away in my hand. I have also seen the genuine materialization of a friend of mine who was a native of Calcutta. Very few people understand the process of materialization[2]. There have been many instances in every country where spirits have materialized themselves without the help of any medium.

---

solidify, and be used for material purposes, and yet could be re-absorbed, leaving absolutely no trace even upon the clothes which it had traversed in leaving the body.

This substance was actually touched by some enterprising investigators, who reported that it was elastic and appeared to be sensitive, as though it was really an organic extrusion from the medium's body."

[2] The materialization process consists of two factors, one of which is the simple spontaneous secretion and formation of this material for the production of forms, images, and living organs.

'** but whatever may be laws and forces governing materializations, the medium's *psyche* must be brought in as a determining, or at least, as a contributing factor'.—B. V. Schrenck Notzing : *Phenomena of Materialization*, p. 282.

The vital and magnetic energies of the medium and also of the sitters give the foundation of all the phenomena that take place in a materializing seance. I have talked with the materializing mediums and have asked them how they felt after the seance was over. Invariably they have answered that as if their whole system was empty, as if there was neither life nor vitality left in them, and as if everything was taken out of their mind and body. They cannot think or show any mental activity in their waking state. Is it not the most pitiable condition ? Undoubtedly these trance mediums may be called martyrs. Through ignorance they sacrifice their vital energy and will-power upon the altar of the spiritualistic phenomena which ultimately wreck them physically, mentally and morally, and which stop the growth and evolution of their souls. There are other kinds of materializing trance like painting mediums, trumpet mediums and independent slate-writing mediums, etc. There is still another kind of trance control which was known in olden times as possession or obsession, but which is now recognized as a kind of insanity by the medical practitioners. All these and various other phenomena of mediumship are now admitted and are scientifically demonstrated facts. Various theories have been formulated to explain these phenomena.[3] Most of theories outside of the spiritualistic theory however have proved to be insufficient.

---

[3] "The most important objective performances of the mediumship may be divided into two main groups :

(1) TELEKINETIC PHENOMENA : This class comprises every sort of action upon inanimate objects without contact, such as oscillations, the moving of tables (attraction and repulsion), the levitation of objects (raising and suspension), inflations and motions of a curtain, the mechanics of motion connected with the so-called 'apports', and finally the generation of musical notes and noises at a distance (including raps and other auditory impressions). Also effects upon musical instruments, direct writing in a word, all forms of action at a distance no matter whether in their case the manner of production by the mediumistic force was the same.

The majority of people who have experienced the phenomena manifested through the genuine mediums, cannot deny that the disembodied spirits can communicate with the living mortals, can materialize themselves under certain conditions, and can perform various other phenomena. Now the question arises whether it is beneficial for the mortals to develop mediumship and become mediums and shall we encourage the spiritualists who develop mediumship. We have already seen that mediumship means a receptive or negative state of the mind and the body. If a person be positive, it will be extremely difficult for him or her to become a good medium. Therefore all persons under all circumstances cannot develop mediumship. It is true that there are some who are born mediumistic, or naturally negative, and they can easily throw themselves under the control of any living or disembodied being. Mediumship does not signify any gift or special talent or power from higher spiritual intelligence. Those who think so are mistaken. Strictly speaking, the world 'development' should not be used in connection with mediumship. Because mediumship is a subjective process of making the mind and the body passive and of surrendering the will and the volitional powers to some external influence which controls the organism of the medium, while 'development' means a gradual unfolding of the positive powers which are latent in the soul by the natural process of evolution. The latter is constructive, while the former is destructive. A medium who appears to be inspired in a semi-trance or full trance condition, does not show any power of his or her own which may be called a gift or

---

(2) TELEPLASTIC PHENOMENA : This group includes the so-called materialization phenomena of the spiritists, i.e., the production of forms and materials of organic or even inorganic matter, in accordance with definite conception and thought images of the medium, which may have their origin in the memory, or in the psychic under-currents of the medium, in the mentality of one of the witnesses, or (in the spiritistic sense) in forces and intelligences outside the medium."—Notzing : *Phenomena of Materialization*, p. 13.

inspiration. It is not the power of the medium that makes him or her appear as inspired, but, on the contrary, the will-power and the intellectual faculties of the medium are suspended, controlled, and kept in abeyance by the controlling spirit who uses the mind and the organism which are passively surrendered to the will of the spirit. It is not a gift of the medium of the spirit. Therefore it cannot be called development.

A medium who becomes absolutely negative or passive in mind and body, becomes subject to all surrounding influences of the earth-bound spirits who are constantly seeking opportunity to control and make some victims and thus through ignorance a medium opens a psychic field which is dominated by the will of these earth-bound spirits. Many of us have seen scores of spirits who manifest themselves in a single seance and how eager they seem to manifest ! If that door is once opened, it will be difficult to prevent those foreign influences from tormenting and eating up the vital energy of the innocent and foolish medium. I know several cases of persons who were at one time mediumistic, but who now suffer terribly from foreign influences and find it hard to overcome them even after constant efforts. Therefore mediumship under no circumstances is a desirable state, nay, it is criminal to surrender one's own will and mind and body to the whims of some earth-bound spirits. Some of the mediums are tempted by the idea that they may develop the power of seeing or hearing at a distance, or things which will happen in future. But they forget that those who have become clairvoyant by the subjective process of mediumship, do not and cannot see or hear whatever they desire to see clairvoyantly or hear clairaudiently. They can see only those things which their controls wish them to see or hear. They are absolutely at the mercy of their controls, just as the hypnotic subjects are at the mercy of their operator's will and suggestion. It is a well-known fact that the mediums gradually lose their power of self-control. They become more and more nervous and this nervousness sometimes culminates into nervous prostration. Brain-diseases of various kinds, the loss of vital energy, the animal magnetism, the continuous insanity, and short life are the evil effects of mediumship.

A high state of mediumship means therefore a degenerated mental condition on the part of the medium. The mediums generally suffer from the loss of memory. They cannot concentrate their minds on one subject for any length of time. They cannot think or reason consecutively. They lose the strength of their will-power and show irritable disposition. They become vain and egoistic and extremely selfish. They become strong in animal passions and animal desires. Some of the mediums become immoral, dishonest and untruthful. Statistics have shown that 74 per cent of the professional mediums develop abnormal animal passions. Nearly 60 per cent become hysterical, 85 per cent suffer from nervous irritability, 58 per cent develop fraud and dishonesty, and 95 per cent show lack of moral discrimination and courage, while 70 per cent develop vanity and selfishness.

Such are some of the evil effect of the mediumistic development. Shall we now wonder why the seers of Truth in India so strongly object to one's becoming a medium ? Shall we wonder why the Vedanta philosophy does not approve of spiritualistic mediumship ? The yogis in India never allow their students to go into the negative or passive condition. They do not deny that we can communicate with the earth-bound spirits or departed ancestors, must they know that to become a medium is a destructive process, and not a constructive one. They discovered a system called the Raja Yoga, in which they describe all these wonderful phenomena, which can be obtained scientifically without going into a negative state, or without surrendering the will and mind to any disembodied spirit.

A Yogi develops his power of clairvoyance and clairaudience by a positive method through the practice of concentration and meditation. He can see or hear anything at any time and anywhere. When he attains to the superconscious state, all the bright and intelligent spirits come to serve him and obey his commands. He is not a slave of the discarnate spirits, but he is a master. A true Yogi is a medium of the supreme universal Spirit who is omnipotent and omniscient, while a spiritualistic medium is under the control of an earthbound spirit who is ignorant and imperfect. No medium has ever gained spiritual wisdom, nor has he understood the higher laws which govern our souls through the communication of departed spirits, while a true Yogi, who has reached superconscious state, has attained perfect knowledge and reached God-consciousness. He is the ideal of nations. He is like Christ, Buddha and Ramakrishna. He attains to perfection even in this life, while a spiritualistic medium loses all self-control and sacrifices a great opportunity of unfolding the spiritual nature and remains in the darkness of ignorance, and after death joins with their controls and enjoy or suffer, according to their thoughts and deeds. A true Yogi, on the other hand, having reached perfection in this life, transcends the realm of the departed spirits, goes beyond heaven, and attains to omniscience and everlasting bliss.

CHAPTER XIV

THE AUTOMATIC SLATE-WRITING

In the year 1899, I was invited to lecture before the Spiritualistic Camp Meeting at Lily Dale near Chattaqua in the State of New York, U.S.A. I spoke on *The Religion of the Hindus* and on *Reincarnation*. The meeting was held in the auditorium, the sides of which were open and the seats were occupied by those who were interested in spiritualism. I was the speaker on the anniversary day, when, according to the number of tickets sold at the gate, the attendance was calculated to be seven thousand who came to hear me. Among this vast audience there were mediums of all kinds present at my lecture. After hearing my lectures, many of the mediums said that their spirit-guides taught the same truth which I was teaching, and they extended their courtesy to me by inviting me to their seances. On the 4th of August, 1899, I attended a seance, where I saw automatic typewriting on a typewriter. Everybody gave the names of their departed friends, who might communicate with them. I also gave the name of my departed *gurubhai*, Jogen. In reply I received the name 'Jogen' written with a blue pencil. This aroused my curiosity and I wanted to find out who wrote it.

Next morning, on August 5th at 10 o'clock, I had the invitation to pay a visit to the famous independent slate-writing medium Mr. Keeler. After a few minutes I went in the sitting room and sat near the window in front of Mr. Keeler on a rocking chair. The sunlight was coming through the window. In the space between us was a small square table, covered with a carpet-like cloth. Mr. Keeler brought out two slates both sides of which I sponged with my own hands. Then he wiped them with his handkerchief. Then he asked me to write some questions addressing the spirit with whom I wished to communicate. I asked him whether I could write my questions in the native tongue of my friend. He replied : 'Yes, you can do so'. Then I wrote in Bengali on a slip of paper, folded it, and put it on the top of those two slates, between which Mr. Keeler had already placed a small bit of a slate-pencil about one half of an inch long. He put his handkerchief loosely around the slates. I held two corners of the slates with both hands, and the medium held the other two corners with his hands. This way the slates were raised above the table in the air between our hands. We sat for a few minutes, and chatted a little, for he said that conversation did not interfere with the writing at all. Mr. Keeler then said : 'I do not know whether your friend will come or not, but I shall do my best'. After a few minutes I asked him whether it was necessary to put my name on the paper. He replied : 'Yes'. He then asked me whether I wrote the name of my friend in English or not. I answered in the negative. He replied : 'Perhaps my spirit guide will not be able to call whom you want, as he cannot read your language.' Hearing this I wrote the following on another slip of paper in English :

'Jogen are you here ? Answer my questions written in Bengali.'

and signed my name—SWAMI ABHEDANANDA. Then I folded this slip of paper and placed it on the top of the slates. Holding the slates again between our hands we talked on various subjects. Mr. Keeler asked me whether my departed friend had ever communicated before. I replied : 'Last evening at Mr. Campbell's seance I asked my friend some questions, but in reply I received a piece of paper on which his name 'Jogen' was written with blue pencil and nothing else. That is all.' Then within a few minutes Mr. Keeler put the slates on the table and wrote with a pencil 'Jogen is here' on one corner of the top slate. He asked me to read it. I read it, and said that the name was correct. Again he held two corners of the double slate with both hands and asked me to hold the other two corners, as stated above. The slates were nearly six inches above the table suspended in the air between our hands, as we sat on either sides of the table with arms stretched. Then I heard the scratching noise of the moving pencil coming from inside of the slates. Mr. Keeler said : 'Do you hear the noise of the pencil ?' I said : 'Yes'. It was over in about two seconds. I felt an electric shock in my arms while the pencil was moving, Mr. Keeler said that he also felt a gentle shock. We opened the slates and found the following words written in legible handwriting :

'I find no one here who can answer the questions of this gentleman', signed G. C.

Then I asked Mr. Keeler who this G. C. was and he replied : 'G. C. is my spirit guide. His full name is George Cristi'. Then Mr. Keeler said : 'Why, your friend is here, he must write'. He wiped the slates, and fixed them again as before. He held the slip of paper with questions in his own hands for a few seconds, and asked me to do the same. I did so. Then we held the slates again as before. Again I felt a gentle electric shock in my arms after a few minutes, and heard the scratching noise of the pencil, coming from inside of the double slates. The noise stopped in a few seconds, and the result was that the slate-writing was in four different languages : Sanskrit, Greek, English and Bengali. Seeing the writing Mr. Keeler was very much surprised, for he could not read or write Sanskrit, Greek and Bengali. Here I must mention that at Lily Dale there was not a single person outside myself who could read or write Sanskrit and Bengali. I was also surprised to see that the handwriting in Bengali resembled the handwriting of my friend 'Jogen' (Swami Yogananda), when he was in his earthly body.

I thanked Mr. Keeler for this extraordinary phenomenon, which I could not explain, and begged of him to give me those slates, as I wanted to find out how it was done by showing the slate-writing to other mediums or spiritualists. Mr. Keeler said that he never had such a slate-writing before. I took the slates and bade him good-bye. Thus ended the seance.

Let me mention here that neither my friend nor myself knew Greek. However, in another seance, I was told by the spirit that my friend brought with him the spirit of a Greek philosopher who wrote the Greek verse. At first I did not believe in the truth of this statement, but when I showed those lines to the Professor of Greek at Columbia University in New York, he said that this verse was a familiar gem of Plato, that every word was correctly written. He then translated the literal meaning of the verse.

In another seance, when I wanted to see Jogen materialized, he replied that he did not like it. But I was surprised to see the spirit of Babu Balaram Basu of 57, Ramkanta Bose Street, Calcutta fully materialized in the seance of Mrs. Moss at Lily Dale in the state of New York. He wore his familiar white turban on his head, as he used to wear it while in his mortal body. But now it was illuminated as it were with tiny electric bulbs all around the folds of his headdress. My eyes were dazzled to look at this brilliant figure with flowing beard and majestic appearance. He did not speak but answered my questions by nodding his turbaned head. He put his right hand on my head and silently blessed me. At that time I could see the medium Mrs. Moss (who was very stout) sitting unconscious in dead trance on a rocking chair. After blessing me, the whole materialized figure of Balaram Basu melted away in a mistlike white substance (ectoplasm) and disappeared.[1]

I wondered why he did not speak and on questioning I received the answer that he did not speak, because he could not speak before he passed out of his earthly life. This statement corroborated with the fact that before he died Balaram Basu had suffered from double pneumonia and could not speak for over a week.

In another seance I heard Jogen's voice in Bengali when he spoke to me through a tin trumpet. He said to me : 'Do you like this country (America)?', to which I replied : 'Yes'. Then he said : 'I do not like this place, I am going to India to see our Holy Mother'.

Here I must mention that while on earth Jogen served our Holy Mother, the consort of Bhagavan Sri Ramakrishna, with his whole heart and soul. I had also seen in America protrait-painting, painted by the invisible hand of a discarnate spirit done in my presence.

---

[1] We have also heard from the Swami that he saw the Holy Mother Sarada Devi, Swami Vivekananda, Swami Adbhutanana (Latu Maharaj), the Poet Girish Chandra Ghose and Sister Nivedita in materialized bodies just after the moments of their passing away. In every case, immediately after those psychic visions were over, the Swami received cablegrams from India bearing the sad news of their passing away.

CHAPTER XV

WHAT IS THERE BEYOND THE GRAVE

It has been discussed already what is there beyond the grave is the question that often rises in our minds and we like to know what will happen to us after we pass out of the body at the time of death. When we read different scriptures of the world, we find that the same question was discussed and various answers were received, either through their intellect, through their conception of the world or through revelations. Among the answers which have been handed down to us from time immemorial, we find that in the Old Testament, when this question arose in the mind of Job, he answered in a negative form. He longed for death, thinking that it would end his mental agony. In Psalms we read :

'Wilt thou shew wonders to the dead ? Shall the dead arise and praise thee'.[1]

Again we read :

'In death there is no remembrance of thee : in the grave who shall give thee thanks ?'[2]

'His breath goeth forth, he returneth to this earth; in that very day his thoughts perish'.[3]

'The dead praise not the Lord, neither any that go down into silence'.[4]

---

[1] Psalm 88, *Verse* 10.
[2] Psalm 6, *Verse* 5.
[3] Psalm 146, *Verse* 4.
[4] Psalm 115, *Verse* 17.

Solomon spoke boldly as :

'All things come alike to all : there is one event to the righteous, and to the wicked ; to the good and to the clean, and to the unclean; * * * as is the good, so is the sinner'.[5] 'Go thy way, eat thy bread with joy and drink thy wine with a merry heart ; * * * Live joyfully with the wife for there is no work, nor device, nor knowledge, nor wisdom, in the grave, whither thou goest'.[6] 'The dead know not anything, neither have they any more reward ; for the memory of them is forgotten.'[7]

Furthermore we read :

'For that which befalleth the sons of men befalleth beasts ; even one thing befalleth them : as the one dieth, so dieth the other ; yea, they have all one breath. So that a man hath no pre-eminence above a beast.

'All go unto place ; all are of the dust, and all turn to dust again'.

'Who knoweth the spirit of man that goeth upward and the spirit of the beast that goeth downward to the earth.'[8]

There are many such passages that create a great deal of confusion in our minds. Which of these answers is true : whether after entering into the grave we continue to live, or is it true that we perish in the grave ?

It has already been discussed that many Christians believe that Jesus the Christ brought eternal life into light. Of course, he did bring eternal life into light among the Jewish tribes who did not believe in the life after·death, or, in the truth, that

---

[5] Ecclesiastes, Ch. IX, *Verse* 2.
[6] Ecclesiastes, Ch. IX, *Verses* 7, 9, 10.
[7] Ecclesiastes, Ch. IX, *Verse* 5.
[8] Ecclesiastes, Ch. III, *Verses* 19-21.

life continues even after we enter into the grave. The Jews from the ancient times down to the time of the Babylonian Captivity did not believe in the existence of a soul which could live separately from the material body. They had an idea that the breath of life came from Jehovah, and at the time of death the same breath of life went back to Jehovah. What happens to the beasts, happens also to the saints and sinners alike. Those passages which I have quoted, referred to that state of belief, that state of mind which existed at that time. But during the Babylonian Captivity, which lasted from 586 to 536 B.C., the Jews came in touch with a highly civilized nation, the Zoroastrians or the Parsees from Persia who believed in the resurrection after death. They believed in a heaven and a hell, in the angels and the archangels, and in the last Day of Judgement. All these ideas were unknown to the Jews of ancient times. But some of the Jews accepted that belief, and others denied it. Those among the Jews who accepted that belief in resurrection, in angels, in archangels, were known as Pharisees. The very word 'Pharisee' is a Hebraic form of the word 'Parsee'. The Pharisees who lived in Persia, were the followers of Zoroastrianism. But the others were orthodox Jews, who did not accept these new ideas. They considered those ideas as heretical, and they were known as Sadducees. So the Sadducees were the orthodox Jews who did not believe in resurrection. Even in the New Testament, we find mention of a Sadducee who came and questioned whether there was such a thing as resurrection. But the idea of resurrection that we find among the ancient Zoroastrians is different from the conception of the resurrection of the body that has been accepted by the Christians. The resurrection of the physical body was not meant by the resurrection when the ancient Zoroastrians believed in that conception.

They believed in the resurrection of the spiritual body which continues to live after the gross physical body is destroyed. After the third day, according to them, the body is laid in the grave and on the morning of the fourth day, all souls rise, and this is the spiritual rise of the souls. And those who are righteous go into the Paradise, the Paradise of the good thought, the good word, and the good deed. Those who are not righteous also rise, and they go to hell of the evil thoughts, the evil word, and the evil deed. There they remain in darkness, until the time of the last Day of Judgement when Ahura Mazda, the Creator of good, would conquer Ahriman, the Creator of evil. Ahriman was at first friendly to Ahura Mazda, but afterwards he rebelled against Ahura Mazda and came down to this earth to take revenge, because he was expelled from the heavens. And this Ahriman by the way became Satan in Christianity. The conception of Satan is what we find in the Zoroastrian scriptures, known as the Zend Avesta. So this Ahriman is the Lord of this world, just as Satan is described as the prince of this world in the fourth Gospel. So he is trying to destroy the good work of the Creator, Ahura Mazda, and he has brought sin and death into this world. He is constantly fighting against the works of Ahura Mazda, the Creator of good, and his power will eventually be overcome and conquered by the Creator of good, and then the Lord will create a new world free from the influence or the power of Ahriman. That is the time when the last Day of Judgement will come. They also believed in a Messiah. That Messiah will appear in the heavens, in the clouds. His name is Saoshyant, and he will help those righteous souls to enter into Paradise, and enjoy eternal celestial pleasures. But those who are in the darkness of ignorance will also be forgiven for their sins, and will be allowed to enter into the celestial regions. That was the original belief among the Zoroastrians.

Now comparing the Christian belief with that of the Zoroastrians, we find how similar the Christian belief is to this old Zoroastrian belief of resurrection, the last Day of

Judgement, and going into heaven. All these conceptions existed in Persia long before the time of Christ, and it was noticed and accepted by the Pharisees during that period of Captivity, which lasted from 586 to 536 B.C. So their conception of resurrection was not absolutely dependent upon the resurrection of the body of Christ. These are all historical facts.

Then how can we admit that Christ brought the conception of eternal life into light in its literal sense, when we know that conception of eternal life existed not only among the Zoroastrians, but also among the Egyptians, Chaldeans, Babylonians, Chinese, Hindus, and all other ancient nations like the Romans, Greeks, and the Scandinavians. They all had a belief in an eternal life. As early as 12000 B.C. we find the records among the Egyptians. The Egyptian writers during the period from 12000 to 8000 B.C. recorded that there was a belief in the resurrection of the gross physical body among the ancient Egyptians and they also believed that the soul of the righteous would go into the celestial regions and enjoy all the pleasures that are to be found in those regions. They would have physical forms almost like the physical form we have on earth and that crude idea of resurrection of the gross physical body was afterwards given up when they came to understand the subtle powers and the subtle forces of nature and when they realized that each human body has its double which is made up of finer elements of matter. When their belief became strong in that double which had exactly the same form as the gross physical body had, they gave up the idea of the resurrection of the gross physical body. The writers among old Egyptians who lived in the 5th dynasty, that is, about 3400 years before Christ, emphatically declared 'the heaven hath thy soul and the earth hath thy body'. The soul belongs to the heaven and the body belongs to the earth. Since that day there arose the idea of preserving the body, because they had another belief that this double which is similar in shape and form with the gross physical body, continues to remain intact so long as the gross physical body is preserved intact, and that idea gave rise to the thought of mummifying the physical body. That was at the foundation of that practice, and the belief that if any arm or any limb of the physical body was mutilated, then that particular part or limb of the double would also be mutilated. For that reason they tried to keep the whole body intact by that peculiar process of mummifying.

They had also this belief that the souls of the righteous would go into heaven, and would live with the gods and eat and drink with the gods. They would have their physical body ; although consisting of finer particles of matter like the etherial body, still those bodies were physical, and they needed food and drink. For that reason, some of the friends and relatives of the departed ones used to keep food and drink in the grave. That practice was continued for sometime. Some of them went so far as to put amulets and charms in the graves, because they had the belief that the departed friends and relatives needed those charms to counteract the evil influences. It was also written that these souls of the righteous ones would go into heavens and walk in the fields of peace, wearing the celestial apparel of white linen and white sandals. There are canals where they bathe in pleasure. The deepest of pleasures that we have on this earth also exist in the Egyptian heaven.

Then when we read the writings of the Babylonians and the Chaldeans, we find that the Chaldeans also had a belief in resurrection of the corpse and for that reason, they embalmed the body and buried it in the grave underground in order to preserve them. That custom has been handed down to the Christians who bury the dead following the same custom of the ancient Chaldeans and the Babylonians. That shows that among the Chaldeans and the Babylonians there was a belief in eternal life. And the ideas that we have today, we did not get from the time of Christ, but they existed centuries before the advent of the illustrious Son of Man.

If we read the Greek and the Roman histories, there we find that the Greeks had a belief in the Elysian Fields that the souls of the righteous would go into the Elysian Fields and there take up the occupations of their life on earth. They would meet their friends, the husband would meet the wife, the parents would meet their children, and they would continue to live there and enjoy all the blessings of life. The Scandinavians had a belief in Valhalla. They were warriors and fighters, and they carried on their fight in the heavens in the presence of Odin. There the brave soldiers who had fallen in the battlefield would go and fight with their enemies and they would get hurt and wounded ; but by the miraculous powers of Odin their wounds would be healed, and they would take their arms again and fight. After fighting in the fields, they would hunt a wild boar and kill it and bring it and roast it and have a great banquet and feast. And this process will continue every day throughout eternity. Now remember that eternity does not mean a thousand years, ten thousand years, a million years, or trillions of years, but it means time without end.

But there are other believers like the American Indians. They have the happy hunting grounds in the heavens. Then we find among the Mohammedans that there is another conception of heaven. They say that the souls of the righteous who follow the commandments of Allah, would go to their Mohammedan heaven where there is plenty of shade, the rivers of pure water running, the rivers of milk, wine, and honey, all running in heavens. And there are maidens (*houris*) who pour wine into the goblets of the pious ones, and the pious ones drink and enjoy the company of those maidens. They have trees, under which they rest and enjoy the taste of the delicious fruits which those trees bear. You know that the

Arabs lived in a desert, where there was a great need of water and shade. The Arab people wanted water, and that was their idea of heaven with plenty of shade, delicious fruits, and all the enjoyments that they could imagine on this earth they projected and made a heaven that contained all such delightful things. It is a kind of heaven which is damp and wet and full of water. But I come from a country where the annual rainfall is five hundred forty inches. I would not care to go to a wet heaven.[9]

So, from these descriptions we learn that each nation and each tribe project their highest ideals of heaven and create one like a dreamland and the conception of heaven is the place where we can enjoy all the pleasures without having any break or sorrow or separation. That is, the souls of each nation and each tribe continue to enjoy these pleasures throughout eternity. Such is their belief. Some people believe that their occupation in heaven will be singing and playing upon the harp. They will sing the eternal music and will be listening to music. There is a verse in a hymn which was sung at one time in the orthodox churches describing the pleasures in heaven : "Where congregations ne'er break up, and Sabbaths never end". Of course, such a heaven will exist for those who believe in such an ideal. There would be a place or a realm where those souls who believe and have same faith in the Lord, will congregate and will sing the praise of their Saviour, and the Saviour might be Jesus the Christ, or Buddha, or a Prophet, or some other Saviour as among the Hindus. They will go and gather around their ideal, just as satellites whirl around a planet. So these faithful believers will be held together by their faith to the centre of their ideal which is the Saviour, and he may be Christ or Buddha or any other incarnation of Divinity. So that would be the heaven, the ideal place where the great righteous saints will go.

---

[9] Cf. Swami Abhedananda : *Path of Realization,* pp. 149-160.

But these beliefs that have been handed down to us do not convince us and do not make us feel sure that after the grave we are going into heaven or to eternal perdition. We want to know more about it, and we want more proofs. Now the spiritual seance will tell you that the souls, after passing through the grave, enter into various conditions and become the angels. It is believed that the angels know everything, and they can help humanity, their friends and relatives. But that is a question, whether they can help us in any way. Many people believe that they can, and others deny it. But they do not deny the existence of the souls after death. They believe in the existence of the discarnate souls, but whether they can help us in any way through communications is another point, and that point should be understood. But who are the departed ones who communicate with us and who can help us ? The popular belief is that no matter how a man lived his life on this earth, but as soon as he passes through the gates of the grave, he will enter into a realm of activity and will become conscious of everything, will know all the laws, and become perfect; and they have the power to help mankind, by giving messages in various other ways. But those who believe in this kind of ideal do not understand that our life in future, or after death, will be the continuation of this life. Death is not an enemy of this life, as it has been popularly understood in the orthodox Christianity. Because the orthodox Christianity has made death a terrible enemy of life, and they believe that as soon as one has entered into the realm of death, his life is stereotyped and he is doomed either to enjoy all the pleasures, or to go to eternal perdition and suffer for ever. Therefore death is not such an enemy of life, but is only a state.

Now we can easily understand that it is a stage or passage through which we can go somewhere else if we study the condition of dying man. Now what happens to a man who is dying ? We find that his body and senses are becoming weak. The sensations are getting dim. The physical body does not move. But his psychical powers are becoming keener and stronger. Some of them would develop perhaps the power of clairvoyance and clairaudience. They would see things at a distance. They would hear sounds from a distance. Their keen psychic senses would be developed, and all the powers that are latent now in our subconscious plane, will rise in the conscious plane. Memory will become then stronger. There have been cases where the dying persons went to a distance in the form of an apparition and gave a message, asking the relative to take care of their orphan children or continue to do certain things which they have left unfulfilled and unfinished. Such cases have been recorded. In Europe, only a few years ago these statistics were kept, giving all the particular of the time, the hour with proper verifications. You will also find in the records and the annals of the Psychical Research Society that have kept such records.

Now what do these records prove ? The records prove that there is a power in us which is latent at present perhaps, but at the time of death that power becomes stronger and acute. It has already been discussed before that the dying persons can communicate with their friends and relatives who have passed out long before their death and who are living in the other world. They cannot only communimate with them, but also can communicate with those who are on this earth.[10] Then after their death they pass through a state ; that is, the souls contract their powers that are scattered in the waking state, just as we do when we go to sleep. Our central life, the source of intelligence, centralized in one point, withdraws all the powers that are scattered all over the body, the sense powers, and all these powers are concentrated in that centre, which is like a nucleus. This nucleus holds those powers at the time of sleep, and at the time of death the same thing

---

[10] The departed souls can communicate with both the souls who have already passed and who are living in this phenomenal world.

happens.[11] It is only a deeper sleep than our ordinary sleep. At the time of death the soul contracts and becomes concentrated into that central nucleus where the sense powers, the thought powers, the reasoning faculties, the memory and all other powers are held together by that life-force which is an inherent property of the individual soul. By that individual soul I mean here the thinker, that which thinks, that which feels, that which perceives, and that which knows. Then that individual soul withdraws his powers just as you have noticed perhaps in the case of a turtle. Now when a turtle is frightened, what does it do ? It withdraws its limbs within the shell. That very illustration had been given in the *Bhagavad Gita* (2-58) :

यदा संहरते चायं कूर्मोऽङ्गानीव सर्वशः ।

'The soul withdraws its limbs inside its shell, just as a turtle when frightened would withdraw its limbs within its shell'.

You can imagine that the process takes place just before the time of death and then that entity or that thinker has a subtle form, which is called in Sanskrit the *sukshma-sharira*. It may be called the spiritual body or the astral body, and that spiritual or astral body goes out of the physical body at the time of death like a mist. It is an imperceptible mist. There are some psychists who have the power to see that mist, and by sensitive photographic plates they have taken the photographs of that mist although it is imperceptible to human eyes. The scientific experiments have also proved that the dead, if placed upon a very sensitive scale and weighed

---

[11] This nucleus is called the *prana* or the *mukhya-prana* (the life-force). "As the *prana* leaves the body it takes with it all the sense-powers, which are dependent upon it. The dying man carries with him the powers of seeing, hearing, smelling, tasting, touching, seizing, moving, speaking, excreting, generating and the power of thinking as well as self-consciousness. All the vital forces and subconscious activities of the organs are also withdrawn when *prana* leaves the body."—Swami Abhedananda : *Self-knowledge*, p. 63. Cf. *Kausitaki Upanishad* (III. 4).

just before death and immediately after death, a decisive difference in the weight will be found. The body will lose about one-half or three quarters of an ounce. That three-quarters of an ounce is the weight of that mist that goes out of the body, and it has been photographed. There have been cases which have been recorded. I have mentioned before the case of a young girl who was standing beside her dying brother and she said : 'Mother, mother, look at the mist around the body.' But the mother could not see the mist around the body.

This mist is only the inner garment of the soul. It is not the soul. The soul is the centre or nucleus, and mist is the finer garment. It is the subtle body and that subtle body remains after death. Where does it go after death ? Then it hovers around the body which is left behind for a long time. If the body is preserved in the grave, the attraction of the physical body which is loved so dearly and which he took care of for so many years with so much love, attracts the soul, or rather the soul clings to that body. For that reason the Hindu belief is that it is better to destroy the body. The destruction of the gross body releases the soul from its attachment to the material body. But, if it is put into the grave, the soul has the desire to come and look at the body and even after it has passed out for a long time, it has that desire and curiosity to see what is happening in the grave. That is a very undesirable state, and it makes the soul unhappy. It is agony for the departed soul to see his beautiful body decaying and disintegrating. It is very undesirable that the souls should suffer even in the other world. For that reason, cremation has been considered as the best way of disposing of the body. The Hindus say that sooner it is destroyed, the quicker the soul forgets its existence which is better for the soul to forget the existence of the dead body which is left behind.

Then what happens to the soul ? The soul, remaining clothed with the finer garment of the subtle body, enters the borderland where this earth ends and the new spirit-world begins. That is called the borderland. But really it is not a land, and there is no time of demarcation in the external space like the horizon. It is the different state of vibration. It is another dimension. Now we are living in the third dimension where we have the knowledge of the length, breadth and height. But we do not know all these things after death. That is the fourth dimension. In that fourth dimension these things like the time and space-divisions do not exist, and yet it occupies the same space. You imagine that the earth is a hollow form, just as an outline, and it has no solid substance in it. There the souls exist, and they come out from that plane of that fourth dimension to our third dimension, and we can see and feel them. Our soul's coming on the earth is like going down to the bottom of the ocean. But when you go there, what will you have to do ? You will have to put on a diver's suit, which weighs tons. If you do not put it on, you cannot go down. If you have a finer body, you cannot come and remain on this plane. You will go into a different plane where the vibration will harmonize with your physical form. For that reason we say that the borderland is not like a place or a corridor leading from this room to other room behind the wall. It has been said that it is a different kind of vibration. The same vibration may be continued, but we have not the power to perceive that vibration. If we have the finer senses, we shall be able to see them and perceive their existence. For instance, there may be music, a concert, and there are different notes which represent different vibrations of sound, or vibration of air, in a different scale with different keys. Now all might be combined into a beautiful harmony, but if you want to hear distinctly each sound or note which is on a different key, you must be conscious of it. Imagine that in this space there are wireless messages that are going on, but one does not interfere with the other, because each one has a different vibration. So each individual soul which passes out of the body, takes his own vibrations with him which are no other than the thoughts and the ideas of the soul. The thoughts and ideas of the soul are nothing but vibrations, and he is the centre, radiating all these vibrations constantly. He takes them with him, and, therefore, he does not interfere with any other centre of vibration. He carries them in his own realm, and there he remains for some time until he may go into a state of slumber which is a sleep state, because the exhaustion, after doing all his physical labour while living on this earth, is so great that the soul likes to rest and remains in that restful sleep. Nothing can disturb the soul when it enters into that sleep. Even God cannot disturb the sleeping soul. But those who have passed away in anxiety, sorrow and suffering, will have a disturbed sleep. They cannot go into a perfect rest. But, on account of attachment, they dream that their earthly friends and relatives weep and wail and grieve. They walk, as it were, in sleep like a somnambulist, a half sleeping and drowsy state. That is why you find many of their manifestations in seances are dreamy, half sleeping and idiotic. They are dragged down by the invocations of their friends, and they come and try in their dream state to help them, but they do not know what they are doing. There are certain souls who do not know that they are dead. They are in a state of confusion. It requires some time for them to realize that they are dead. They remain some time earth-bound i.e. if they have strong attachment for their friends and relatives whom they loved so much on earth, they hover around them. But it causes them great sorrow and suffering when their friends and relatives do not recognize their presence and do not treat them properly. So each soul will make his own environment and condition according to his thoughts and deeds.

So we understand that there is not a general law for everybody. Just as two individuals are not equally alike, so two souls will not be in the same state of vibration after death. After entering into that borderland, the souls will go into that slumber and remain there indefinitely. Some souls will remain longer in that sleep, and stay of others will be shorter. Those that are strongly attached to immoral and animal desires, will not have a long sleep, because they will wake up by their desires which will sprout in that state. Some will remain earth-bound, and they will remain in that state, and gratify their earthly desires, and will perhaps pick out some mediums through whom they can gratify their desires of drinking and immorality, and this is why you find a great many mediums have turned out to be drunken and immoral. It is not the fault of the mediums, but it is the fault of the spirit who is trying to gratify his immoral tendencies and desires through the sense organs of the medium. And, for that reason, it is very dangerous to allow these spirits to come and take possession of our physical forms and organs. There is one law about it and that law should be understood very clearly. We have taken this body as the result of our thoughts and deeds which we had in the past ; we have manufactured this body to rise higher to gain more experience for ourselves, not for anybody else. Suppose we allow other spirits to come and manifest through us, but what do we gain by it ? Really we gain nothing by it. We have sacrificed our opportunity, and that is our loss. We may say that we are helping humanity, but we are not doing so. We have been put into a hypnotic sleep and we are unconscious.

Our organs have been used by somebody else, or by some other force, and this other force is gaining experience through us and we are depriving us of our own opportunity for the good of that spirit who is manifesting through us. That consideration has been overlooked by great many of those who are interested in the spirit-manifestations and in communications with the departed ones. The Hindus are the people who from time immemorial have studied the spiritual side and have recorded the result and have left their knowledge which has been handed down to us through generations. There is no other nation in the world which has so perfect a knowledge in these lines, as we have in India. For that reason, you will notice that we do not allow our friends to go into that trance or mediumistic condition, because there is a great danger in it. If you once open your psychic door, you cannot close it very easily. There are some spirits who are fraudulent and can impersonate as somebody else and fool the people. Such cases have been recorded. Some one will appear as a great soul, but, in reality, he is not great. How are you going to distinguish them ? Of course, not by their apparent wise counsels which they can borrow from the subconscious mind of anybody. That discrimination should be made, and we must realize the difference between the higher and the lower spirits, and also that whenever we allow them to come to us for any message, we are dragging them to the earth plane. It is not helpful to them. For that reason, the Hindus believe that it is better in every way to leave these spirits alone, and if they have gone into slumber, let them rest there, and send them the good thoughts, because only good thoughts will be useful and beneficial to them.

The funeral ceremonies among the Hindus are different from those of the Christians. The difference lies in these that the services for the departed ones are performed, the good acts and the charitable works are done in their name, with the thought that the result of these works will go to them. That will release them from their earth-bound condition. We can help the spirits more than they can help us, because they are nearer to our thought realm.[12] If we send them a good thought, we are helping them, because thought is the product of the mind, and the departed souls remain in the mental world, and so thought can easily reach them. So, if we do any good act in their name and if we concentrate our mind with

---

[12] Vide Notes.

the thought that the result of this good work will go to them to help them in their onward progress, we are doing good to them. They can give us sometimes certain messages. Some of them who are advanced and have understood the law of cause and effect and are conscious of the causes, can trace the results.

For instance, you have a certain thought in your mind and that is the seed of a future result which is bound to come to you. If anyone can read that thought that you have in a seed from just now, he can tell what will happen in the future. The psychometrists can do that, rolling in that idea and producing an effect like the blossoming of a flower. It is all there in the mind. It is a vibratory state of the mind. That vibratory state can be realized by those who are advanced in the psychic planes and have developed the psychic powers. So we cannot make one rule for everybody. Some will sleep in that slumber for a long time, and those souls who are spiritually advanced and highly developed will throw off these subtle forms which are like the sheaths (kosha)[13] of the soul. These are the limitations. These are also the animal desires and tendencies, jealousy and love for material things. All those are the limitations of the soul. The soul, after sleeping for some time when realizing that it is under limitations, discards them. These discarded shells are sometime called the astral shells, and these astral shells float around. There is no soul in them. They are like thought forms, and these thought-forms might be reanimated by the thought of the medium or of any individual. So you may see some ghosts or elementals. They are all like them. There are other elementals of lower animal spirits i.e. they have not yet become human beings. They are rising in the process of evolution. These might come and might be perceived after waking from the soul-slumber, and then these souls enter into the astral plane. They might have

---

[13] In truth, the sheaths or koshas are the coverings, and they are the assuming coverings of the mind, or of the consciousness.

a very peaceful rest, and then they go into those planes where they can realize the fulfilment of their desires. Those are the planes which we call the heavens where we have fulfilment of our desires, thoughts and deeds. If we have performed good deeds, those impressions are left there and those impressions will gradually sprout and produce the result by the law of cause and sequence. Those results are reaped by the individuals in those different realms which are called the heavens (*svargas*), and those are the ideals of different nations. So you see that those who have a desire to enjoy pleasures like the pleasures in a particular heaven where there is plenty to eat and drink, and shade and a cool place, will dream of such a state. Their ideals will be materialized, as it were. The realm of thought-form is like the realm where their thought is realized as truth, just as in a dream. When you dream a dream, you do not know that it is a dream, but you know that it is real and it is thought-form that you are perceiving. You may look at it, you may touch it, you may hear the sound, but they are all in the realm of thoughts. So there are no real scenes or trees or different roads and canals except in the thought-forms. They are like a dreamland, and there the soul remains and enjoys those pleasures, because it wanted them. It is the plane for fulfilment of thoughts and desires. After a while when those desires are fulfilled, the souls get tired of that condition. Then the soul wants change and it gets out of those conditions. It wants something different. There are many souls in the other realm who are tired or exhausted. They want a more tangible and sensible or perceptible realization of their ideals and thoughts. So they like to go to different planes or realms. Some of them would like to come down on this earth to enjoy more pleasures and develop more powers, and so they are born and reincarnated. Some of them have the power to choose their parents. Some will go to sleep again.

The sleep after death is like the sleep before birth. Then they have a second sleep. Before they come to this plane, they go into that sleep and gravitate towards the proper environment. If I have a strong desire to be the best artist and if I do not succeed or pass away before I fulfil my desire, that desire will remain in me even in that soul-slumber. It will sprout again. Perhaps I will be drawn into the heaven of the artists where I would have communication and communion with the other artists who are living there and exchange our thoughts perhaps. Then I will try to manifest that desire again once more on this plane, and I will gravitate under the proper conditions and environments where I will have the physical body which will be the instrument through which I would realize my ideal. That is the process that takes place.

So there is no eternal heaven or eternal place of any punishment. If there be any punishment at all, it is like the punishment as we have on the earth plane. That punishment you will get. When you desire a thing and cannot get it, that is hell. That state you may go through on account of strong attachment. A miser who has formed the habit of handling dollars and cents enjoys it and loves it. Now, if he goes into that plane or astral plane, he will carry that desire with him. But he will have no dollars and cents to handle and he will be hankering after that and that will be his punishment. So it is very difficult for us to know exactly what would be the hell or that state of punishment for any individual who has committed something wrong. It is all that we draw towards ourselves by our thoughts and deeds. These dreams might be real for the time being, as all dreams are true, so long as we are dreaming. But, in reality, when compared with the eternal time, or when compared with the highest standard, they last only for a short period. So no heaven is eternal, and no hell is eternal : For that reason, it is said in the *Bhagavad Gita* (8.16) :

आब्रह्मभुवनाल्लोकाः पुनरावर्त्तिनोऽर्जुन ।

'O Arjuna, none of these heavens from the highest heaven of the Creator downward is permanent. The inhabitants thereof are sure to return from them sooner or later'.

They are ephemeral. They do not last throughout eternity in one state. So this is a progress that the soul makes after entering into the grave. Either he will go to heaven, or suffer according to the law of justice. The law of justice is very strict. There is no such thing as forgiveness, but it is the justice that balances compensation. The well-balanced state of the law of cause and effect is inexorable. 'Whatsoever thou sowest thou shalt reap'. That is as strong and as real as you are sitting here now. You may deny it, but you cannot get out of it. You may deny through ignorance the force of gravity, but at every step you cannot move, and cannot even exist on the surface of the earth, if it were not for the force of gravity. A child does not know whether there is such a thing as gravity, and his ignorance does not affect the law in any way. Our childish denial does not make a thing non-existence, and it simply shows that we do not know better. So this law of cause and sequence, called the law of *karma*, does not wait for widow's tears, or orphan's cries. What we have sown, we must reap either on this plane, or in some other realm. So after death we may enjoy the pleasures of our thoughts and deeds in the heavenly regions too.

The occupations may be according to the belief that we will continue to do certain things. It is not true however that all the types of our earthly occupations will be reproduced there. That is not possible. If it were so, then life would not be worth-living. Suppose a street-cleaner has to clean the streets of heaven throughout eternity, a cook or a seamstress will have to continue to do the same work throughout eternity ; so what kind of heaven would that be ? It would be the

opposite place, according to our conception. But there are
works and activities of the physical body on the unconscious
plane which help the souls who are suffering in the darkness,
and give a certain light of knowledge, but even that cannot be
done without violating a law, because no one can give us
anything unless we deserve it. Those souls which deserve any
help will receive the help. For that reason, the widely known
common maxim, 'heaven helps those that help themselves,'
is absolutely true. Because those who help themselves, have
made themselves ready for receiving the help from the universe
and if we have not made ourselves ready to receive the help
from the universe, the unvierse does not help us. It depends
entirely upon our own worth and attitude. And, for that
reason, the great teachers have always told us to be prepared
to receive help and to live on this earth a life that will bring
to us peace and happiness, and that will never make us repent
even for a second, because we must feel the responsibility
that we have upon our shoulders. By coming on this earth and
living this earthly life, we have taken the whole burden of the
responsibility of our future as well as of whatever we are
going to do on this earth, because our character and future are
made or created by ourselves. These is no other soul that will
mould our future for us, but we are little creators, and as the
creators on a dimunitive scale we are making our future,
creating our destiny, and building up our character by our
thoughts and deeds. And, therefore, we must do it consciously
and knowingly, and by understanding the laws that govern
our lives, not only on the physical plane, but also on the
mental, moral, intellectual, and spiritual planes.

If we understand those laws, then we are opening up
vistas of our future progress. We have nothing to be sorry for,
when we have nothing to repent. Our earthly life would be a
series or a continuous chain of pleasure and happiness, if we
know the real conditions and truths that underlie our beings.
But these truths are hidden from us, because we have not

become ready to know them. We are just playing on the surface, but the time is bound to come for each individual soul when there will be an awakening of a desire to know the real truth. No soul will be lost. Each soul will attain eventually to the highest knowledge or realization, and enter into that state where there is no birth, no death, and no change of any kind but the eternal being, the eternal bliss and the eternal knowledge. So we must not be afraid of death. Death is nothing but a change. We may throw off this old body, because we may put on another new body, if we have such a desire. We also find in the *Bhagavad Gita* (2.13) :

देहिनोऽस्मिन् यथा देहे कौमारं यौवनं जरा।

तथा देहान्तरप्राप्तिर्धीरस्तत्र न मुह्यति ॥

'As in our physical body, we survive the death of the baby body, and of the young body, so we live after throwing off the form of the subtle body, as we throw off the old garments and put on new ones.'

So at the time of death we throw off the old physical body which has served its purpose, and put on a new and finer one. Therefore the wise ones will never be afraid of death, but always will remember that there is an eternal life for everybody, and no soul will be lost. Those who have attained to the highest spiritual realization will eventually come face to face with the Infinite, and attain to that peace and happiness which have been attained by Sri Krishna, Buddha, Chirst, Ramakrishna, and by all the other Saviours of the world. Really the attainment of the supreme knowledge is the goal of spiritualism, and it is the be-all and end-all of all human beings.

CHAPTER XVI

DISCUSSIONS THAT WERE PRIVILEGED TO HAVE WITH THE SWAMI

QUESTIONS AND ANSWERS

Q. In the realm after death, will the soul continue to evolve into a state of perfection, or is it necessary to gravitate back to the earth and reincarnate?

Ans. It depends upon the desire of the soul.

Q. If the soul can evolve without coming back, would it not be better not to come back?

Ans. They cannot get the same experience in the other realm, as they would get here in the physical form.

Q. Are there enough bodies for all souls that wish to gravitate back and become reincarnated?

Ans. Well, you have got hold of an idea that the bodies are waiting for the souls. That is not correct. The souls manufacture the bodies. The idea that you have expressed is the old belief in transmigration and that the bodies are made ready to recèive the migrating souls, but that does not mean reincarnation. I have explained that in my lecture on *Transmigration*. The soul manufactures the body by obeying the physical laws of evolution.

Q. When the angel was cast out of heaven, did he incarnate?

Ans. Well, that is a mythological belief. By the angel from heaven, you mean him who became Satan. That is a mythological belief that the angel disobeyed the personal Creator. Then He expelled him, and so he fell on this earth. That is a crude kind of explanation, which was given by the primitive minds. There was no actual truth about it. They tried to explain good and evil in nature by that mythology. It was not an actual fact.

Q. You say the dead do not know that they are dead.

Ans. They do not know. It takes a long time for them to realize that they had passed out.

Q. What assurance have we that we are alive ?

Ans. There is no proof. We may call ourselves dead.

Q. How are you going to stop the spirits that are drunk from making the mediums drunk ?

Ans. The spirit who has been a drunkard on this earth has carried that desire with him, and he wants to drink. But he cannot find drinks there, and he wants to hover around the brothels. So he takes possession of a medium or some friend or relative, and drives him to drink, so that he enjoys the flavour of it.

Q. How is the obsessed man going to stop it ?

Ans. Well, you would have to dehypnotize him. The medium should be exorcised, that is, the obsession could be cured by a higher spirit of higher development. If you know somebody who has a familiar spirit of higher nature, that higher spirit will drive him out by command or by will-power, but the patient might not have that will-power ; he requires freedom from another soul to be cured.

Q. Can a soul remain in one particular physical body idefinitely ?

Ans. Yes, it can, if it has understood the laws and lived the right life.

Q.   Why did the ancients take out heart and place there a scarab ?

Ans. That was their belief. The scarab was the symbol of creation.

Q.   You stated that if the body lay in the grave, the soul would suffer when it returns and sees that body. Would not the soul suffer more if the body were burnt ?

Ans. It might do for a while, if they are conscious that their body is destroyed. It might shock them for a little, but after it is destroyed they would forget. It would be the easiest way to make them forget, because they cannot come and look at it. But if the body is preserved, then that attraction of the body will attract the soul down, and it may occur many times. So there is an advantage in cremation.

Q.   What is the shortest time in years that a spirit soul would remain in dream or in an unconscious state ?

Ans. Our time does not affect them. Our five thousand years might be five seconds to them.

Q.   But how long would it be ? Ten years ?

Ans. Well, that I have already told you.

Q.   The Hindus have a way that when somebody dies they put a jar of water and a towel, and they believe that the soul comes for them eight times. Where did that originate ?

Ans. I never saw anything like that. There might be some superstitious belief, but we never saw anything like that, that the souls need food, that the souls of the departed ones require nourishment. Some people offer food once a year and our one year may be one day to them ; so once a year they offer food in their name, but the poor people get the benefit.

Q.   Do we know our friends there ?

Ans. Yes, we do.

Q. What is the difference between reincarnation and transmigration ?

Ans. Our religion teaches reincarnation, which is a little different from transmigration. Reincarnation is more scientific. It does not teach that we come back from the human plane to the animal bodies indiscriminately simply to gratify our whims.

Q. Do I understand that the soul divides itself into two parts ?

Ans. No, it is what we call the subtle body. It is the body which the soul has manufactured already. It is there now in you and in me. It is not divided, only it takes shelter in the finer spiritual form, and it remains with it while it goes into that slumber and in that astral shell.

Q. What is this mist you were talking about ?

Ans. That mist is only the finer elements like electrons going out of the body.

Q. Has it anything to do with the soul after death ?

Ans. The soul is the centre which contains life, mind, and intelligence, and the mist is not that. Mist is only the particles of matter amassed together like a cloud or vapour.

Q. Is that the ego ?

Ans. The ego is in the centre. It is not manifested but it is in a causal state like a nucleus, like an atom.

Q. What becomes of the ego ?

Ans. It is there, only it is potential, unmanifested.

Q. Is the soul given a power over the physical body ?

Ans. Yes, the healing power is in the soul.

APPENDIX A

A SUMMARY OF SWAMI ABHEDANANDA'S SPEECH AT AN ANNIVERSARY MEETING OF THE PSYCHICAL RESEARCH SOCIETY OF CALCUTTA

In 1925, the anniversary meeting of the Psychical Research Society of Calcutta was held in the Arya Samaj Hall, located at the Cornwallis Street,[1] Calcutta. His Highness Maharaja the late Kameshwar Singh Bahadur of Darbhanga presided over the meeting. It was a distinguished gathering. Many prominent persons like Maharaja Sir Pradyot Kumar Tagore, Maharaja Manindra Chandra Nundy of Cossimbazar, Pandit Shyam Sunder Chakravarty, Editor of the Servant (now defunct), and a number of veteran physicians, physicists, and scholars of the great city of Calcutta were present on that occasion. SWAMI ABHEDANANDA was also invited to deliver there a speech on Spiritualism. Long before the hour announced for the meeting the spacious hall was packed to suffocation.

SWAMI ABHEDANANDA, in his flowing ochre-coloured garments, entered the hall a few minutes before the meeting. His noble figure, his bright countenance beaming with inward spiritual light and his serenity made a deep impression on the minds of the audience. It was a sight not to be easily forgotten.

---

[1] At present Bidhan Sarani.

238

At the outset of the meeting the late Babu Piyush Kanti Ghosh of the Amrita Bazar Patrika and one of the chief organizers of the meeting, moved a resolution that SWAMI ABHEDANANDA might be requested to become the President of the Psychical Research Society of Calcutta, during the coming year. The resolution was unanimously carried. After the delivery of the Presidential Address, the President respectfully requested SWAMI ABHEDANANDA to deliver his speech.

The Swami in his speech first gave a brief account of the origin, growth and development of the spiritualistic movement in America, and its gradual spread in other countries of the world. He said that during his long stay in America he came in contact with this movement and some of its leaders well-known in that Continent. Then he very charmingly described his novel experiences as an eye-witness of some famous spiritualistic seances. There he had the opportunity to receive messages from the spirits of many distinguished persons, such as Prof. William James of Harvard, Prof. Myers and others.

The Swami said many things about the various conditions of men after death. After death men have to go through various stages in spirit-life. The man who led here a vicious life must undergo pains and sufferings in a place where absolute darkness reigns in perpetuity. But the case of a man, pious and virtuous, is entirely different.

The Swami continued to describe his various experiences of spirit-communications. At one time he was present in a spiritualistic seance, and a very striking event took place there. A music-box, coated with phosphorus at its bottom, was placed on a table within a dark room. The room was kept for holding a spiritualistic seance. Its doors and windows were all tightly shut up. Hardly had the seance begun when the music-box was suddenly and visibly lifted up and gradually touched the ceiling. Then like a flying bird, it began to move along the four walls of that room with the full play of some particular musical tune. Once there was heard a high sound and the box went outside penetrating through the wall. From outside of the room it began to move in the same way and the flow of the music went on. Then after some fifteen minutes another high sound was heard and the music-box was found in the room. The same tune was still being played. The whole event took only about a quarter of an hour.

There happened an incident in another seance which was no less striking. As the Swami was listening there to the message of some spirit, he suddenly felt the touch of a number of hands all over his body. But he found that there were no such persons around him. He was a little surprised when he heard the voices of some spirits addressing him : 'Do you think the medium is doing all these things ?

Then in that very seance there took place another event which was still more surprising. As the Swami was coming back from the dark screen to resume his seat, he was surprised to find that his chair was occupied by a lady. It was not at all a human being but the materialized body of some spirit. As soon as he came near her, the spirit got up and shook hands with him. He felt that her touch was as tangible and warm as that of a living human body. But in a moment the hand of the spirit, held by him, melted away.

The Swami said that it was possible for some spirits to appear in materialized form without the help of the mediums and they could directly communicate with all. He also said that he had heard how an independent voice in a seance, held in the house of Sir Alfred Turner, addressed him and others present there, with these words : 'Good evening, brother'.

But this power of materializing the body is not possessed by all spirits. Only the spirits advanced in psychic powers are able to do this. One thing should be made clear that though the spirits may assume the materialized bodies, they are not conscious of their material state of existence. So they cannot retain such bodies of theirs for long.

In continuation of his speech, the Swami said that the spiritualistic movement had done much towards dispelling many erroneous and superstitious beliefs from the minds of a large number of bigoted and fanatic Christians. It had given a death blow to the queer belief in the confinement of the departed persons under the grave till the last Day of Judgement. The inquisitive minds in America and in other countries no longer believe that the dead are subject to lie beneath the graves and will be resurrected on the Doomsday to go to an unknown place to receive the judgement for their virtues and vices. The unscientific doctrine of eternal hell-fire upheld by the Christian churches is gradually losing its hold on the learned and thinking people in the West. Now it sounds quite ludicrous to all who have thoroughly rationalized their views.

But in spite of all his interest in spiritualistic movement, the Swami did not hesitate to expose its demerits and dark sides. He denied its unjust claim that it solved the problems of the religious life of man. It has by no means been helpful to any spiritual aspirant in finding out the way of salvation. It has always proved futile in shaping the religious character of any person. On the contrary, it has misled him. Under the influence of the spiritualistic movement people have been subject to error, and failed to distinguish religion from spiritualism. Spiritualism and religion were things quite contrary in their very nature. The function of spiritualism is to deal with the ghosts and spirits while religion always inspires and enables man to tear off his bonds of miseries and imperfection and to realize his higher Self. Obsession with ghosts and the ghost-world degrades the mind, while contemplation of God helps man to raise himself at last to the plane of life divine. In matters spiritual, the spiritualistic movement never comes to any use. The practice of spirit-communication has brought, in many cases, sad results. Spiritualism never elevates the minds of the mediums either intellectually, or morally, or spiritually. Rather it lowers them to a pitiful state. The constant practice of mediumship weakens the mind, destroyes the brain-power and the consequence often is insanity and other incurable diseases. Men and women who regularly sit as mediums in spiritualistic seances become like passive and thoughtless creatures. People who come under the evil and pernicious influence of the evil spirits often become like toys in their hands. They are gradually deprived of the power of reasoning and the blessing of human life, and they come to a miserable end. One should not therefore confuse spiritualism with religion. The former may satisfy some of our curiosities ; at best it ensures us of the survival of human soul after death. It cannot do anything higher. But the nature of religion is quite different. The practice of religion leads man to the state of unending peace. Religion enables us to transcend the bonds of repeated births and deaths.

In order to transcend the limits and bonds of earthly life, and in order to go beyond ignorance, error and untruth, one has to be fully acquainted with the theory and practice of the Vedantic *sadhana,* generally known as the system of Yoga. Without the practice of Yoga no person would be able to set himself free from the bonds of repeated births and deaths. The sincere and systematic practice of Yoga alone can enable a man to unveil the mystery of his own being. This alone is the way to solve all the problems of the soul, of its birth and death, and its existence before and after its appearance in human form. It is religion, and not spiritualism that can help us to know the true nature of our own being, which is essentially all-wise, all-pervading, immutable and Divine. The religious history of the world since ages past has been bearing witness to this fact. All the great seers of Truth,

Prophets and Incarnations, who are regarded today as the living embodiments of the spiritual ideal of mankind, had to go through this path of spiritual practice. Their ceaseless and sincere efforts made them free forever from untruth, ignorance and illusion. In attaining to this state of Self-realization they had overcome all sorrows, sufferings and miseries.

It is wrongly believed by many people that the teachings of the Vedanta make human life dry and monotonous and that we become pessimists. Vedanta, they say, is all rationality. Yes, the Vedanta supports nothing unreasonable. Nor does it indulge in anything without the process of rational analysis. For, without reason there is no other way to distinguish truth from untruth. This process should be applied in order to know the highest Truth ; and we cannot help this. But it is far from truth that the practice or *sadhana* as enjoyed by the Vedanta makes our life dry and pessimistic. On the contrary, it sweetens life with ineffable joy. It leads man to the perennial source of unbounded happiness. The teachings of Vedanta inspire and guide us to realize our oneness and identity with the Infinite. This is the highest goal of all religion. Whosoever realizes this state attains to eternal Bliss even in this life.

APPENDIX B

AN INTERESTING DISCOURSE UNDER THE AUSPICES OF THE CALCUTTA PSYCHICAL SOCIETY

(Saturday, January 23, 1926)

The fourth monthly meeting of the Society was held sometime in 1926, at the Ramakrishna Vedanta Society Hall, at 40, Beadon Street, under the presidency of His Holiness Swami Abhedananda Maharaj. Long before the appointed hour, the hall and the adjoining rooms were packed up. There was a crowded and appreciative audience, and amongst those present were Mr. G. S. Dutta, I.C.S., Rai Jatindra Nath Chowdhury of Taki, Dr. E. G. H. Bowering, B.S.C.(O), M.B.(H), Babus Jogendra Nath Mitter, Basanta Kumar Mitter, Bhut Nath Mukherjee, Dr. M. M. Basu, Babus Balai Chand Mullick, Satish Chandra Sen Gupta, Saroj Kumar Choudhury, Shyama Charan Paul and others. Babu Piyush Kanti Ghosh could not attend on account of illness.

At the commencement, Dr. M. N. Basu in a few well chosen words, proposed Swami Abhedananda Maharaj to the chair. In doing so he said that the meeting had been organised in order that both the members of the Calcutta Psychical Society and the Ramakrishna Vedanta Society would have the privilege of hearing the personal experience of the seances of the Western countries from their revered and common president. Both the Societies have the same object in view viz. the realization of their selves. The spiritualists and psychists are being looked down in this country, because it is said that they dabble with ghosts only and have no higher aims. But one cannot be a good psychic unless he leads a pure religious life and practises Yoga.

The Joint Secretary, Babu Saroj Kumar Chaudhuri seconded Dr. Basu's proposal and Swamiji took the presidential chair amidst cheers. The President thereupon introduced Dr. Bowering, a spiritualist, who delivered an interesting address on "Spiritualism". In the course of his address he said that the scriptures adduce three historical instances as a proof of life after death. They are :

(1) The prophet Samuel, 4 years after death at the bidding of the woman at Endor confronts the guilty panic-stricken soul and speaks to him.

(2) Moses, apart from the thronging multitudes, but in the sight of wandering disciples, the bodiless for ages steps out of the unseen world to hold converse with Christ on the Mount of Transfiguration so real and man-like that St. Peter wanted to make a Tabernacle for him.

(3) The Master Jesus Christ himself tells us in his Epistle (1 Peter III ? 18-20) that when the body of Jesus was stiffening in death on the Cross the departed tenant was preaching unto "Spirits".

All three of these persons had died and all had left behind the earthly body and yet they stand forth on the page of the divine inspiration as living, thinking and speaking.

There is sufficient proof in the Bible about the existence of life after death and more convincing in the words : "He is not a God of the dead but of the living" (Lukes XX, 38). As regards the state of unconsciousness between death and judgement, the utterances of Christ, St. Peter and St. Paul together with a conscience of belief of all races and creeds for centuries are against it. With regard to life after death, the Bible proclaims it, Jesus confirms it and our reason approves it.

"Tell me at the time of dissolution, I shall lose my consciousness that I shall practically pass to nothingness until the Resurrection morn and I shiver at the thought of being thus chloroformed by death. Tell me that there is an unseen life, but it is dim and shadowy, nebulous and intangible, a world of strangers and unreality and I dread the knock of death which will summon me to such a sphere. But on the other hand, make the new life what the Bible shows it to be— a real life when I shall be the same man as I am now. Oh ! what a difference will it make, my real self will undergo no change except that of environment and when my Heavenly Father shall call me, I shall learn that for myself there is no death ; what seems so is transition".

Babu Satish Chandra Sen Gupta then related his personal experiences of how he talked with a spirit.

PRESIDENTIAL ADDRESS

The President Swami Abhedananda then delivered a most interesting address which was greatly appreciated by the audience. In narrating his experiences of spiritualistic phenomena he showed photographs of automatic slate writings of discarnate spirits and described in detail the phenomena of slate writings, materialization of spirits and spirit-photography. The President then said : "In America there are very good mediums of all kinds and places where they give demonstrations of spirit communications**".

Then the Swami said that he had seen in America portrait painting done by invisible hand of a discarnate spirit in his presence.

He then concluded by saying "you cannot get all by reading. Through the practice of Raj-Yoga you can be like Sankaracharya and Ramakrishna who were mediums of the Divinity himself. It is said that the spirit of Vyasa came and discussed with Sankaracharya.

If you wish to communicate with the spirits of higher order you will have to lead a holy life and become pure and virtuous, living on the same plane of vibration with them. You may question, "Why do not the spirits come to you ? Why do not the debates come to you ?" The answer is because you are on another plane of vibration. You will have to raise yourself so that your prayer and desire will reach them. You may have desire for communicating with them, but your desire does not reach them, for you are on a lower plane of vibration, that is, *"tamasic plane"*.

Therefore, you have to pray and practise Yoga in order to purify yourself. Through purity of heart you will be able to converse with the departed souls and unless your heart is pure you will not be able to approach them.

In conclusion, Swamiji said that while in America he saw the astral form of Ramakrishnadeva's wife at the time when she left her mortal coil. He also had the good fortune to see from America Babu Girish Chandra Ghosh and other friends the moment they left this world. Rai Jatindra Nath Choudhury thanked the President for his very able and interesting address.

APPENDIX C

QUESTIONS AND ANSWERS

WE HAVE GIVEN HERE FROM OUR MEMORY, SOME OF THE DISCUSSIONS THAT WE WERE PRIVILEGED TO HAVE WITH THE SWAMI :

Q. Swamiji, what becomes of the souls immediately before and after death ?

Ans. The soul immediately before death contracts and withdraws all sense-powers gradually. The physical senses grow dimmer and dimmer as a flickering candle-flame gradually approaches ultimate extinction ; but the senses and powers grow keen and strong. The soul just before leaving the body lives in an unconscious state like slumber and in that state the astral or spiritual body passes out like a mist.

Q. Then is the condition of the souls beyond their grave awful indeed ?

Ans. Yes. The earth-bound spirits suffer much. They do not know that they are dead. In that slumber state the souls carry concentrated records of their entire lives. When the souls wake from sleep they enter into an astral plane. This astral plane is nothing but the projection of the souls' own ideas. Their dimensions are in vibrations. The disembodied souls find their ideas realized in that astral plane. They sleep, but their periods of sleeps vary.

248

Q. Do they not enter then into a lonely and foreign realm ?

Ans. Yes. Just to make it clear, let us take an example. Suppose you are an inhabitant of a large and thickly populated city like Calcutta. There happens a terrible earthquake in a dead dark night resulting a total devastation of the whole city. The houses fall to pieces and the whole city appears like a vast desert enveloped with deep darkness. Then if you are allowed to move and walk freely with your eyes blind-fold, what will be your condition ? Just imagine. Such is the wretched condition of the earthbound spirits after death.

Q. Is it the same condition with all the spirits ?

Ans. No. Ordinary earthbound souls only suffer from it. The case of the virtuous souls is entirely different. They move easily and freely, and can see their ways with the light of their own knowledge and purity.

Q. Swamiji, may we ask you again where the souls really go after death ?

Ans. They go where they already are. Where do you stay when you fall asleep ? You then stay in the mind. After death the souls need not go to any other place. They continue to stay in the same mental plane just as we do in our state of sleep or dream (*svapna*). The souls then live in the mental plane or *manomaya jagat*. They move and do everything mentally in that state. Nothing of the material plane remains for them. The bodies in which they dwell at that time are subtle and are made of seventeen subtle elements. They are : five *pranas*, five *karmendriyas*, five *jnanendriyas*, the *manas* and the *buddhi*. The composite subtle body of seventeen elements is called by the *Sankhya* and other Hindu philosophies, *sukshmasarira*.

Q. How do the prayers and good thoughts of the living become helpful to the souls departed ?

Ans. I have already said that just after death souls cannot realize themselves as detached from their previous material bodies. They remain in a swoon and are unconscious immediately after death. In that condition prayers of any kind by the well-wishers help the spirits a good deal. Good thoughts from the relatives and the nearest and dearest ones bring alleviating reaction in their mental planes. Thus they create a certain vibration in their stupefied condition of mind, restore their veiled consciousness, and thereby the souls come to know that really they are not in their material bodies. The weeping and wailing of their relatives afflict them with pain and thereby some are dragged down from their astral planes. But good prayers bring back their consciousness and then they try to cross the *borderland.* This borderland in vibration is like a narrow river of ether which can be compared to a neutral zone. It has been called by the Hindus the *Baitarani,* by the Parsis (Zoroastrians) *Chinnat-bridge* and *Sirat* by the Mohammedans.

Ordinary or earthbound spirits cannot cross the borderland easily. They generally go to a region where prevails permanent darkness. This dark astral plane has been described in the *Upanishad* as :

"Asuryā nāma te lokā andhena tamasāvritah; tāmaste pretyabhigacchanti ye ke chātmahano janhhā."—Isha Upanishad, 1.3 :

'There are the regions of permanent darkness ; the light of the sun or other luminaries is never seen there. Those who have not realized their true Self or do not strive for Self-realization, must go to that dark region after death.'

The sun, the moon and the stars cannot shine in the spirit-world as they belong to this material world of ours. There is no room for any earthly or material thing in that subtle world beyond death.

Q. Is then the condition of the earthbound spirits worse after death ?

Ans. Yes. In the case of the earthbound souls, desires are not fulfilled and so their sufferings become worse and worse. They dig their own graves. All desires for material enjoyment then reach the most acute form. The souls then suffer from the burning flames of those unfulfilled passions.

In fact, what you will sow you will reap. The desires remain in the form of impressions or *samskaras.* The death of the body cannot destroy the *samskaras.* After death they remain as seed-forms in the mind.

Q. Swamiji, what is meant by the *double* or astral body ?

Ans. Double or astral body is nothing but an exact counterpart of the physical body. The astral body leaves or goes out of the physical body at the time of death, and when it leaves the latter, there remains still a slender thread or cord of astral or vapourlike substance. Finally it also melts away. The soul remains then in a state of coma resembling the condition of an unborn child in the mother's womb.

Q. It is possible to communicate with the dead ?

Ans. Certainly. Generally the half-awakened souls manifest themselves in spiritualistic circles through the channel of the medium. Some are dragged down from their peaceful sleep to answer our selfish calls and some themselves are eager enough to communicate. They appear in a dreamy state. Sometimes it has been found that, seeing the mediumistic channel open, they lose their self-control.

Q. Can the disembodied spirits take any material form ?

Ans. Yes, they can. Astral shells or astral corpses of the departed spirits may be materialized temporarily by means of the vitality of the mediums in their unconscious state. They appear in shadowy forms, move and even speak sometimes.

Men who have psychic powers can see these shadowy forms of the spirits. Experiments have been made by the spiritualists many a time, proving that the psychical corpses can be aroused into apparent life by a strong mediumistic current.

Q. Do the departed souls incarnate again on earth ?

Ans. Yes. Until and unless they are able to break the bonds of desire and transcend the cycles of birth and death, they are born again and again on earth. Sooner or later the departed souls feel a strong desire to manifest themselves again in new life. The seeds of their unsatisfied desires compel them to be born again on earth. So they select their fit parents, circumstances and surroundings before being born. They fall again into a state of soul-slumber, and die on the astral plane as they did before on earth. By the same cyclic process of evolution and involution they are born in a state of partial slumber. They awake gradually from the dream-like states to the consciousness of the earth-plane.

Q. Is it not good to culture spiritualism for the knowledge of the world beyond death ?

Ans. It is no good, I think, for those who really aspire to realize the supreme knowledge of the *Atman.* It is our aim of life not to acquire knowledge of things fleeting and unreal, but to reach the goal which is the absolute Truth and Blessedness. Spirit-worlds may be true from the empirical point of view, but really they are nothing but the imageries of the human minds. Spirits are unborn and uncreated and are immortal in their nature. Birth and death, coming and passing are merely the appearance. Only through the veil of ignorance a man thinks himself to be dead or born. When his darkness of ignorance is dispelled by the self-effulgent radiance of the *Atman,* he realizes himself as the immortal Bliss. Spiritualism does not help us to transcend the cycles of death and birth ; the knowledge of the Absolute alone can make us free from it.

WE REPRODUCE HERE SOME REPORTS OF THE SPEECHES BY THE SWAMI ON THE SUBJECT PUBLISHED IN VARIOUS JOURNALS OF AMERICA

I

FREE RELIGIOUS ASSOCIATION OF AMERICA IN SESSION

Intellectual leaders from all over New England present— Opening Address by Dr. Janes—'Conception of Immortality' the topic of this morning.

'Large and typically Bostonian audience filled the floor and first gallery of the Hollis Street Theatre this morning, at the 32nd annual convention of the Free Religious Association of America, to which delegates have come from many parts of the Continent, but most of the members live in this city and vicinity. A glance through the audience showed that a good portion of the intellectual leaders of New England were present.

'Former President, Thomas Wentworth Higginson being absent on account of illness, Dr. Legis G. Janes of Cambridge, the newly elected President, occupied the Chair at the morning session of the convention, and made a brief opening address, saying that having attended the first meeting of the Free Religious Association as a young man, 32 years ago, he had been profoundly influenced by it, and his whole life changed. He said that he would like to see the whole world under the banner of free religion and the sects cease to strive against each other. 'I would like', he continued, 'to see political reforms brought about. When I heard Emerson and Lucretia Mott speak at the initial meeting I thought the presidency of this Society was a position of greater honour than the presidency of the United States ; and there has been nothing in the recent conduct of the present incumbent of the latter office to modify my youthful opinion.'

'The subject of the morning conference was *The Conception of Immortality,* and the first paper, discussing the philosophical argument, was presented by PROF. JOSIAH ROYCE, Ph.D. of the Harvard University. His thesis was a scholarly argument for immortality from the standpoint of a mental philosopher.

'We have no empirical foundation for a belief', said he, 'that so great an ill as death is to be compensated by a resurrection. Life is full of ills that seem unaccountable, as far as our direct human observation can go. The Teutonic Socrates said that a future life must be believed, if at all, because of its reasonableness in view of what is known and supposed of divine attributes. Certain arguments are becoming humorous from the Society of Psychical Research, but I cannot accept as conclusive the evidence thus collected. Neither the newspapers nor the records of the Society just named, have attempted authentic reports of happenings in the world of spirits. The investigators are honest, but the supply of connected facts is limited, and precludes the possibility of deducing broad scientific conclusions.

'That the dead exist, and that they hold communications with the living is incapable of being demonstrated to the world. If the supposed communications are such as could not come from living men, they are naturally ascribed to subjective hallucinations. If, on the other hand, the communications are such as might come from living men, imparting knowledge in their possession of this world, they are to be explained by telepathy, or some kind of natural influence. Even if spiritual communications could be definitely proved, it would only leave us where savage folklore leaves its votaries in the assurance that some souls exist somehow—not a specially valuable belief.

'PROF. ROYCE then proceeded to say what he considered a solid philosophical basis for a full belief in immortality, but in language rather too technical to be appreciated by those not well-grounded in psychology. But he made a stout defence of his statement that, as he expressed it, *the ethical individual is not limited to the present form of consciousness.*

'The argument from psychical research was presented by. Prof. James H. Hyslop of Columbia University, the head of the American Society of Psychical Research.

'Our researches have been handicapped', said the speaker, 'by erotic and inane deceptions perpetrated upon willing dupes by Spiritualism, and our Society has been called in question because we undertake to apply scientific methods to the investigation of psychical problems. But after a period of struggle for existence the Society of Psychical Research now looks the materialists boldly in the face, challenging them to battle. Our method is the only rational one that can secure the results desired. The business of the philosophers is only to classify and arrange the results we can obtain. All the known facts of physiology seem to point toward the conclusion that consciousness is merely a result of physiological processes, and must have something more than *a priori* reasoning to disprove the arrangements of materialists, among whom I once numbered myself.

'Philosophers since the time of Kant cannot well accept any knowledge not based on some form of experience, and it is this experience that our Society is engaged in collecting. Even if we receive as genuine all the table-tipping, clairvoyance and the like, it would not even prove the existence of soul, much less its immortality. We must have full knowledge of conditions of isolation in apparent cases of communication from spirits, and know that there is a survival of personal identity in the manifestation which is said to have been received. There must be something learnt by the subject that could not have been known naturally.

'When I consider the sins and general *cursedness* of humanity, I wonder that men are allowed to live as long as they do. Why would it not be fitting to cleanse the universe by a general and sweeping annihilation ? The only objection I would make to this is that it would be too great a reward for the hypocrisy and deceit of some men.

'I do not hesitate to accept the spiritualistic theory, even if it should let loose a madhouse upon the world. I only insist upon the application of scientific methods to the study and settlement of the great problems of immortality.

'A brief recess gave the treasurer an opportunity to canvass the audience for funds, and then Miss Anna Boynton Thompson of Boston explained the views of the transcendentalists upon immortality.

'The transcendental theory', said Miss Thompson, 'considers the consciousness as the gateway of knowledge. God, the uncaused first cause, is freedom, and we are each created in His image ; immortality is quantitative, and lies in power of every one who wills to have it, working right for the sake of right. The individuality working the right is as really immortal as God's life, of which it is a part. Only when I will do right for its own sake, do I really exist, and in that case my existence is eternal.

'I believe that the ego is God uncreated, and that itself creates, seeing the divine will in its constant progress, doing the will actualizing the divine vision. Be ye yourselves the Christ and ye are yourselves immortal life.'

'Because of the lateness of the hour, President Janes omitted his paper, which included the scientific argument, and introduced as the last speaker SWAMI ABHEDANANDA of India, now working in the United States as a Hindu missionary.

'The Swami said that the doctrine of immortality had its origin among the Aryans of ancient India. He quoted from the Book of Ecclesiastes to show that Solomon had no faith in a future life after death and said that the world is still full of agnostics, who deny that after a man dies he can live again. The miraculous resurrection of a single person no longer is enough to make a living hope in a future life. Those who believe in that resurrection may deny hope for the future to us who doubt it, but their words no longer strongly influence the world.

'The impenetrable wall that seems to surround those who would look beyond the grave is simply the idea men have that the soul is produced by the body and that when the body is destroyed, the soul is also ended. The Hindus believe that each individual soul has existed before, meaning by soul the subtle body or ego, the germ of life. When this germ has finished its work in one physical body, it drops the old envelope and manufactures a new one. This ego is imperishable. As to death, we may say that there is no annihiliation in the universe, but, it is full of change, and the subtle body continues to change through evolution, until the purposes of life are fulfilled, perfection is attained, and all the inherent powers are fully developed. We understand that this subtle body is not our true nature but a receptacle for that spirit which forms a part of the universal Spirit, like a circle whose centre is everywhere and its circumference nowhere. This inclusive Spirit is the ultimate absolute God, worshipped in different parts of the world as Allah, Christ, Buddha, or

Father in heaven. He is free from all changes, and subject to no limitations. This Spirit fills all the universe, embraces all life, and is the source of all actions.

'The object of all religions is the same, the attainment of immortality, the cultivation of the soul. Christianity misses its ideal when it turns to dogmas and beliefs, instead of pursuing soul culture.'

—BOSTON HERALD, JUNE 2, 1899.

II

NEW ENGLAND CREMATION

THEY LISTEN TO TALKS BY JOHN STORER COBB, THEIR FOUNDER, AND BY SWAMI ABHEDANANDA

(A)

'A public meeting was held under the auspices of the New England Cremation Society yesterday afternoon in Wesleyan Hall. Harrison Otis Apthorp, President of the Society, presided, and brief addresses were made by Rev. Paul Revere Forthingham of New Bedford, Rev. Samuel M. Crothers of Cambridge, the SWAMI ABHEDANANDA of India, who spoke on *Cremation in India,* John Storer Cobb, founder of the Society, and others.

'Rev. Mr. Forthingham spoke of the great antiquity of the practice of cremation. It was formerly a sort of religious ceremony, and very sacred, and a distinguished honour to the bodies of the dead to be burned. There had always been something deeply religious about flame, and even now there was something sacred about the use of fire. The practice of cremation strengthened spirituality in man, in his opinion, for it emphasized the distinction between the spirit and the body.

'Rev. Samuel M. Crothers of Cambridge also spoke strongly in favour of cremation.

'The SWAMI ABHEDANANDA told of the practice of cremation in his country, which, he said, dated from prehistoric times. It has been deemed the most beautiful way of disposing of the bodies of the dead. It was believed by the Parsees that the body should be destroyed as soon as possible after the spirit had left it. The Hindoos believed the spirit was entirely separate from the body. The spirit was the real man, and the body was but the shell in which it was kept.'

—BOSTON JOURNAL, JUNE 2, 1899.

(B)

'A native Hindoo, SWAMI ABHEDANANDA of India, a young man with an intelligent face and a command on the choicest English, spoke most interestingly of cremation in India, saying that it dated from prehistoric times. There was no need of cremation societies. The Hindoos know this way of disposing of the dead.

'Unlike the Egyptians who associated the body and soul so closely that they could not conceive of the one existing without the other, and so were driven to the embalming of the one to make sure the happy existence of the other. The Hindoos held the higher view that the soul was everything and the body was nothing—only the house in which the man lived and is reduced to nothingness as soon as possible after its immortal tenant had gone out of it.'

—BOSTON TRAVELLER, JUNE 2, 1899.

III

DELIVERED IN THE OUTLOOK CLUB, NEW YORK

'We think that at birth, the soul comes from God. The Hindu believes that the soul exists before and after the death of the body. This belief solves many problems of life ; it explains all the inequalities that we often find. Happiness and misery are a result of past incarnation. We create our own destiny. The soul takes its future form according to its desires. The desire to see produced the eye, to hear the ear. The soul must reach perfection sooner or later, for no soul can be lost. Heaven and hell are mental conditions, and the ultimate goal is the manifestation of divinity. The word 'Buddha' means enlightened, and there are many types of Buddha. To work and not to think of the results is the highest form of action. Love, when true, seeks no return.'

—DAILY EVENING ITEM, LYNN : MASS, TUESDAY, APRIL 10, 1900.

IV

PURE IDEALISM THE BASIS :

SWAMI ABHEDANANDA SPEAKS ON :

Indian mystics and their methods of attaining perfection demonstrated.

The Swami said that * * the human soul was immortal being an emanation from the Infinite Spirit, and always had existed and always will. The immortal must be so at the beginning as well as at the end. No religion was of any use that did not teach the past immortality of the soul, as well as the future.

'The present state of the spirit depends on the past, and the future upon the present. We take character with us through death, and nothing else. That character was made up of every act and thought, that inevitably react upon the doer. 'What thou thinkest, that shalt thou become.' This was the great law of *karma*, which was merely the scientific law of causation * * '

—THE MALL AND EMPIRE, THURSDAY, FEBRUARY 4, 1905.

V

EAST INDIAN TALKS ON SPIRITUALISM
FROM HIS OWN EXPERIENCE

'*Spiritualistic Mediumship* was the subject of a lecture delivered yesterday by SWAMI ABHEDANANDA of India, at the Vedanta Society's room, 62, West Seventy-first Street. He said that he had seen materialization and had received spirit messages both in Sanskrit and Bengali about which he believed there was no mistake.

'Admitting the fundamental facts of Spiritualism, he denounced the practice of mediumship, declaring that the negative state essential to it led in many cases to the loss. of memory, loss of the power of reasoning and self-control, to the dulling of the moral sense and not infrequently to insanity. For this reason, in India from ancient times the Yogis and the spiritual teachers have always guarded their pupils and disciples from becoming mediums and have instead taught them how they could develop the psychic powers which would make them masters of themselves and the realm of spirits.'

—NEW YORK HERALD, FEBRUARY 13, 1905.

VI

'There is some good in Spiritualism,' said the Swami. 'Why did we come into life all of a sudden if we did not live before and will not live after life leaves the human body ?' he asked.

'Treating the question of immortality scientifically, the Swami declared : *Science shows that something cannot come out of nothing, that life must have existed in substance before it came into the human body.*'

—PITTSBURGH POST, JANUARY 26, 1907.

VII

'Vedanta, it is claimed, explains the fundamental principles of Spiritualism, tells us how the soul exists after death, what kind of soul can communicate with us, and how the earth-bound souls, being subject to the law of *karma* and causation, reincarnate on this earth taking human form again and again.'

—CHICAGO INTER-OCEAN, OCTOBER 26, 1908.

VIII

WEST CORNWALL SWAMI DISCUSSES

HIS PHILOSOPHY :

'* * What is the Vedanta theory of the transmigration of the soul ? Let me say first that we believe that the souls of the departed take up the new life in human bodies, as opposed to the Platonic view that the soul sometimes takes up the new existence in the body of an animal.

'The Indian version of transmigration is that each soul is bound to receive its body as a natural consequence of its former deeds and misdeeds, and not to have free choice of its lot. This is the law of cause and effect. The universal law of cause and effect, let me add, was discovered by the great thinkers of India. They gave it the Sanskrit term *karma*. The law of *karma* has become one of the fundamental truths of modern science. Scientists gave it different names. They variously term it the law of causation, the law of compensation, the law of action and reaction, etc. But they all have the same idea in mind, namely that every cause is productive of a corresponding result, that every action is productive of a corresponding reaction.

'The law of *karma* controls our birth and re-birth. Our belief is that the parents do not create the souls. They are merely the channels through which the migrating souls receive their material forms. The souls come with their desires.

'When death comes, the soul does not manifest until the surroundings become favourable for a manifestation.

'Our belief that the soul takes up new life in the human body, and never in the body of an animal, makes our theory one of re-incarnation rather than of mere transmigration. Why should the soul choose to become an animal ? We argue, by the process of evolution the human soul has already passed through different stages of animaldom. It would not want to revert to animalism. It is unscientific to think otherwise.

'A noted professor has said of the theory of transmigration : *None but hasty thinkers will reject it on the ground of inherent absurdity. Like the doctrine of evolution itself that of transmigration has its roots in the world of reality.*'

—WATERBUT HERALD, 'CONN.' (Editorial Sec.), OCT. 14, 1917.

IX

THE SWAMI ARRIVES :

'Five miles from West Cornwall the SWAMI ABHEDANANDA, Hindu philosopher and well-known writer on Vedantism, holds forth. * *

'I am a teacher of philosophy,' said the Swami, 'the Vedanta philosophy, or religion, as you choose to call it. The fundamental principle of this school of thought is a belief in the immortality of the soul. After the death of the body, the soul continues to live, but for sometime it goes neither to heaven nor to hell. It gravitates. Take the souls of the soliders who die on the battlefields. For the most part these men are so suddenly killed that they are not conscious of their corporeal non-existence. For a time their souls remain on different planes of the spiritual world. Then, according to the worth that each man displayed on earth, his soul is dealt with. The worthy are rewarded, the unworthy punished. But there is no eternal damnation. We consider such ideas foolish. Not only shall we all be saved, but eventually we shall all, like God, be perfect.

'We believe that there is a heaven to meet the desires of each and every one of us ; in other words, that there is a musician's heaven, an artist's heaven, a heaven for the mechanically inclined, etc. When I speak of heaven and hell, I do not speak of them as being definite destinations of the soul. Heaven and hell are merely mental conditions. Suppose, for instance, a man was a miser all of his life. After death his punishment would be a continuation of his earthly longing for gold, with the attendant impossibility of gratifying this desire.

'It is our idea that one's present existence on earth is an expression of the past lives that one has led. We believe that there is an indefinite series of births and re-births ; that through this process enlightenment comes to us.'

—NEW YORK HERALD, SUNDAY, OCT. 14, 1917.

APPENDIX E

NOTES ON DIFFERENT CHAPTERS

1. * * * The Lokayata school believes consciousness or soul to be the product of physical elements. It says that the soul is nothing but a by-product of the four physical elements, earth, water, fire and air,—"*prithivya apaha tejo vayuh iti chattari tattavani tebhya chaitanyam iti.*" According to the Lokayatas the existence of the soul or consciousness ceases to function with the death of the physical body.—"*paralokinobhavat paralokabhava iti.*" Therefore, there is no such thing like the world after death. The soul means, according to them, the physical body which dies.

2. * * * 'When Ralph Waldo Emerson went to meet Carlyle in London, Carlyle presented to Emerson a copy of the English translation of the *Bhagavad Gita* by Charles Wilkins and said, 'I have been inspired by the teachings of *Bhagavad Gita* and I hope that you will be similarly inspired by them. 'Emerson after reading the *Gita* wrote that beautiful poem on *Brahm.*'—Swami Abhedananda : *Leaves from My Diary*, p. 38.

3. * * * The resurrection of the corpse was one of the earliest beliefs about the soul after death. Some say that the belief in, and the conception of the soul, or a 'double' apart from the body grew out of the sun's daily rise and setting. As the sun sets and rises again in the sky in the next morning, so the soul of a man leaves the body to enter it again after the interval of a certain length of a specified time.

This early conception of the Vedic Aryans was transmitted through the trade route to Egypt, Babylon, Phoenicia, and other countries lying on either coast of the Mediterranean sea giving rise to the kindred allegorical stories of Tammuz, Attis, Adonis, Osirs, Demeter, Istar, Cybele, Apphrodite, Hermes, Mithras and other legends of the kind. The solar origin of these deities as well as of Jesus the Christ has been recognized by J. M. Robertson, Arthur Drews, Conybeare and a whole host of European scholars. Sir Frazer on the other hand ascribes the phenomena of resurrection upon the annual suspension and the rejuvenation of the plant-life in the seasons of winter and spring respectively.

4. *   *   * Embalming is a method of preserving bodies by injections and dressings, either internally or externally applied.

'This term is generally given to the process employed by the ancient Egyptians and others, by which corpses were preserved as mummies * *. The most elaborate process was somewhat as follows :

'A deep cut was made beneath the ribs on the left side, and through the opening thus made, the internal organs were removed, with the exception of the heart and kidneys. The brain was also extracted through the nose by means of a bent iron instrument. The cavities of the skull and trunk were washed out with palm-wine, and filled with raisins, Cassia, and similar substances ; and the skull was dressed by injecting drugs of various kinds through the nostrils. The body was then soaked in natron for seventy days. It was then removed and wrapped carefully in linen cloth, cemented by gum.

'The less expensive process consisted in removing only the brains and injecting the viscera with cedar oil. When the body was soaked in natron for the same period of time (seventy days), the viscera and soft parts came away *en masse*, and only the skin and bones were left. The very poor, who could not afford either of the above methods, embalmed their dead by washing the body in myrrh and salting it for seventy days.'—W. H. Carrington & Meader : *Death,* pp. 85-86.

5.   *   *   *   We find in the Rig Veda, both the customs of burial (*anagnidhāna*) and cremation (*agnidhāna*) are mentioned in the same 10th Mandala. From the 14th to the 18th Mandala, Yama and Agni are mentioned. In the 1st Mantra of the 16th Sukta there is mentioned : *"mainamagne bi daho mābhi śocho, māsya tvachang chikṣipo mā śarīram ; yadā śrtam kṛṇavo jātavedo'themenam pra hiṇutāt pitṛbhyah."* That is, 'O Agni, do not burn the dead body completely, do not give him pain, do not scatter his skin or body. When his body will be burnt well with your flames, do send him to the *pitriloka*.'

This invoking Mantra bears testimony to the fact not of complete but of partial cremation. In the 18th Sukta from 10th to 14th Mantras it is found again that there are the customs of complete burial : *"upa sarpa mātaram bhūmimetā-muruvyachasam pṛthivīm suśevām"* etc. The fractional burial was also in vogue amongst the ancient Vedic peoples. In the 14th Mantra of the 15th Sukta of the Rig Veda we find again : *"ye agnidagdhā ye anagnidagdhā"* etc. This no doubt indicates both the customs of cremation and burial.

6.   *   *   *   The early Buddhists held that there is no such thing as *soul* in the sense 'a permanent unchangeable entity.' Prof. Stcherbatsky : 'A personality (*pudgal*) in which other systems imagine the presence of a permanent spiritual principle, a soul (*Ātman*), is in reality a bundle of elements or forces (*samskārasamūha*). It contains nothing permanent or substantial, it is *anātmā*.' (*Conception of Nirvāṇa*, p. 8). Instead of *Atta* or *Ātmā* only the *shandhasantana* which has been compared to the flame of a lamp, is admitted by some of the schools of the Buddhists. They maintain a changing group of entities called the five *skandhas* which alone constitute a being regarded as *Atta* or soul. These *skandhas* may be of the grossest or the subtlest form, but they are in the continual flux of elements.

The philosophy of *Lankāvatāra* also explains this theory in the following manner : 'The Skandhas, Dhatus, and Ayatanas have nothing personal in them ; there is no 'me and mine' in them * *. The material world as well as the physical body are manifestations of the mind known as *Alayavijnana*, and when they are discriminated as particular existence, we are discriminating our own mind. When thus created they are seen in constant transmigration, they never remain even for a moment as they are, they flow like a stream, they change like a seed, they flicker like a candle-light, they move like the wind or like a cloud. Owing to the habit-energy (*vasana*) * * we now transmigrate from one state to another revolving like a wheel, like a machine, like a phantom creation, or like a walking ghost'.—D. T. Suzuki : *Studies in the Lankāvatāra-Sutra*, p. 167.

7.   *   *   *   In the Avesta of the Parsees we find the words : *Astabanta* (*Astibat*) and *Manahya* (*Manasya*) : i.e., the worlds, visible and invisible. There we also come across the word Yima (Sanskrit *Yama*), the son of Bibingghat (Sanskrit *Vaivasvat*). According to the Avesta, the soul remains swooned just after death. For continuous three days and nights, the soul begins to think of its deeds, good or bad, done during its life-time. The attachment for its nearest and dearest ones remains only for three days and nights, and after that it departs from there either for heaven or hell. We find in the Zend Avesta (Yast XII) : Zarathustra asked Ahura Mazda : 'O Ahura Mazda, when one of the faithfuls departs from his life, where does his soul abide on that night ?' Ahura Mazda answered : 'It takes its seat near the head singing the *Ushtavati Gatha*' etc. Vide Swami Abhedananda : *Great Saviours of the World*, (new edition), pp. 65-113.

8.   *   *   *   Dr. Inge says that transmigration or rebirth is incorrectly called 'metempsychosis.' He says that *Metemsomatosis* or *Palingenesia* are right words, since it is the bodies, not the soul that are changed to rebirth.

9. * * * Except Pythagoras and Plato other celebrated Greek philosophers and historians maintained the same belief regarding it. As we find 'according to Herodotus (II, 123)', J. F. Clarke quotes, 'the soul must pass through all animals, fishes, insects, and birds ; in short, must complete the whole circuit of animated existence, before it again enters the body of a man ; and this circuit of the souls is performed in three thousand years.'—*The Great Religions*, p. 226.

Empedocles believed that the cause of transmigration was sin and the full term of transmigration covered 30,000 years. But he said that finally the soul would become a god. This view more or less coincides with the pauranic theory of the Hindus. The Pauranic theory says that soul transmigrates from the lower to the higher births 84,00,000 times and ultimately returns to human form again. Pinder believed that only the bad were condemned to transmigration and the good went to the sky, the air, Elysium or Olympus. But 'Porphyry and Iamblichus,' as Dr. Inge reminds us, 'refuse to believe that human souls are even sent to inhabit the bodies of beasts and birds.' 'The earliest Hermetic document, the *Kore Kosmou*, is dated probably to 510 B.C., and certainly within a century after that, by an allusion to the Persian rule, * * metempsychosis is assumed between human and animal bodies, the soul is individual, and at death it returns to its proper position in the sixty regions between the earth and moon. Thence it seems to have been conducted to earth again for a reincarnation.'—Cf. W. M. Felinders Petric : *Aspects of Egyptian Religion,* (Oxford : *History of Religions,* Vol. I, p. 196) : Most of the poets, philosophers and celebrated historians of ancient Greece believed in the existence and immortality of the human soul beyond grave. Erwin Rohde in his celebrated book *Psyche* has shown clearly how the cult of souls and the beliefs in the immortality of the soul were prevalent among the Dionysic Religion, the Orphics, the philosophers, and the poets in Greece of the glorious past days. Dr. Inge states :

'* * belief in immortality was less general in the first century than it is among ourselves, and decidedly less general than it became two hundred years later. * * the Romans were disposed to believe in some sort of shadowy survival, which justified family meetings at the grave and the customary tributes to the departed spirit. * * But the belief in ghosts and apparitions * * seems to have been almost universal in the second century, except among the 'godless Epicureans', Plutarch, Dion Cassius, the younger Pliny, and Suetonius all believed in spiritualism ; and neo-Platonism, with its doctrine of 'daemous' did nothing to discourage it. The decay of Aristotelianism removed obstacles to free belief in immortality * * The main doctrine of Orphism were the probation of the soul in this life as a preparation for eternity, * * and the rebirth of souls in higher or lower forms, determined by the merits and demerits of the subject in its previous state of existence.'—(*Plotinus*, Vol. I, pp. 52-53).

10. In the *Upanishads* we find the following passages which mention the retrogression of human souls to lower and animal bodies :

(*i*) "*Atha.... ya etau panthānau na viduste kītah pataṅgā yadidam dandaśūkam.*"—(Brihadaranyaka Upanishad, 6.2.16). That is, 'those who do not know these two paths (*dakshinayana* and *uttarayana*), become insects and moths, and these frequently biting things (gnats and mosquitoes).'

(*ii*) "*Tat ya iha ramaṇīyacharaṇā abhyasho ha yatte ramaṇīyam yonimapadyeran brāhmaṇayonim va kṣatriyayonim va vaiśyayonim va atha ya iha kapūyacharaṇā abhyasho ha yattekapūyam yonimāpadyerañshvayonim va sūkarayonim va chaṇḍālayonim va.*"—Chhandogya Upanishad, 5.10.7). This is, 'those who have been of good conduct here, would quickly attain good birth—birth of Brahmana, birth of Kshatriya, or birth of Vaisya. And those who have been of bad conduct here attain evil birth,—the birth of a dog, the birth of a hog, or the birth of Chandala.'

(*iii*) "*Yonimanye prapadyante śariratvāya dehinah ;
sthanumanye'nusamyanti yathākarma yathāśrutam.*"—(Katha
Upanishad, 2.2.7). That is, 'some souls according to their
karma and inclination of mind receive another birth, and
some others again are degenerated into the states of trees and
stones.'

(*iv*) In the *Sankhayana Aranyaka* (Ch. II, 2) and *Kausitaki
Brahmana Upanishad*, (1.1-6), we find it is mentioned :
"* *chandramastham yah pratyāha * * sa iha kito va patango
vā shakunirvā shārdūlo vā simho vā matsyo vā parashvā vā
* * pratyājāyate.*" That is, 'those who depart from this world
shall go to the moon. * * He is born on earth as a worm, or
a grasshopper, or a fish, or a bird, or a lion, or a boar, or a
snake, or a tiger or a man, or another creature, in one or other
station according to his deeds and his knowledge.'

11. * * * Grant Allen mentions : 'It is the
universal Catholic custom to place the relics of saints or
martyrs under the altars in churches. Thus the body of St.
Mark the evangelist lies under the high altar of St. Mar's at
Venice ; and in every other Italian Cathedral, or Chapel, a
reliquary is deposited within the alter itself. So well understood
is this principle in the Latin Church that it has hardened into
the saying, 'No relic no altar.' The sacrifice of the Mass takes
place at such an altar, and is performed by a priest in
sacrificial robes. The entire Roman Catholic ritual is a ritual
derived from the earlier sacerdotal ideas of ministry at an
altar, and its connection with the primitive form is still kept
up by the necessary presence of human remains in its holy
places.

Furthermore, the very idea of a church itself descended
from the early Christian meeting-places in the catacombs or
at the tombs of the martyrs, which are universally allowed to
have been the primitive Christian altars. * * Thus Christianity
is linked on to the very unique custom of worship at tombs,
and habit of ancestor-worship by altars, relics, and invocation

of saints, even revolutionary Protestantism still retaining some last faint marks of its origin in the dedication of churches to particular evangelists or martyrs, and in the more or less disguised survival of altar, priesthood, sacrifice, and vestments.'—*The Evolution of the Idea of God*, pp. 24-26.

12.   *   *   * In *Shrāddha* ceremony of the Hindoos an effigy (*Brāhmaṇa*) made of Kusa-grass (*darbhamaya-Brāhmaṇa*) is placed and worshippped as an image or a representative of the dead. In the *Brishotsarga-shrāddha* ceremony, there is used again a *Yūpa* made of the *Vilva* tree which is called the *Brishakāshtha* in the shape of a man or woman. This idol or the wooden post is preserved after the *Shrāddha* ceremony is over as the symbol or image of the deceased.

We find again that there is a current custom of burning the effigy which is called the *parnanaradāha* or *kuśaputtalikā* as a different kind of cremation ceremony of the Hindus. This ceremony is observed when the dead body of the deceased is not found. This effigy is made of 360 leaves of *palāśa* or *śara* according to the *Suddhitattva*.

The similar custom is found in many other ancient nations of the world. Cf. Frazer : *Golden Bough*, p. IV. Vol. I, pp. 250-259 : Grant Allen : *Evolution of the Idea of God*, p. 94 ; R. M. Dorman : *The Origin of Primitive Superstitions*, p. 117 ; Dr. E. O. James : *Comparative Religion*, pp. 311-312 ; Elliot Smith : *Egyptian Mummies*, F. E. A., 1914, p. 192 ; A. W. Benn : *The Greek Philosopher*, p. 503 ; W. Budge : *Book of the Death*, Ch. VI ; L. A. Waddell : *Buddhism in Tibet or Lamaism*, p. 405.

13.   *   *   * This statement of Swami Abheda-nanda reminds us two of the instances which we were privileged to hear from him. He said that when he was in America, he saw one evening a face of a discarnate spirit floating in the air before him. The face of the spirit looked

pale marked with pain and agony. The Swami asked the
spirit : 'What ails you ?' The voice came. 'Help me. Help me.
I am suffering. I have committed suicide.' The Swami blessed
him by saying : 'If you think my prayers and blessings will
help you, you have my good wishes, I am praying for you.
Peace be unto you.' The Swami saw that the pale and gloomy
face of the spirit lighted up, who then melted away smiling.
The other instance was of a spirit of a sailor who was
drowned in the sea. He too appeared before him like one
groping in darkness. The Swami asked him : 'What's wrong
with you ?' The spirit replied that he did not know, he was
drowned. He requested the Swami to help him. The Swami
then prayed for him, and he melted away with his look bright
and peaceful.

It will not be out of place to mention here again that
Swami Abhedananda heard also the voice of his brother
disciple Swami Adbhutananda (Latu Maharaj) immediately
after his passing away in India. The Swami heard one day a
heavy voice in the air : 'Kali Kali.' He immediately looked
around, but found no body. He asked who he was, and the
voice came : 'I am Latu. I have came to see you'. The Swami
apprehended the passing away of his beloved brother and it
came to be true as he received the cablegram next day bearing
the sad news of Swami Adbhutananda's demise.

The Swami also saw the materialized spirit of the poet
Girish Chandra Ghosh, who was spitting on all sides as he
appeared. The explanation of that act of Girish Chandra was
given by the Swami as : As we spit on a useless ephemeral
thing, so the Poet being free from the bondage of his earthly
body spat on the ephemeral worldly things, which bears no
actual value of reality in comparison with the absolute
existence.

—THE EDITOR.

APPENDIX F

EXTRACTS FROM THE SACRED WRITINGS OF THE ANCIENT HINDUS AND THOSE OF THE MYSTICS, POETS AND PHILOSOPHERS, AS REGARDS THE PRE-EXISTENCE AND IMMORTALITY OF THE SOUL :

"O Agni, make warm that part of this deceased which is birthless and eternal with thy heat. Let thy brightness and thy flame make that part of him heated. O Jataveda Agni, take this departed soul to the spheres of the pious and virtuous with thy forms of walfare."

—RIG VEDA, X, 16.4.

"This man has only two abodes, this and the next world." (4.3.9). "Exhausting the results of whatever work he did in this life, he returns from that world to this for (fresh) work." Thus does the man who desires to transmigrate." (4.4.6) :

"The Self is taintless, beyond the (subtle) ether, birthless, infinite and constant." (4.4.20).

—BRIHADARANYAKA UPANISHAD.

"Mortal is the body, held by death ;—it is the abode of that Immortal (unbodied) Self. The bodied one is held by pleasure and pain ; * * but pleasure and pain do not touch the unbodied Self."

—CHHANDOGYA UPANISHAD.

'The soul must be a thing both uncreated and immortal. * * And then it is that a human soul passes into the life of a beast, and from a beast who was once a man, the soul comes back into a man again.'

—PLATO.

'It (soul) is an absolute reality. * * it exists before ever it belongs to a body.'

—PLOTINUS.

'The human mind cannot be absolutely destroyed with the body, but something of it remains which is eternal.'

—SPINOZA.

'The soul is always joined with the aggregate of subordinate Monads, though not always with the same ones. * * not the soul only, but every living thing is imperishable. * * Death is decrease and involution, birth increase and evolution. The dying creature takes only a portion of its bodily machine and returns to the slumberous or germinal condition of *evolution*, in which it existed before birth. * * Pre-existence as well as post-existence must be conceded both to animals and men.'

—LEIBNITZ.

'The soul is indivisible, incorporeal, unextended, and it is consequently incorruptible. * * Such a being therefore is indissoluble by the force of nature ; that is to say, the *soul of man is naturally immortal.*'

—BERKELEY.

'Now, this endless progress (*progress ad infinitum*) is only possible on the supposition of an *endless* duration of the *existence* and personality of the same rational being (which is called the immortality of the soul). The *summum bonum*, then, practically is only possible on the supposition of the immortality of the soul.'

—IMMANUEL KANT.

'Man as Spirit is immortal, is an object of God's interest, is raised above finitude and dependence, * * that he has freedom to abstract himself from everything, and this implies that he can escape mortality.'

—HEGEL.

'The immortal *psyche* remains, with fettered pinions, fastened to the earth.'

'Death in Nature is Birth, and in Death itself appears visibly the exaltation of Life. There is no destructive principle in Nature, for Nature throughout is pure, unclouded Life ; * * Death and Birth are but the struggle of Life with itself to assume a more glorious and congenial form. * * and what mortals call Death is the visible appearance of this second Life. * * Death is the ladder by which my spiritual vision rises to a new Life and a new Nature.'

—FICHTE.

'The finite self is plainly a partial world, yet possesses within it the principle of infinity, taken in the sense of the nexsus towards absolute unity and self-completion.'

—B. BOSANQUET.

'I communicate my view, not of course in order to convert any one to my opinion, but because I am convinced that a serious study of these phenomena is of the greatest importance to psychology, and because I think that my personal confession may lead a reader or two to approach the region of investigation which is usually treated with contempt by socalled men of science.'

—PROF. WILLIAM JAMES.

'We never become, for our own rational consciousness, perfect individual selves. Yet all our empirical life has meaning, and constitutes the life of one Self, just in so far, but only in so far, as this our empirical life is consciously viewed by ourselves as a process of progressing towards the fulfilment of our individual and consciously chosen ideal.'

—PROF. JOSIAH ROYCE.

'Any evidence which will prove immortality will also prove pre-existence. * * each of us exists through all time—past and future.

'Human selves are among the fundamental differentiations of the universe, and that they are therefore, *sub specie tempors,* immortal.'

—Dr. MacTaggart.

'It is the spirit, it is Reality, in so far as it is truly real, in so far as it is unity of thought and willing ; it is Life in so far as realized in its profundity as this unity itself ; it is Freedom, if a reality so conceived be perpetual development, creation, progress.'

—B. Croce.

'I do not hesitate to accept the spiritualistic theory. * * I only insist upon the application of scientific methods to the study and settlement of the great problems of immortality.'

—Prof. James H. Hyslop.

'Let us not forget that we here have to deal with a science of today and yesterday, which is still groping for its utensils, ways, methods, and aims, and that in the midst of a night which is darker than the earthly night. * * Most sciences have centuries of useless effort and barren uncertainty behind them, and among the youngest of them there are probably few which promise such a harvest, even in the first stages—a harvest which may not correspond to what we believe ourselves to have sown, but which already shows many buds of a strange and unknown fruit.'

—Maeterlinck.

'* * it seems to me that the spiritualistic hypothesis may be mentioned with the same right as the other, for all discussions on it have not proved that it is untenable.'

—C. Flammarion.

'A life after death is not a matter of speculation or conjecture of hope and fear ; it is a practical certainty which the individual has little dreams of doubting as he doubts the reality of his conscious existence.'

—J. G. FRAZER.

'The burial customs of many peoples afford the best evidence that the disembodied soul is conceived as like in all essential respects to the living of soul and body. * * And the even more widely spread custom of burying or burning with the dead man his most valued possessions, especially weapons and ornaments, is due to the belief that even these things have their shadowy duplicates or ghost-souls, which can be carried away by the departing soul and used by it as the real objects, were used by the living man.'

—PROF. McDOUGALL.

'The faith in immortality may be less widespread than the belief in a God, though this is doubtful.'

—PROF. PRATT.

'It (spirit) is a thin, unsubstantial human image, in its nature a sort of vapour, film, or shadow : * * continuing to exist and appear to men after the death of that body : able to enter into, possess, and act in the bodies of other men, of animals, and even of things.'

—PROF. TYLOR.

'The soul is not in time ; time is rather in this soul. Values are eternal and indestructible. * * we are sure of our immortality.'

—DEAN INGE.

'What is true of our apprehension of the divine is true also of its counterpart in the creature—soul and spirit.'

—RUDOLF OTTO

'The man who has let things pass away in their lower forms where they are mortal, receives them again in God, where alone they are real. All that is dead here, is life there. And all that is here gross and tangible is there (*sub specie ydeali*) spirit.'

—MEISTER ECKHART.

'Death has no power the immortal soul to slay,
That, when its present body turns to slay,
Seeks a fresh home, and with unlessened might,
Inspires another frame with life and light.

*   *   *   *

Death, so called, is not older matter stressed
In some new form. And in a varied vest,
From tenement to tenement though tossed.
The soul is still the same, the figure only lost.'

—DRYDEN.

'The soul that rises with us, our life's Star,
Hath had elsewhere its setting
And cometh from afar.'

—W. WORDSWORTH.

'Support the fervour of the heavenly morn ?
No. No. The energy of life may be
Kept on after the grave, but not begun ;
And he who flagged not in the earthly strife,
From strength to strength advancing—only he,
His soul well-knit, and all his battles won,
Mounts, and the ardly, to eternal life.'

—MATTHEW ARNOLD.

(a)   Alas ; What is life, what is death,
            What are we,
        That when the ship sinks we no
            longer may be

What to see thee no more, and to feel
        thee no more,
To be after life what have been before.'

(b)   'The One remains, the many change and pass ;
Heaven's light for ever shines, Earth's shadows fly ;
Life, like a dome of many-coloured glass,
Stains the white radiance of Eternity,
Until Death tramples it to fragments.—Die,
If thou wouldst be with that which thou dost seek.'

                                    —P. B. SHELLEY.

'For the journey is done and the summit attained,
        And the barriers fall,
        *   *   *   *
Shall change, shall become first a peace out of pain,
        Then a light, then thy breast,
O Thou Soul of my soul I shall clasp Thee again,
        And with God be the rest.'

                                    —R. BROWNING.

'Form is born of that which is without form,
And goes again, for *verily to Him do we return.*'

                                    —AL-GHAZALI : *Masnavi.*

'Of my soul's union with this fleshly frame,
Of life and death Thou art the end and aim.
        *   *   *   *
'The forms which clothe existence only stay
One moment, in the next they pass away ;
This subtle point is proven by the text ;*
Its fashion altereth from day to day.'

                                    —JIMT : *Lawa'th.*

* *Koran* : Iv. 29.